This book was very loved
But we needed room for new.
We hope you will enjoy it
Just as much as we did, too.

NEW HAVEN FREE PUBLIC LIBRARY

DATE DUE

MAR 06 2013			

The Britannica Guide to
The History of
Mathematics

MATH EXPLAINED

The Britannica Guide to
The History of
Mathematics

EDITED BY ERIK GREGERSEN,
ASSOCIATE EDITOR, ASTRONOMY AND SPACE EXPLORATION

Educational Publishing

IN ASSOCIATION WITH

EDUCATIONAL SERVICES

Published in 2011 by Britannica Educational Publishing
(a trademark of Encyclopædia Britannica, Inc.)
in association with Rosen Educational Services, LLC
29 East 21st Street, New York, NY 10010.

First Edition

Britannica Educational Publishing
Michael I. Levy: Executive Editor
J.E. Luebering: Senior Manager
Marilyn L. Barton: Senior Coordinator, Production Control
Steven Bosco: Director, Editorial Technologies
Lisa S. Braucher: Senior Producer and Data Editor
Yvette Charboneau: Senior Copy Editor
Kathy Nakamura: Manager, Media Acquisition
Erik Gregersen: Associate Editor, Astronomy and Space Exploration

Rosen Educational Services
Hope Lourie Killcoyne: Senior Editor and Project Manager
Bethany Bryan: Editor
Nelson Sá: Art Director
Cindy Reiman: Photography Manager
Matthew Cauli: Designer, Cover Design
Introduction by John Strazzabosco

Library of Congress Cataloging-in-Publication Data

The Britannica guide to the history of mathematics / edited by Erik Gregersen.—1st ed.
    p. cm.—(Math explained)
"In association with Britannica Educational Publishing, Rosen Educational Services."
Includes bibliographical references and index.
ISBN 978-1-61530-127-0 (lib. bdg.)
    1. Mathematics—History. I. Gregersen, Erik. II. Title: History of mathematics.
QA21.B84 2011
510.9—dc22

                                                                        2010008356

Manufactured in the United States of America

On the cover: Hands with abacus, an old-fashioned counting device. *Jed Share/Photodisc/
Getty Images*

On page 12: Illustrating Pythagoras's theorem, this diagram comes from a mid-19th-century
edition of the *Elements* of Euclid, a seminal multi-book series incorporating the findings of
both mathematicians. *SSPL via Getty Images*

On page 20: A page from Newton's annotated copy of *Elements*, Euclid's treatise on geometry. *Hulton Archive/Getty Images*

On pages 21, 84, 182, 217, 256, 282, 285, 294: This diagram from Newton's *Principia
Mathematica* concerns hourly variations of the lunar orbit. *SSPL via Getty Images*

CONTENTS

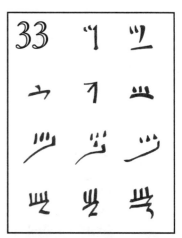

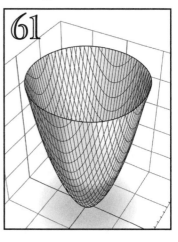

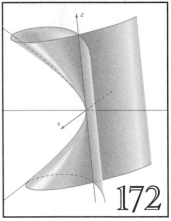

199

220

221

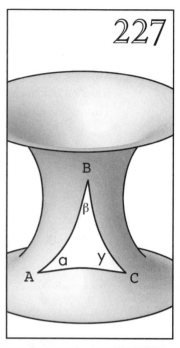

265

INTRODUCTION

It seems impossible to believe that at one point in ancient time, human beings had absolutely no formal mathematics—that from scratch, the ideas for numbers and numeration were begun, applications found, and inventions pursued, one layered upon another, creating the very foundation of everyday life. So dependent are we upon this mathematic base—wherein we can do everything from predict space flight to forecast the outcomes of elections to review a simple grocery bill—that to imagine a world with no mathematical concepts is quite a difficult thought to entertain.

In this volume we encounter the humble beginnings of the ancient mathematicians and various developments over thousands of years, as well as modern intellectual battles fought today between, for example, the logicians who either support the mathematic philosophy of Platonism or promote its aptly named rival, anti-Platonism. We explore worldwide math contributions from 4000 BCE through today. Topics presented from the old world include mathematical astronomy, Greek trigonometry and mensuration, and the ideas of Omar Khayyam. Contemporary topics include isomorphic structures, topos theory, and computers and proof.

We also find that mathematic discovery was not always easy for the discoverers, who perhaps fled for their lives from Nazi threats, or created brilliant mathematical innovation while beleaguered by serious mental problems, or who pursued a mathematic topic for many years only to have another mathematician suddenly and quite conclusively prove that what had been attempted was all wrong, effectively quashing years of painstaking work. For the creative mathematician, as for those who engage in other loves or conflicts, heartbreak or disaster might be encountered. The lesson learned is one in courage and the pure guts of those willing to take a chance—even when most of the world said no.

Entering into math history is a bit like trying to sort through a closet full of favourite old possessions. We pick up an item, prepared to toss it if necessary, and suddenly a second and third look at the thing reminds us that this is fascinating stuff. First thing we know, a half hour has passed and we are still wondering how, for instance, the Babylonians (*c.* 2000 BCE) managed to write a table of numbers quite close to Pythagorean Triples more than 1,000 years before Pythagoras himself (*c.* 500 BCE) supposedly discovered them.

The modern-day math student lives and breathes with her math teacher's voice ringing in her ear, saying, "Memorize these Pythagorean triples for the quiz on Friday." Babylonian students might have heard the same request. Their triples were approximated by the formula of the day, $a^2 + b^2/2a$, which gives values close to Pythagoras's more accurate $a^2 + b^2 = c^2$. Consider that such pre-Pythagorean triples were written by ancient scribes in cuneiform and sexagesimal (that's base 60). One such sexagesimal line of triples from an ancient clay tablet of the time translates to read as follows: 2, 1 59, 2 49. (The smaller space shown between individual numbers, such as the 1 and the 59 in the example, are just as one would leave a slight space if reporting in degrees and minutes, also base 60). In base 10 this line of triples would be 120, 119, 169. The reader is invited for old time's sake to plug these base 10 numbers into the Pythagorean Formula $a^2 + b^2 = c^2$ to verify the ancient set of Pythagorean triples that appeared more than 1,000 years before Pythagoras himself appeared.

An equally compelling example of credit for discovery falling upon someone other than the discoverer is found in a quite familiar geometrically appearing set of numbers. Most math students recognize the beautiful Pascal's Triangle and can even reproduce it, given pencil and paper. The triangle yields at a glance the coefficients of a binomial expansion, among many other bits of useful mathematics information. As proud as Blaise Pascal (1600s) must have been over his Pascal's triangle, imagine that of Zhu Shijie (a.k.a. Chu Shih-Chieh), who first published the triangle in *his* book, *Precious Mirror of Four Elements* (1303). Zhu probably did not give credit to Pascal, as Pascal would not be born for another 320 years.

Zhu's book has a gentle kind of title that suggests the generous sort of person Zhu might have been. Indeed, he gave full credit for the aforementioned triangle to his predecessor, Yang Hui (1300), who in turn probably lifted the triangle from Jia Xian (*c.* 1100). In fact, despite significant contributions to math theory of his times, Zhu unselfishly referred to methods in his book as *the old way* of doing things, thus praising the work of those who came before him.

We dig deeper into our closet of mathematic treasures and imagine mathematician Kurt Gödel (1906–1978). His eyes were said to be piercing, perhaps even haunting. Like a teacher of our past, could Mr. Gödel pointedly be asking about a little something we omitted from our homework, perhaps? We probably have all been confronted at one time or another for turning in an assignment that was incomplete. Gödel, however, made a career out of incompleteness, literally throwing the whole world into a tizzy with his incompleteness theorem. Paranoid and mentally unstable, his tormented mind could nonetheless uncover what other great minds could not. It was 1931, a year after his doctoral thesis first announced to the world that a young mathematics great had arrived.

Later an Austrian escapee of the Nazis, Gödel with his incompleteness theorem proved to be brilliant and on target, but also bad news for heavyweight mathematicians Bertrand Russell, David Hilbert, Gottlob Frege, and Alfred North Whitehead. These four giants in the math world had spent significant portions of their careers trying to construct axiom systems that could be used to prove all mathematical truths. Gödel's incompleteness theorem ended those pursuits, trashing years of mathematical work.

Russell, Hilbert, Frege, and Whitehead all made their marks in other areas of math. How would they have taken this shocking news of enormous rejection? Let's try to imagine.

Bertrand Russell might stare downward upon us, shocks of tufted white hair about his face, perhaps asking himself at the tragic moment, can it be possible, all that work, gone in a moment? Would he have thrown math books around the office in anger? How about David Hilbert? Can we imagine his hurt, his pain, at having the whole world know that his efforts have simply been dashed by that upstart mathematician, Gödel? Consider Frege and then Whitehead, and then we realize that another half hour has passed. But our mental image of Gödel's stern countenance calls us back for yet more penetrating thought.

Gödel was called one of the great logicians since Aristotle (384–322 BCE). Gödel's engaging gaze captivated the attention of Albert Einstein, who attended Gödel's hearing to become a U.S. citizen. Einstein feared that Gödel's unpredictable behaviour might sabotage his own cause to remain in the U.S. Einstein's presence prevailed. Citizenship was granted to Gödel. In 1949 Gödel returned the favour by mathematically demonstrating that Einstein's theory of relativity allows for possible time travel.

The story of Gödel did not end well. Growing ever more paranoid as his life progressed, he starved himself to death.

Our investigative journey is far from complete. Yet we take a few sentimental minutes to ponder Gödel and maybe ask, how could his mind have entertained these mathematical brilliancies that shook the careers of the world's brightest and yet feared ordinary food so that his resulting anorexia eventually took his life? How could the same mind entertain such opposing thoughts? But there's so much still to be tackled yet in math history.

How about this 13th century word problem? Maybe we always hated word problems in math class. How might we have felt seven or eight hundred years ago?

Suppose one has an unknown number of objects. If one counts them by threes, there remain two of them. If one counts them by fives, there remain three of them. If one counts them by sevens, there remain two of them. How many objects are there?

Even if we detest word problems we can hardly resist. After a bit of trial and error we find the answer and chuckle as though we knew we could do it all along; we just were sweating a little at first, and now feel that deeper sense of satisfaction at having solved a problem. Perhaps at some point we might wonder if our slipshod method might have been improved upon. Did it have to be trial and error? That same dilemma plagued Asian mathematicians in the 1st through 13th centuries CE. Where were the equations that might easily solve the problems? In China, probably around the 13th century, the concept of equations was just coming into existence.

In Asia the slow evolution of algorithms of root extraction was leading to a fully developed concept of the equation. But strangely, for reasons not clear now, a period of progressive *loss* of achievements occurred. The 14th through 16th centuries of Asian math are sometimes referred to as the "fall into oblivion." Counting rods were out. The abacus was in. Perhaps that new technology of the day led to sluggish development, until the new abacus caught on. By the 17th century counting rods had been totally discarded. One can imagine a student with his abacus before math class, sliding the buttons up and down to attack a math problem. In this math closet of history we, too, touch the smooth wooden buttons and suddenly a tactile sense has become a part of our math experience, the gentle clicking as numbers are added for us by this ingenious advancement in technology, giving us what we crave—speed and accuracy—relieving the brain for other tasks while we calculate.

If much of this mysterious development in math sounds like fiction, then we have arrived in contemporary mathematical times. For while you might think that cold, rigid, unalterable, and concrete numbers seem to make up our world of mathematics, think again. Remember Gottlob Frege, whose years of math pursuit with axiomatic study was abruptly rejected by Kurt Gödel's incompleteness theorem? Frege was a battler, developing the Frege argument for Platonism. Platonism asserts that math objects, such as numbers, are nonphysical objects that cannot be perceived by the senses. Intuition makes it possible to acquire knowledge of nonphysical math objects, which exist outside of space and time. Frege supports that notion. Others join the other side of the epistemological argument against Platonism.

What we are engaging in here is called mathematics philosophy. If this pursuit seems like a waste of time, recall that other "wastes of time" such as imaginary numbers, which later proved crucial to developing electrical circuitry and thus our modern world, did become important. But we began in pursuit of the aforementioned term fiction, which is where we are now headed. One philosophy of math beyond Platonism is nominalism. And one version of nominalism is fictionalism. Fictionalists agree with Platonists that if there really *were* such a thing as the number 4, then it would be an abstract object. The American philosopher Hartry Field is a fictionalist.

Mathematics philosophers have forever undertaken mental excursions that defy belief—at first, that is. As with the other objects we have come across in this closet, we might not even recognize nor understand it immediately, but we pick it up for examination anyway. Then we read for a while about Platonism, Nominalism, Fictionalism— arguments for and against—and we have been launched into a modern-day journey, for this is truly new math. Topics such as these are not from the ancients but rather from modern mathematicians. The ideas are still in relative infancy, waiting to find acceptance, and it is hoped, applications that might one day change our world or that of those who follow us.

Perhaps the trip will take us down a dead-end road. Perhaps the trip will lead to significant discovery. One can never be certain. But there's this whole closet to go through, and we select the next item....

1. *Hyp.* Si fieri poteſt, ſit D ipſarum AC,
AB communis menſura. ᵃ ergò D metitur
AC — AB (BC). ᵇ ergò AB ⊓ BC, contra
Hypoth.

   2. *Hyp.* Dic AB ⊓ BC, ᶜ ergò AC ⊓
AB, contra Hypoth.

ᵃ 3. ax. 10.
ᵇ 1. def. 10.
ᶜ 16. 10.

Coroll.

Hinc etiam, ſi tota magnitudo ex duabus
compoſita, incommenſurabilis ſit alteri ipſarum, eadem & reliquæ incommenſurabilis erit.

Prop. XVIII.

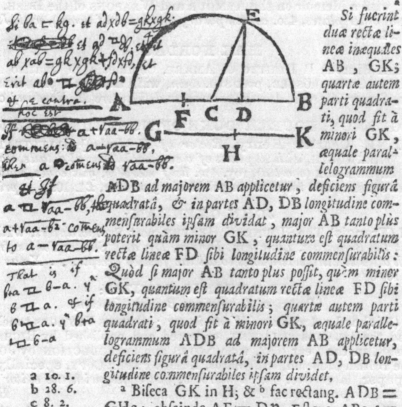

Si fuerint
duæ rectæ li-
neæ inæquales
AB, GK;
quartæ autem
parti quadra-
ti, quod fit à
minori GK,
æquale paral-
lelogrammum

ADB ad majorem AB applicetur, deficiens figurâ
quadratâ, & in partes AD, DB longitudine commenſurabiles ipſam dividat, major AB tanto plus
poterit quàm minor GK, quantum eſt quadratum
rectæ lineæ FD ſibi longitudine commenſurabilis:
Quòd ſi major AB tanto plus poſſit, quàm minor
GK, quantum eſt quadratum rectæ lineæ FD ſibi
longitudine commenſurabilis; quartæ autem parti
quadrati, quod fit à minori GK, æquale paralle-
logrammum ADB ad majorem AB applicetur,
deficiens figurâ quadratâ, in partes AD, DB longitudine commenſurabiles ipſam dividet,

   ᵃ Biſeca GK in H; & ᵇ fac rectang. ADB =
GHq: abſcinde AF = DB. Eſtque AB] ᶜ =
4 ADB ᵈ (4 GHq, vel GKq) + FDq. Jam
primò

ᵃ 10. 1.
ᵇ 28. 6.
ᶜ 8. 2.
ᵈ conſtr. &
4. 2.

CHAPTER I
ANCIENT WESTERN MATHEMATICS

Mathematics is the science of structure, order, and relation that has evolved from elemental practices of counting, measuring, and describing the shapes of objects. It deals with logical reasoning and quantitative calculation, and its development has involved an increasing degree of idealization and abstraction of its subject matter. Since the 17th century, mathematics has been an indispensable adjunct to the physical sciences and technology, and in more recent times it has assumed a similar role in the quantitative aspects of the life sciences.

In many cultures—under the stimulus of the needs of practical pursuits, such as commerce and agriculture—mathematics has developed far beyond basic counting. This growth has been greatest in societies complex enough to sustain these activities and to provide leisure for contemplation and the opportunity to build on the achievements of earlier mathematicians.

All mathematical systems (for example, Euclidean geometry) are combinations of sets of axioms and of theorems that can be logically deduced from the axioms. Inquiries into the logical and philosophical basis of mathematics reduce to questions of whether the axioms of a given system ensure its completeness and its consistency.

As a consequence of the exponential growth of science, most mathematics has developed since the 15th century CE. This does not mean, however, that earlier developments have been unimportant. Indeed, to understand the history of modern mathematics, it is necessary to know its history at least in Mesopotamia and Egypt, in ancient

Greece, and in Islamic civilization from the 9th to the 15th century. These civilizations influenced one another and Greek and Islamic civilization made important direct contributions to later developments. For example, India's contributions to the development of contemporary mathematics were made through the considerable influence of Indian achievements on Islamic mathematics during its formative years.

ANCIENT MATHEMATICAL SOURCES

It is important to be aware of the character of the sources for the study of the history of mathematics. The history of Mesopotamian and Egyptian mathematics is based on the extant original documents written by scribes. Although in the case of Egypt these documents are few, they are all of a type and leave little doubt that Egyptian mathematics was, on the whole, elementary and profoundly practical in its orientation. For Mesopotamian mathematics, on the other hand, there are a large number of clay tablets, which reveal mathematical achievements of a much higher order than those of the Egyptians. The tablets indicate that the Mesopotamians had a great deal of remarkable mathematical knowledge, although they offer no evidence that this knowledge was organized into a deductive system. Future research may reveal more about the early development of mathematics in Mesopotamia or about its influence on Greek mathematics, but it seems likely that this picture of Mesopotamian mathematics will stand.

From the period before Alexander the Great, no Greek mathematical documents have been preserved except for fragmentary paraphrases, and, even for the subsequent period, it is well to remember that the oldest copies of Euclid's *Elements* are in Byzantine manuscripts dating from the 10th century CE. This stands in complete contrast to the situation described above for Egyptian and Babylonian documents. Although in general outline the present account of Greek mathematics is secure, in such important matters as the origin of the axiomatic method, the pre-Euclidean theory of ratios, and the discovery of the conic sections, historians have given competing accounts based on fragmentary texts, quotations of early writings culled from nonmathematical sources, and a considerable amount of conjecture.

Many important treatises from the early period of Islamic mathematics have not survived or have survived only in Latin translations, so that there are still many unanswered questions about the relationship between early Islamic mathematics and the mathematics of Greece and India. In addition, the amount of surviving material from later centuries is so large in comparison with that which has been studied that it is not yet possible to offer any sure judgment of what later Islamic mathematics did not contain, and therefore it is not yet possible to evaluate with any assurance what was original in European mathematics from the 11th to the 15th century.

MATHEMATICS IN ANCIENT MESOPOTAMIA

Until the 1920s it was commonly supposed that mathematics had its birth among the ancient Greeks. What was known of earlier traditions, such as the Egyptian as represented by the Rhind papyrus (edited for the first time only in 1877), offered at best a meagre precedent. This impression gave way to a very different view as Orientalists succeeded in deciphering and interpreting the technical materials from ancient Mesopotamia.

Owing to the durability of the Mesopotamian scribes' clay tablets, the surviving evidence of this culture is substantial. Existing specimens of mathematics represent all the major eras—the Sumerian kingdoms of the 3rd millennium BCE, the Akkadian and Babylonian regimes (2nd millennium), and the empires of the Assyrians (early 1st millennium), Persians (6th through 4th centuries BCE), and Greeks (3rd century BCE to 1st century CE). The level of competence was already high as early as the Old Babylonian dynasty, the time of the lawgiver-king Hammurabi (c. 18th century BCE), but after that there were few notable advances. The application of mathematics to astronomy, however, flourished during the Persian and Seleucid (Greek) periods.

THE NUMERAL SYSTEM AND ARITHMETIC OPERATIONS

Unlike the Egyptians, the mathematicians of the Old Babylonian period went far beyond the immediate challenges of their official accounting duties. For example, they introduced a versatile numeral system, which, like the modern system, exploited the notion of place value, and they developed computational methods that took advantage of this means of expressing numbers. They also solved linear and quadratic problems by methods much like those now used in algebra. Their success with the study of what are now called Pythagorean number triples was a remarkable feat in number theory. The scribes who made such discoveries must have believed mathematics to be worthy of study in its own right, not just as a practical tool.

The older Sumerian system of numerals followed an additive decimal (base-10) principle similar to that of the Egyptians. But the Old Babylonian system converted this into a place-value system with the base of 60 (sexagesimal).

The reasons for the choice of 60 are obscure, but one good mathematical reason might have been the existence of so many divisors (2, 3, 4, and 5, and some multiples) of the base, which would have greatly facilitated the operation of division. For numbers from 1 to 59, the symbols 𒁹 for 1 and 𒌋 for 10 were combined in the simple additive manner (e.g., 𒌍𒁹𒁹 represented 32). But, to express larger values, the Babylonians applied the concept of place value: for example, 60 was written as 𒁹, 70 as 𒁹𒌋, 80 as 𒁹𒌋𒌋, and so on. In fact, 𒁹 could represent any power of 60. The context determined which power was intended. The Babylonians appear to have developed a placeholder symbol that functioned as a zero by the 3rd century BCE, but its precise meaning and use is still uncertain. Furthermore, they had no mark to separate numbers into integral and fractional parts (as with the modern decimal point). Thus, the three-place numeral 3 7 30 could represent $3\,1/_8$ (i.e., $3 + 7/60 + 30/60^2$), $187\,1/_2$ (i.e., $3 \times 60 + 7 + 30/60$), 11,250 (i.e., $3 \times 60^2 + 7 \times 60 + 30$), or a multiple of these numbers by any power of 60.

The four arithmetic operations were performed in the same way as in the modern decimal system, except that carrying occurred whenever a sum reached 60 rather than 10. Multiplication was facilitated by means of tables; one typical tablet lists the multiples of a number by 1, 2, 3,..., 19, 20, 30, 40, and 50. To multiply two numbers several places long, the scribe first broke the problem down into several multiplications, each by a one-place number, and then looked up the value of each product in the appropriate tables. He found the answer to the problem by adding up these intermediate results. These tables also assisted in division, for the values that head them were all reciprocals of regular numbers.

Regular numbers are those whose prime factors divide the base. The reciprocals of such numbers thus have only a finite number of places (by contrast, the reciprocals of nonregular numbers produce an infinitely repeating numeral). In base 10, for example, only numbers with factors of 2 and 5 (e.g., 8 or 50) are regular, and the reciprocals (1/8 = 0.125, 1/50 = 0.02) have finite expressions; but the reciprocals of other numbers (such as 3 and 7) repeat infinitely (0.$\overline{3}$ and 0.$\overline{142857}$, respectively, where the bar indicates the digits that continually repeat). In base 60, only numbers with factors of 2, 3, and 5 are regular. For example, 6 and 54 are regular, so that their reciprocals (10 and 1 6 40) are finite. The entries in the multiplication table for 1 6 40 are thus simultaneously multiples of its reciprocal 1/54. To divide a number by any regular number, then, one can consult the table of multiples for its reciprocal.

Babylonian mathematical tablet. Yale Babylonian Collection

An interesting tablet in the collection of Yale University shows a square with its diagonals. On one side is written "30," under one diagonal "42 25 35," and right along the same diagonal "1 24 51 10" (i.e., $1 + 24/60 + 51/60^2 + 10/60^3$). This third number is the correct value of $\sqrt{2}$ to four sexagesimal places (equivalent in the decimal system to 1.414213..., which is too low by only 1 in the seventh place), while the second number is the product of the third number and the first and so gives the length of the diagonal when the side is 30. The scribe thus appears to have known an equivalent of the familiar long method of finding square roots. An additional element of sophistication is that, by choosing 30 (that is, 1/2) for the side, the scribe obtained as the diagonal the reciprocal of the value of $\sqrt{2}$ (since $\sqrt{2}/2 = 1/\sqrt{2}$), a result useful for purposes of division.

GEOMETRIC AND ALGEBRAIC PROBLEMS

In a Babylonian tablet now in Berlin, the diagonal of a rectangle of sides 40 and 10 is solved as $40 + 10^2/(2 \times 40)$. Here a very effective approximating rule is being used (that the square root of the sum of $a^2 + b^2$ can be estimated as $a + b^2/2a$), the same rule found frequently in later Greek geometric writings. Both these examples for roots illustrate the Babylonians' arithmetic approach in geometry. They also show that the Babylonians were aware of the relation between the hypotenuse and the two legs of a right triangle (now commonly known as the Pythagorean theorem) more than a thousand years before the Greeks used it.

A type of problem that occurs frequently in the Babylonian tablets seeks the base and height of a rectangle, where their product and sum have specified values. From the given information the scribe worked out the difference, since $(b - h)^2 = (b + h)^2 - 4bh$. In the same way, if the product and difference were given, the sum could be found. And, once both the sum and difference were known, each side could be determined, for $2b = (b + h) + (b - h)$ and $2h = (b + h) - (b - h)$. This procedure is equivalent to a solution of the general quadratic in one unknown. In some places, however, the Babylonian scribes solved quadratic problems in terms of a single unknown, just as would now be done by means of the quadratic formula.

Although these Babylonian quadratic procedures have often been described as the earliest appearance of algebra, there are important distinctions. The scribes lacked an algebraic symbolism. Although they must certainly have understood that their solution procedures were general, they always presented them in terms of particular cases, rather than as the working through of general formulas and identities. They thus lacked the means for presenting general derivations and proofs of their solution procedures. Their use of sequential procedures rather than formulas, however, is less likely to detract from an evaluation of their effort now that algorithmic methods much like theirs have become commonplace through the development of computers.

As mentioned above, the Babylonian scribes knew that the base (b), height (h), and diagonal (d) of a rectangle satisfy the relation $b^2 + h^2 = d^2$. If one selects values at random for two of the terms, the third will usually be irrational, but it is possible to find cases in which all three terms are integers: for example, 3, 4, 5 and 5, 12, 13. (Such solutions are sometimes called Pythagorean triples.) A tablet in the Columbia University Collection presents a list of 15 such triples. Decimal equivalents are shown in parentheses at the right. The gaps in the expressions for h, b, and d separate the place values in the sexagesimal numerals:

h	b	d			
2	1 59	2 49	(120	119	169)
57 36	56 7	1 20 45	(3,456	3,367	4,825)
1 20	1 16 41	1 50 49	(4,800	4,601	6,649)
3 45	3 31 49	5 9 1	(13,500	12,709	18,541)
1 12	1 5	1 37	(72	65	97)
...	...	...	...	...	...
1 30	56	1 46	(90	56	106)

(The entries in the column for h have to be computed from the values for b and d, for they do not appear on the tablet, but they must once have existed on a portion now missing.) The ordering of the lines becomes clear from another column, listing the values of d^2/h^2 (brackets indicate figures that are lost or illegible), which form a continually decreasing sequence: [1 59 0] 15, [1 56 56] 58 14 50 6 15,..., [1] 23 13 46 40. Accordingly, the angle formed between the diagonal and the base in this sequence increases continually from just over 45° to just under 60°. Other properties of the sequence suggest that the scribe knew the general procedure for finding all such number triples—that for any integers p and q, $2d/h = p/q + q/p$ and $2b/h = p/q - q/p$. (In the table the implied values p and q turn out to be regular numbers falling in the standard set of reciprocals, as mentioned earlier in connection with the multiplication tables.) Scholars are still debating nuances of the construction and the intended use of this table, but no one questions the high level of expertise implied by it.

MATHEMATICAL ASTRONOMY

The sexagesimal method developed by the Babylonians has a far greater computational potential than what was actually needed for the older problem texts. With the development of mathematical astronomy in the Seleucid period, however, it became indispensable. Astronomers sought to predict future occurrences of important phenomena, such as lunar eclipses and critical points in planetary cycles (conjunctions, oppositions, stationary points, and first and last visibility). They devised a technique for computing these positions (expressed in terms of degrees of latitude and longitude, measured relative to the path of the Sun's apparent annual motion) by successively adding appropriate terms in arithmetic progression. The results were then organized into a table listing positions as far ahead as the scribe chose. (Although the method is purely arithmetic, one can interpret it graphically: the tabulated values form a linear "zigzag" approximation to what is actually a sinusoidal variation.) While observations extending over centuries are required for finding the necessary parameters (e.g., periods, angular range between maximum and minimum values, and the like), only the computational apparatus at their disposal made the astronomers' forecasting effort possible.

Within a relatively short time (perhaps a century or less), the elements of this system came into the hands of the Greeks. Although Hipparchus (2nd century BCE) favoured the geometric approach of his Greek predecessors, he took over parameters from the Mesopotamians and adopted their sexagesimal style of computation. Through the Greeks it passed to Arab scientists during the Middle Ages and thence to Europe, where it remained prominent in mathematical astronomy during the Renaissance and the early modern period. To this day it persists in the use of minutes and seconds to measure time and angles.

Aspects of the Old Babylonian mathematics may have come to the Greeks even earlier, perhaps in the 5th century BCE, the formative period of Greek geometry. There are a number of parallels that scholars have noted: for example, the Greek technique of "application of area" corresponded to the Babylonian quadratic methods (although in a geometric, not arithmetic, form). Further, the Babylonian rule for estimating square roots was widely used in Greek geometric computations, and there may also have been some shared nuances of technical terminology. Although details of the timing and manner of such a transmission are obscure because of the absence of explicit documentation, it seems that Western mathematics, while stemming largely from the Greeks, is considerably indebted to the older Mesopotamians.

MATHEMATICS IN ANCIENT EGYPT

The introduction of writing in Egypt in the predynastic period (*c.* 3000 BCE) brought with it the formation of a special class of literate professionals, the scribes. By virtue of their writing skills, the scribes took on all the duties of a civil service: record keeping, tax accounting, the management of public works (building projects and the like), even the prosecution of war through overseeing military supplies and payrolls. Young men enrolled in scribal schools to learn the essentials of the trade, which included not only reading and writing but also the basics of mathematics.

One of the texts popular as a copy exercise in the schools of the New Kingdom (13th century BCE) was a satiric letter in which one scribe, Hori, taunts his rival, Amen-em-opet, for his incompetence as an adviser and manager. "You are the clever scribe at the head of the troops," Hori chides at one point:

> *a ramp is to be built, 730 cubits long, 55 cubits wide, with 120 compartments—it is 60 cubits high, 30 cubits in the middle... and the generals and the scribes turn to you and say, "You are a clever scribe, your name is famous. Is there anything you don't know? Answer us, how many bricks are needed?" Let each compartment be 30 cubits by 7 cubits.*

This problem, and three others like it in the same letter, cannot be solved without further data. But the point of the humour is clear, as Hori challenges his rival with these hard, but typical, tasks.

What is known of Egyptian mathematics tallies well with the tests posed by the scribe Hori. The information comes primarily from two long papyrus documents that once served as textbooks within scribal schools. The Rhind papyrus (in the British Museum) is a copy made in the 17th century BCE of a text two centuries older still. In it is found a long table of fractional parts to help with division, followed by the solutions of 84 specific problems in arithmetic and geometry. The Golenishchev papyrus (in the Moscow Museum of Fine Arts), dating from the 19th century BCE, presents 25 problems of a similar type. These problems reflect well the functions the scribes would perform, for they deal with how to distribute beer and bread as wages, for example, and how to measure the areas of fields as well as the volumes of pyramids and other solids.

The Numeral System and Arithmetic Operations

The Egyptians, like the Romans after them, expressed numbers according to a decimal scheme, using separate

Ancient Egyptian hieroglyphic numeral system

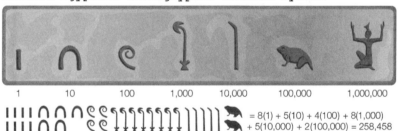

Ancient Egyptians customarily wrote from right to left. Because they did not have a positional system, they needed separate symbols for each power of 10. Encyclopædia Britannica, Inc.

symbols for 1, 10, 100, 1,000, and so on. Each symbol appeared in the expression for a number as many times as the value it represented occurred in the number itself. For example, ∩∩|||| stood for 24. This rather cumbersome notation was used within the hieroglyphic writing found in stone inscriptions and other formal texts, but in the papyrus documents the scribes employed a more convenient abbreviated script, called hieratic writing, where, for example, 24 was written ⅄—.

In such a system, addition and subtraction amount to counting how many symbols of each kind there are in the numerical expressions and then rewriting with the resulting number of symbols. The texts that survive do not reveal what, if any, special procedures the scribes used to assist in this. But for multiplication they introduced a method of successive doubling. For example, to multiply

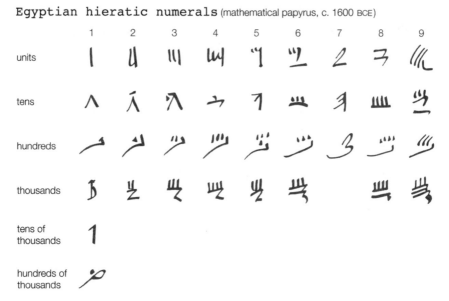

Egyptian hieratic numerals (mathematical papyrus, c. 1600 BCE)

Encyclopædia Britannica, Inc.

28 by 11, one constructs a table of multiples of 28 like the following:

1	28
2	56
4	112
8	224
16	448
...	...

The several entries in the first column that together sum to 11 (i.e., 8, 2, and 1) are checked off. The product is then found by adding up the multiples corresponding to these entries; thus, 224 + 56 + 28 = 308, the desired product.

To divide 308 by 28, the Egyptians applied the same procedure in reverse. Using the same table as in the multiplication problem, one can see that 8 produces the largest multiple of 28 that is less then 308 (for the entry at 16 is already 448), and 8 is checked off. The process is then repeated, this time for the remainder (84) obtained by subtracting the entry at 8 (224) from the original number (308). This, however, is already smaller than the entry at 4, which consequently is ignored, but it is greater than the entry at 2 (56), which is then checked off. The process is repeated again for the remainder obtained by subtracting 56 from the previous remainder of 84, or 28, which also happens to exactly equal the entry at 1 and which is then checked off. The entries that have been checked off are added up, yielding the quotient: 8 + 2 + 1 = 11. (In most cases, of course, there is a remainder that is less than the divisor.)

For larger numbers this procedure can be improved by considering multiples of one of the factors by 10, 20, ... or even by higher orders of magnitude (100, 1,000, ...), as necessary (in the Egyptian decimal notation, these multiples are easy to work out). Thus, one can find the product of 28 by 27 by setting out the multiples of 28 by 1, 2, 4, 8, 10, and 20. Since the entries 1, 2, 4, and 20 add up to

27, one has only to add up the corresponding multiples to find the answer.

Computations involving fractions are carried out under the restriction to unit parts (that is, fractions that in modern notation are written with 1 as the numerator). To express the result of dividing 4 by 7, for instance, which in modern notation is simply 4/7, the scribe wrote 1/2 + 1/14. The procedure for finding quotients in this form merely extends the usual method for the division of integers, where one now inspects the entries for 2/3, 1/3, 1/6, etc., and 1/2, 1/4, 1/8, etc., until the corresponding multiples of the divisor sum to the dividend. (The scribes included 2/3, one may observe, even though it is not a unit fraction.) In practice the procedure can sometimes become quite complicated (for example, the value for 2/29 is given in the Rhind papyrus as 1/24 + 1/58 + 1/174 + 1/232) and can be worked out in different ways (for example, the same 2/29 might be found as 1/15 + 1/435 or as 1/16 + 1/232 + 1/464, etc.). A considerable portion of the papyrus texts is devoted to tables to facilitate the finding of such unit-fraction values.

These elementary operations are all that one needs for solving the arithmetic problems in the papyri. For example, "to divide 6 loaves among 10 men" (Rhind papyrus, problem 3), one merely divides to get the answer 1/2 + 1/10. In one group of problems, an interesting trick is used: "A quantity (*aha*) and its 7th together make 19 — what is it?" (Rhind papyrus, problem 24). Here one first supposes the quantity to be 7: since $1^1/_7$ of it becomes 8, not 19, one takes 19/8 (that is, 2 + 1/4 + 1/8), and its multiple by 7 (16 + 1/2 + 1/8) becomes the required answer. This type of procedure (sometimes called the method of "false position" or "false assumption") is familiar in many other arithmetic traditions (e.g., the Chinese, Hindu, Muslim, and Renaissance European), although they appear to have no direct link to the Egyptian.

Geometry

The geometric problems in the papyri seek measurements of figures, like rectangles and triangles of given base and height, by means of suitable arithmetic operations. In a more complicated problem, a rectangle is sought whose area is 12 and whose height is 1/2 + 1/4 times its base (Golenishchev papyrus, problem 6). To solve the problem, the ratio is inverted and multiplied by the area, yielding 16. The square root of the result (4) is the base of the rectangle, and 1/2 + 1/4 times 4, or 3, is the height. The entire process is analogous to the process of solving the algebraic equation for the problem ($x \times \frac{3}{4}x = 12$), though without the use of a letter for the unknown. An interesting procedure is used to find the area of the circle (Rhind papyrus, problem 50): 1/9 of the diameter is discarded, and the result is squared. For example, if the diameter is 9, the area is set equal to 64. The scribe recognized that the area of a circle is proportional to the square of the diameter and assumed for the constant of proportionality (that is, $\pi/4$) the value 64/81. This is a rather good estimate, being about 0.6 percent too large. (It is not as close, however, as the now common estimate of $3\frac{1}{7}$, first proposed by Archimedes, which is only about 0.04 percent too large.) But there is nothing in the papyri indicating that the scribes were aware that this rule was only approximate rather than exact.

A remarkable result is the rule for the volume of the truncated pyramid (Golenishchev papyrus, problem 14). The scribe assumes the height to be 6, the base to be a square of side 4, and the top a square of side 2. He multiplies one-third the height times 28, finding the volume to be 56; here 28 is computed from $2 \times 2 + 2 \times 4 + 4 \times 4$. Since this is correct, it can be assumed that the scribe also knew the general rule: $A = (h/3)(a^2 + ab + b^2)$. How the scribes actually derived the rule is a matter for debate, but it is reasonable to suppose that they were aware of related rules, such as that for the volume of a pyramid: one-third the height times the area of the base.

The Egyptians employed the equivalent of similar triangles to measure distances. For instance, the *seked* of a pyramid is stated as the number of palms in the horizontal corresponding to a rise of one cubit (seven palms). Thus, if the *seked* is 5¼ and the base is 140 cubits, the

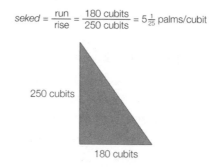

$$seked = \frac{run}{rise} = \frac{180 \text{ cubits}}{250 \text{ cubits}} = 5\tfrac{1}{25} \text{ palms/cubit}$$

250 cubits

180 cubits

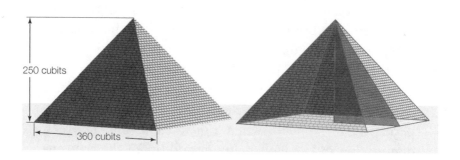

250 cubits

360 cubits

The Egyptians defined the seked *as the ratio of the run to the rise, which is the reciprocal of the modern definition of the slope.* Encyclopædia Britannica, Inc.

height becomes 93⅓ cubits (Rhind papyrus, problem 57). The Greek sage Thales of Miletus (6th century BCE) is said to have measured the height of pyramids by means of their shadows (the report derives from Hieronymus, a disciple of Aristotle in the 4th century BCE). In light of the *seked* computations, however, this report must indicate an aspect of Egyptian surveying that extended back at least 1,000 years before the time of Thales.

Assessment of Egyptian Mathematics

The papyri thus bear witness to a mathematical tradition closely tied to the practical accounting and surveying activities of the scribes. Occasionally, the scribes loosened up a bit: one problem (Rhind papyrus, problem 79), for example, seeks the total from seven houses, seven cats per house, seven mice per cat, seven ears of wheat per mouse, and seven *hekat* of grain per ear (result: 19,607). Certainly the scribe's interest in progressions (for which he appears to have a rule) goes beyond practical considerations. Other than this, however, Egyptian mathematics falls firmly within the range of practice.

Even allowing for the scantiness of the documentation that survives, the Egyptian achievement in mathematics must be viewed as modest. Its most striking features are competence and continuity. The scribes managed to work out the basic arithmetic and geometry necessary for their official duties as civil managers, and their methods persisted with little evident change for at least a millennium, perhaps two. Indeed, when Egypt came under Greek domination in the Hellenistic period (from the 3rd century BCE onward), the older school methods continued. Quite remarkably, the older unit-fraction methods are still prominent in Egyptian school papyri written in the demotic (Egyptian) and Greek languages as late as the 7th century CE, for example.

To the extent that Egyptian mathematics left a legacy at all, it was through its impact on the emerging Greek mathematical tradition between the 6th and 4th centuries BCE. Because the documentation from this period is limited, the manner and significance of the influence can only be conjectured. But the report about Thales measuring the height of pyramids is only one of several such accounts of Greek intellectuals learning from Egyptians. Herodotus and Plato describe with approval Egyptian practices in the teaching and application of mathematics. This literary evidence has historical support, since the Greeks maintained continuous trade and military operations in Egypt from the 7th century BCE onward. It is thus plausible that basic precedents for the Greeks' earliest mathematical efforts—how they dealt with fractional parts or measured areas and volumes, or their use of ratios in connection with similar figures—came from the learning of the ancient Egyptian scribes.

GREEK MATHEMATICS

When mathematics appeared in Greece, the discipline emerged from being a collective endeavour to an activity performed by individuals whose names are known to history. Among the greatest Greek mathematicians were Euclid, Archimedes, and Apollonius.

THE DEVELOPMENT OF PURE MATHEMATICS

It was not until the Greeks that "pure" mathematics arose. As it is known today, some branches of mathematics may have no immediate practical application but are studied only because of the intellectual delight they give to their practitioners. For this we have the mathematicians of ancient Greece to thank.

THE PRE-EUCLIDEAN PERIOD

The Greeks divided the field of mathematics into arithmetic (the study of "multitude," or discrete quantity) and geometry (that of "magnitude," or continuous quantity) and considered both to have originated in practical activities. Proclus, in his *Commentary on Euclid*, observes that geometry—literally, "measurement of land"—first arose in surveying practices among the ancient Egyptians, for the flooding of the Nile compelled them each year to redefine the boundaries of properties. Similarly, arithmetic started with the commerce and trade of Phoenician merchants. Although Proclus wrote quite late in the ancient period

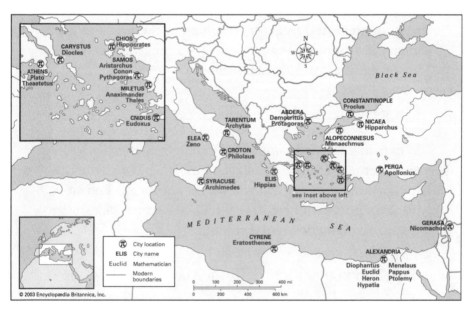

This map spans a millennium of prominent Greco-Roman mathematicians, from Thales of Miletus (c. 600 BCE) to Hypatia of Alexandria (c. 400 CE). Their names are located on the map under their cities of birth.

(in the 5th century CE), his account drew upon views proposed much earlier—by Herodotus (mid-5th century BCE), for example, and by Eudemus, a disciple of Aristotle (late 4th century BCE).

However plausible, this view is difficult to check, for there is only meagre evidence of practical mathematics from the early Greek period (roughly, the 8th through the 4th century BCE). Inscriptions on stone, for example, reveal use of a numeral system the same in principle as the familiar Roman numerals. Herodotus seems to have known of the abacus as an aid for computation by both Greeks and Egyptians, and about a dozen stone specimens of Greek abaci survive from the 5th and 4th centuries BCE. In the surveying of new cities in the Greek colonies of the 6th and 5th centuries, there was regular use of a standard length of 70 *plethra* (one *plethron* equals 100 feet) as the diagonal of a square of side 50 *plethra*. In fact, the actual diagonal of the square is $50\sqrt{2}$ *plethra*, so this was equivalent to using 7/5 (or 1.4) as an estimate for $\sqrt{2}$, which is now known to equal 1.414.... In the 6th century BCE, the engineer Eupalinus of Megara directed an aqueduct through a mountain on the island of Samos, and historians still debate how he did it. In a further indication of the practical aspects of early Greek mathematics, Plato describes in his *Laws* how the Egyptians drilled their children in practical problems in arithmetic and geometry. He clearly considered this a model for the Greeks to imitate.

Such hints about the nature of early Greek practical mathematics are confirmed in later sources—for example, in the arithmetic problems in papyrus texts from Ptolemaic Egypt (from the 3rd century BCE onward) and the geometric manuals by Heron of Alexandria (1st century CE). In its basic manner, this Greek tradition was much like the earlier traditions in Egypt and Mesopotamia. Indeed, it is likely that the Greeks borrowed from such older sources to some extent.

What was distinctive of the Greeks' contribution to mathematics—and what in effect made them the creators of "mathematics," as the term is usually understood—was its development as a theoretical discipline. This means two things: mathematical statements are general, and they are confirmed by proof. For example, the Mesopotamians had procedures for finding whole numbers a, b, and c for which $a^2 + b^2 = c^2$ (e.g., 3, 4, 5; 5, 12, 13; or 119, 120, 169). From the Greeks came a proof of a general rule for finding all such sets of numbers (now called Pythagorean triples): if one takes any whole numbers p and q, both being even or both odd, then $a = (p^2 - q^2)/2$, $b = pq$, and $c = (p^2 + q^2)/2$. As Euclid proves in Book X of the *Elements*, numbers of this form satisfy the relation for Pythagorean triples. Further, the Mesopotamians appear to have understood that sets of such numbers a, b, and c form the sides of right triangles, but the Greeks proved this result (Euclid, in fact, proves it twice: in *Elements*, Book I, proposition 47, and in a more general form in *Elements*, Book VI, proposition 31), and these proofs occur in the context of a systematic presentation of the properties of plane geometric figures.

The *Elements*, composed by Euclid of Alexandria about 300 BCE, was the pivotal contribution to theoretical geometry, but the transition from practical to theoretical mathematics had occurred much earlier, sometime in the 5th century BCE. Initiated by men like Pythagoras of Samos (late 6th century) and Hippocrates of Chios (late 5th century), the theoretical form of geometry was advanced by others, most prominently the Pythagorean Archytas of Tarentum, Theaetetus of Athens, and Eudoxus of Cnidus (4th century). Because the actual writings of these men do not survive, knowledge about their work depends on remarks made by later writers. While even this limited evidence reveals how heavily Euclid depended on them, it does not set out clearly the motives behind their studies.

It is thus a matter of debate how and why this theoretical transition took place. A frequently cited factor is the discovery of irrational numbers. The early Pythagoreans held that "all things are number." This might be taken to mean that any geometric measure can be associated with some number (that is, some whole number or fraction; in modern terminology, rational number), for in Greek usage the term for number, *arithmos*, refers exclusively to whole numbers or, in some contexts, to ordinary fractions. This assumption is common enough in practice, as when the length of a given line is said to be so many feet plus a fractional part. However, it breaks down for the lines that form the side and diagonal of the square. (For example, if it is supposed that the ratio between the side and diagonal may be expressed as the ratio of two whole numbers, it can be shown that both of these numbers must be even. This is impossible, since every fraction may be expressed as a ratio of two whole numbers having no common factors.) Geometrically, this means that there is no length that could serve as a unit of measure of both the side and diagonal. That is, the side and diagonal cannot each equal the same length multiplied by (different) whole numbers. Accordingly, the Greeks called such pairs of lengths "incommensurable." (In modern terminology, unlike that of the Greeks, the term "number" is applied to such quantities as $\sqrt{2}$, but they are called irrational.)

This result was already well known at the time of Plato and may well have been discovered within the school of Pythagoras in the 5th century BCE, as some late authorities like Pappus of Alexandria (4th century CE) maintain. In any case, by 400 BCE it was known that lines corresponding to $\sqrt{3}$, $\sqrt{5}$, and other square roots are incommensurable with a fixed unit length. The more general result, the geometric equivalent of the theorem that $\sqrt{p}$ is irrational whenever p is not a rational square number, is associated with Plato's friend Theaetetus. Both Theaetetus and Eudoxus contributed to the further study of irrationals, and their followers collected the results into a substantial theory, as represented by the 115 propositions of Book X of the *Elements*.

The discovery of irrationals must have affected the very nature of early mathematical research, for it made clear that arithmetic was insufficient for the purposes of geometry, despite the assumptions made in practical work. Further, once such seemingly obvious assumptions as the commensurability of all lines turned out to be in fact false, then in principle all mathematical assumptions were rendered suspect. At the least it became necessary to justify carefully all claims made about mathematics. Even more basically, it became necessary to establish what a reasoning has to be like to qualify as a proof. Apparently, Hippocrates of Chios, in the 5th century BCE, and others soon after him had already begun the work of organizing geometric results into a systematic form in textbooks called "elements" (meaning "fundamental results" of geometry). These were to serve as sources for Euclid in his comprehensive textbook a century later.

The early mathematicians were not an isolated group but part of a larger, intensely competitive intellectual environment of pre-Socratic thinkers in Ionia and Italy, as well as Sophists at Athens. By insisting that only permanent things could have real existence, the philosopher Parmenides (5th century BCE) called into question the most basic claims about knowledge itself. In contrast, Heracleitus (*c.* 500 BCE) maintained that all permanence is an illusion, for the things that are perceived arise through a subtle balance of opposing tensions. What is meant by "knowledge" and "proof" thus came into debate.

Mathematical issues were often drawn into these debates. For some, like the Pythagoreans (and, later, Plato), the certainty of mathematics was held as a model for reasoning in other areas, like politics and ethics. But for others mathematics seemed prone to contradiction. Zeno of Elea (5th century BCE) posed paradoxes about quantity and motion. In one such paradox, it is assumed that a line can be bisected again and again without limit. If the division ultimately results in a set of points of zero length, then even infinitely many of them sum up only to zero, but, if it results in tiny line segments, then their sum will be infinite. In effect, the length of the given line must be both zero and infinite. In the 5th century BCE, a solution of such paradoxes was attempted by Democritus and the atomists, philosophers who held that all material bodies are ultimately made up of invisibly small "atoms" (the Greek word *atomon* means "indivisible"). But in geometry such a view came into conflict with the existence of incommensurable lines, since the atoms would become the measuring units of all lines, even incommensurable ones. Democritus and the Sophist Protagoras puzzled over whether the tangent to a circle meets it at a point or a line. The Sophists Antiphon and Bryson (both 5th century BCE) considered how to compare the circle to polygons inscribed in it.

The pre-Socratics thus revealed difficulties in specific assumptions about the infinitely many and the infinitely small and about the relation of geometry to physical reality, as well as in more general conceptions like "existence" and "proof." Philosophical questions such as these need not have affected the technical researches of mathematicians, but they did make them aware of difficulties that could bear on fundamental matters and so made them the more cautious in defining their subject matter.

Any such review of the possible effects of factors such as these is purely conjectural, since the sources are fragmentary and never make explicit how the mathematicians responded to the issues that were raised. But it is the particular concern over fundamental assumptions and proofs that distinguishes Greek mathematics from the earlier traditions. Plausible factors behind this concern can be identified in the special circumstances of the early Greek tradition—its technical discoveries and its cultural environment—even if it is not possible to describe in detail how these changes took place.

THE *ELEMENTS*

The principal source for reconstructing pre-Euclidean mathematics is Euclid's *Elements*, for the major part of its contents can be traced back to research from the 4th century BCE and in some cases even earlier. The first four books present constructions and proofs of plane geometric figures: Book I deals with the congruence of triangles, the properties of parallel lines, and the area relations of triangles and parallelograms. Book II establishes equalities relating to squares, rectangles, and triangles. Book III covers basic properties of circles, and Book IV sets out constructions of polygons in circles. Much of the content of Books I–III was already familiar to Hippocrates, and the material of Book IV can be associated with the Pythagoreans, so that this portion of the *Elements* has roots in 5th-century research. It is known, however, that questions about parallels were debated in Aristotle's school (*c.* 350 BCE), and so it may be assumed that efforts to prove results—such as the theorem stating that, for any given line and given point, there always exists a unique line through that point and parallel to the line—were tried and failed. Thus, the decision to found the theory of parallels on a postulate, as in Book I of the *Elements*, must have been a relatively recent development in Euclid's time. (The postulate would later become the subject of much study, and in modern times it led to the discovery of the so-called non-Euclidean geometries.)

Book V sets out a general theory of proportion—that is, a theory that does not require any restriction to commensurable magnitudes. This general theory derives from Eudoxus. On the basis of the theory, Book VI describes the properties of similar plane rectilinear figures and so generalizes the congruence theory of Book I. It appears that the technique of similar figures was already known in the 5th century BCE, even though a fully valid justification could not have been given before Eudoxus worked out his theory of proportion.

Books VII–IX deal with what the Greeks called "arithmetic," the theory of whole numbers. It includes the properties of numerical proportions, greatest common divisors, least common multiples, and relative primes (Book VII); propositions on numerical progressions and square and cube numbers (Book VIII); and special results, like unique factorization into primes, the existence of an unlimited number of primes, and the formation of "perfect numbers"—that is, those numbers that equal the sum of their proper divisors (Book IX). In some form Book VII stems from Theaetetus and Book VIII from Archytas.

Book X presents a theory of irrational lines and derives from the work of Theaetetus and Eudoxus. The remaining books treat the geometry of solids. Book XI sets out results on solid figures analogous to those for planes in Books I and VI. Book XII proves theorems on the ratios of circles, the ratios of spheres, and the volumes of pyramids and cones. Book XIII shows how to inscribe the five regular solids—known as the Platonic solids—in a given sphere (compare the constructions of plane figures in Book IV). The measurement of curved figures in Book XII is inferred from that of rectilinear figures. For a particular curved figure, a sequence of rectilinear figures is considered in which succeeding figures in the sequence become continually closer to the curved figure—the particular method used by Euclid derives from Eudoxus. The solid constructions in Book XIII derive from Theaetetus.

In sum the *Elements* gathered together the whole field of elementary geometry and arithmetic that had developed in the two centuries before Euclid. Doubtless, Euclid must be credited with particular aspects of this work, certainly with its editing as a comprehensive whole. But it is not possible to identify for certain even a single one of its results as having been his discovery. Other, more advanced fields, though not touched on in the *Elements*, were already being vigorously studied in Euclid's time, in some cases by Euclid himself. For these fields his textbook, true to its name, provides the appropriate "elementary" introduction.

One such field is the study of geometric constructions. Euclid, like geometers in the generation before him, divided mathematical propositions into two kinds: "theorems" and "problems." A theorem makes the claim that all terms of a certain description have a specified property; a problem seeks the construction of a term that is to have a specified property. In the *Elements* all the problems are constructible on the basis of three stated postulates: that a line can be constructed by joining two given points, that a given line segment can be extended in a line indefinitely, and that a circle can be constructed with a given point as centre and a given line segment as radius. These postulates in effect restricted the constructions to the use of the so-called Euclidean tools—i.e., a compass and a straightedge or unmarked ruler.

THE THREE CLASSICAL PROBLEMS

Although Euclid solves more than 100 construction problems in the *Elements*, many more were posed whose solutions required more than just compass and straightedge. Three such problems stimulated so much interest among later geometers that they have come to be known as the "classical problems": doubling the cube (i.e., constructing a cube whose volume is twice that of a given cube), trisecting the angle, and squaring the circle. Even in the pre-Euclidean period, the effort to construct a square equal in area to a given circle had begun. Some related results came from Hippocrates. Others were reported from Antiphon and Bryson, and Euclid's theorem on the circle in *Elements*, Book XII, proposition 2, which states that circles are in the ratio of the squares of their diameters, was important for this search. But the first actual constructions (not, it must be noted, by means of the Euclidean tools, for this is impossible) came only in the 3rd century BCE. The early history of angle trisection is obscure. Presumably, it was attempted in the pre-Euclidean period, although solutions are known only from the 3rd century or later.

There are several successful efforts at doubling the cube that date from the pre-Euclidean period, however. Hippocrates showed that the problem could be reduced to that of finding two mean proportionals: if for a given line a it is necessary to find x such that $x^3 = 2a^3$, lines x and y may be sought such that $a:x = x:y = y:2a$; for then $a^3/x^3 = (a/x)^3 = (a/x)(x/y)(y/2a) = a/2a = 1/2$. (Note that the same argument holds for any multiplier, not just the number 2.) Thus, the cube can be doubled if it is possible to find the two mean proportionals x and y between the two given lines a and $2a$. Constructions of the problem of the two means were proposed by Archytas, Eudoxus, and Menaechmus in the

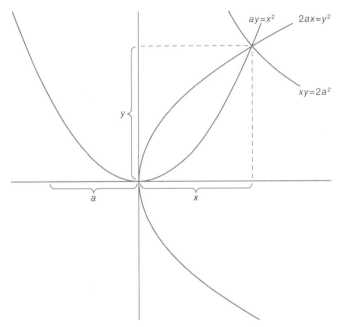

In the 4th century BCE, Menaechmus gave a solution to the problem of doubling the volume of a cube. In particular, he showed that the intersection of any two of the three curves that he constructed (two parabolas and one hyperbola) based on a side (a) of the original cube will produce a line (x) such that the cube produced with it has twice the volume of the original cube. Encyclopædia Britannica, Inc.

4th century BCE. Menaechmus, for example, constructed three curves corresponding to these same proportions: $x^2 = ay$, $y^2 = 2ax$, and $xy = 2a^2$. The intersection of any two of them then produces the line x that solves the problem. Menaechmus's curves are conic sections: the first two are parabolas, the third a hyperbola. Thus, it is often claimed that Menaechmus originated the study of the conic sections. Indeed, Proclus and his older authority, Geminus (mid-1st century CE), appear to have held this view. The evidence does not indicate how Menaechmus actually conceived of the curves, however, so it is possible that the formal study of the conic sections as such did not begin until later, near the time of Euclid. Both Euclid and an older contemporary, Aristaeus, composed treatments (now lost) of the theory of conic sections.

In seeking the solutions of problems, geometers developed a special technique, which they called "analysis." They assumed the problem to have been solved and then, by investigating the properties of this solution, worked back to find an equivalent problem that could be solved on the basis of the givens. To obtain the formally correct solution of the original problem, then, geometers reversed the procedure: first the data were used to solve the equivalent problem derived in the analysis, and, from the solution obtained, the original problem was then solved. In contrast to analysis, this reversed procedure is called "synthesis."

Menaechmus's cube duplication is an example of analysis: he assumed the mean proportionals x and y and then discovered them to be equivalent to the result of intersecting the three curves whose construction he could take as known. (The synthesis consists of introducing the curves, finding their intersection, and showing that this solves the problem.) It is clear that geometers of the 4th century BCE were well acquainted with this method, but Euclid provides only syntheses, never analyses, of the problems solved in the *Elements*. Certainly in the cases of the more complicated constructions, however, there can be little doubt that some form of analysis preceded the syntheses presented in the *Elements*.

GEOMETRY IN THE 3RD CENTURY BCE

The *Elements* was one of several major efforts by Euclid and others to consolidate the advances made over the 4th century BCE. On the basis of these advances, Greek geometry entered its golden age in the 3rd century. This was a period rich with geometric discoveries, particularly in the solution of problems by analysis and other methods, and was dominated by the achievements of two figures: Archimedes of Syracuse (early 3rd century BCE) and Apollonius of Perga (late 3rd century BCE).

ARCHIMEDES

Archimedes was most noted for his use of the Eudoxean method of exhaustion in the measurement of curved surfaces and volumes and for his applications of geometry to mechanics. To him is owed the first appearance and proof of the approximation $3\frac{1}{7}$ for the ratio of the circumference to the diameter of the circle (what is now designated π). Characteristically, Archimedes went beyond familiar notions, such as that of simple approximation, to more subtle insights, like the notion of bounds. For example, he showed that the perimeters of regular polygons circumscribed about the circle eventually become less than $3\frac{1}{7}$ the diameter as the number of their sides increases (Archimedes established the result for 96-sided polygons). Similarly, the perimeters of the inscribed polygons eventually become greater than $3\frac{10}{71}$. Thus, these two values are upper and lower bounds, respectively, of π.

Archimedes' result bears on the problem of circle quadrature in the light of another theorem he proved: that the area of a circle equals the area of a triangle whose height equals the radius of the circle and whose base equals its circumference. He established analogous results for the sphere showing that the volume of a sphere is equal to that of a cone whose height equals the radius of the sphere and whose base equals its surface area. The surface area of the sphere he found to be four times the area of its greatest circle. Equivalently, the volume of a sphere is shown to

Archimedes. Time & Life Pictures/Getty Images

be two-thirds that of the cylinder which just contains it (that is, having height and diameter equal to the diameter of the sphere), while its surface is also equal to two-thirds that of the same cylinder (that is, if the circles that enclose the cylinder at top and bottom are included). The Greek historian Plutarch (early 2nd century CE) relates that Archimedes requested the figure for this theorem to be engraved on his tombstone, which is confirmed by the

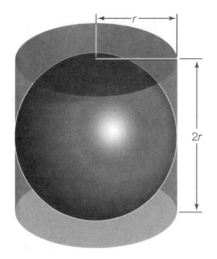

The surface area of a sphere is $4\pi r^2$ and the surface area of the circumscribing cylinder is $6\pi r^2$. Hence, any sphere has two-thirds the surface area of its circumscribing cylinder. Archimedes (d. 212/211 BCE) was so proud of his discovery of this relationship that he had the formula chiseled on his tomb. Encyclopædia Britannica, Inc.

Roman writer Cicero (1st century BCE), who actually located the tomb in 75 BCE, when he was quaestor of Sicily.

APOLLONIUS

The work of Apollonius of Perga extended the field of geometric constructions far beyond the range in the *Elements*. For example, Euclid in Book III shows how to draw a circle so as to pass through three given points or to be tangent to three given lines. Apollonius (in a work called *Tangencies*, which no longer survives) found the circle tangent to three given circles, or tangent to any combination of three points, lines, and circles. (The three-circle tangency construction, one of the most extensively studied geometric problems, has attracted more than 100 different solutions in the modern period.)

Apollonius is best known for his *Conics*, a treatise in eight books (Books I–IV survive in Greek, V–VII in a medieval Arabic translation; Book VIII is lost). The conic sections are the curves formed when a plane intersects the surface of a cone (or double cone). It is assumed that the surface of the cone is generated by the rotation of a line through a fixed point around the circumference of a circle which is in a plane not containing that point. (The fixed point is the vertex of the cone, and the rotated line its generator.) There are three basic types: if the cutting plane is parallel to one of the positions of the generator, it produces a parabola. If it meets the cone only on one side of the vertex, it produces an ellipse (of which the circle is a special case); but, if it meets both parts of the cone, it produces a hyperbola. Apollonius sets out in detail the properties of these curves. He shows, for example, that for given line segments a and b the parabola corresponds to the relation (in

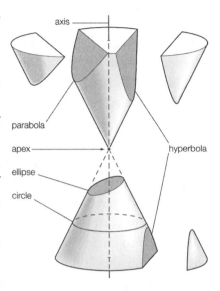

The conic sections result from intersecting a plane with a double cone, as shown in the figure. There are three distinct families of conic sections: the ellipse (including the circle); the parabola (with one branch); and the hyperbola (with two branches). Encyclopædia Britannica, Inc.

modern notation) $y^2 = ax$, the ellipse to $y^2 = ax - ax^2/b$, and the hyperbola to $y^2 = ax + ax^2/b$.

Apollonius's treatise on conics in part consolidated more than a century of work before him and in part presented new findings of his own. As mentioned earlier, Euclid had already issued a textbook on the conics, while even earlier Menaechmus had played a role in their study. The names that Apollonius chose for the curves (the terms may be original with him) indicate yet an earlier connection. In the pre-Euclidean geometry *parabolē* referred to a specific operation, the "application" of a given area to a given line, in which the line x is sought such that $ax = b^2$ (where a and b are given lines). Alternatively, x may be sought such that $x(a + x) = b^2$, or $x(a - x) = b^2$, and in these cases the application is said to be in "excess" (*hyperbolē*) or "defect" (*elleipsis*) by the amount of a square figure (namely, x^2). These constructions, which amount to a geometric solution of the general quadratic, appear in Books I, II, and VI of the *Elements* and can be associated in some form with the 5th-century Pythagoreans.

Apollonius presented a comprehensive survey of the properties of these curves. A sample of the topics he covered includes the following: the relations satisfied by the diameters and tangents of conics (Book I); how hyperbolas are related to their "asymptotes," the lines they approach without ever meeting (Book II); how to draw tangents to given conics (Book II); relations of chords intersecting in conics (Book III); the determination of the number of ways in which conics may intersect (Book IV); how to draw "normal" lines to conics (that is, lines meeting them at right angles; Book V); and the congruence and similarity of conics (Book VI).

By Apollonius's explicit statement, his results are of principal use as methods for the solution of geometric problems via conics. While he actually solved only a limited set of problems, the solutions of many others can be inferred from his theorems. For instance, the theorems of Book III permit the determination of conics that pass through given points or are tangent to given lines. In another work (now lost) Apollonius solved the problem of cube duplication by conics (a solution related in some way to that given by Menaechmus). Further, a solution of the problem of angle trisection given by Pappus may have come from Apollonius or been influenced by his work.

With the advance of the field of geometric problems by Euclid, Apollonius, and their followers, it became appropriate to introduce a classifying scheme: those problems solvable by means of conics were called solid, while those solvable by means of circles and lines only (as assumed in Euclid's *Elements*) were called planar. Thus, one can double the square by planar means (as in *Elements*, Book II, proposition 14), but one cannot double the cube in such a way, although a solid construction is possible (as given above). Similarly, the bisection of any angle is a planar construction (as shown in *Elements*, Book I, proposition 9), but the general trisection of the angle is of the solid type. It is not known when the classification was first introduced or when the planar methods were assigned canonical status relative to the others, but it seems plausible to date this near Apollonius's time. Indeed, much of his work—books like the *Tangencies*, the *Vergings* (or *Inclinations*), and the *Plane Loci*, now lost but amply described by Pappus— turns on the project of setting out the domain of planar constructions in relation to solutions by other means. On the basis of the principles of Greek geometry, it cannot be demonstrated, however, that it is impossible to effect by planar means certain solid constructions (like the cube

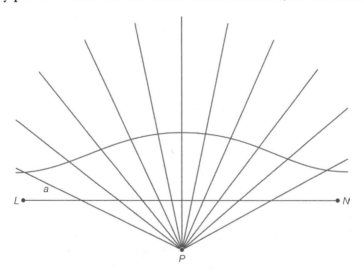

From fixed point P, several lines are drawn. A standard distance (a) is marked along each line from line LN, and the connection of the points creates a conchoid curve. Encyclopædia Britannica, Inc.

duplication and angle trisection). These results were established only by algebraists in the 19th century (notably by the French mathematician Pierre Laurent Wantzel in 1837).

A third class of problems, called linear, embraced those solvable by means of curves other than the circle and the conics (in Greek the word for "line," *grammē*, refers to all lines, whether curved or straight). For instance, one group of curves, the conchoids (from the Greek word for "shell"), are formed by marking off a certain length on a ruler and then pivoting it about a fixed point in such a way that one of the marked points stays on a given line. The other marked point traces out a conchoid. These curves can be used wherever a solution involves the positioning of a marked ruler relative to a given line (in Greek such

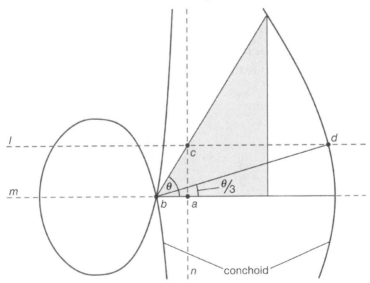

Nicomedes (3rd century BCE) discovered a special curve, known as a conchoid, with which he was able to trisect any acute angle. Given ∠θ, construct a conchoid with its pole at the vertex of the angle (b) and its directrix (n) through one side of the angle and perpendicular to the line (m) containing one of the angle's sides. Then construct the line (l) through the intersection (c) of the directrix and the remaining side of the angle. The intersection of l and the conchoid at d determines ∠abd = θ/3, as desired. Encyclopædia Britannica, Inc.

constructions are called *neuses*, or "vergings" of a line to a given point). For example, any acute angle (figured as the angle between one side and the diagonal of a rectangle) can be trisected by taking a length equal to twice the diagonal and moving it about until it comes to be inserted between two other sides of the rectangle. If instead the appropriate conchoid relative to either of those sides is introduced, the required position of the line can be determined without the trial and error of a moving ruler. Because the same construction can be effected by means of a hyperbola, however, the problem is not linear but solid. Such uses of the conchoids were presented by Nicomedes (middle or late 3rd century BCE), and their replacement by equivalent solid constructions appears to have come soon after, perhaps by Apollonius or his associates.

Some of the curves used for problem solving are not so reducible. For example, the Archimedean spiral couples uniform motion of a point on a half ray with uniform rotation of the ray around a fixed point at its end. Such curves

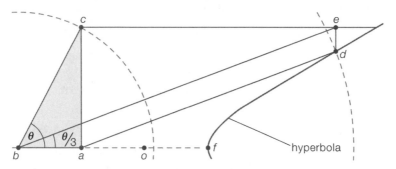

Pappus of Alexandria (c. 320) discovered that a hyperbola could be used to trisect an acute angle. Given ∠θ, construct points along one side such that ba = ao = of, and draw the hyperbola with centre at o and one vertex at f. Next, construct the line perpendicular to side ba such that c lies along the other side of ∠θ. Having established the length of bc, draw the line ad such that d lies on the hyperbola and ad = 2 × bc. Next, draw the line through c that is parallel to ba and the line through d that is perpendicular to ba, labeling the intersection of these lines e. Finally, draw line be, which produces ∠abe = θ/3, as desired. Encyclopædia Britannica, Inc.

have their principal interest as means for squaring the circle and trisecting the angle.

Applied Geometry

A major activity among geometers in the 3rd century BCE was the development of geometric approaches in the study of the physical sciences—specifically, optics, mechanics, and astronomy. In each case the aim was to formulate the basic concepts and principles in terms of geometric and numerical quantities and then to derive the fundamental phenomena of the field by geometric constructions and proofs.

In optics, Euclid's textbook (called the *Optics*) set the precedent. Euclid postulated visual rays to be straight lines, and he defined the apparent size of an object in terms of the angle formed by the rays drawn from the top and the bottom of the object to the observer's eye. He then proved, for example, that nearer objects appear larger and appear to move faster and showed how to measure the height of distant objects from their shadows or reflected images and so on. Other textbooks set out theorems on the phenomena of reflection and refraction (the field called catoptrics). The most extensive survey of optical phenomena is a treatise attributed to the astronomer Ptolemy (2nd century CE), which survives only in the form of an incomplete Latin translation (12th century) based on a lost Arabic translation. It covers the fields of geometric optics and catoptrics, as well as experimental areas, such as binocular vision, and more general philosophical principles (the nature of light, vision, and colour). Of a somewhat different sort are the studies of burning mirrors by Diocles (late 2nd century BCE), who proved that the surface that reflects the rays from the Sun to a single point is a paraboloid of revolution. Constructions of such devices remained of interest as late as the 6th century CE, when Anthemius of Tralles, best known for his work as architect of Hagia Sophia at Constantinople, compiled a survey of remarkable mirror configurations.

Mechanics was dominated by the work of Archimedes, who was the first to prove the principle of balance: that two weights are in equilibrium when they are inversely proportional to their distances from the fulcrum. From this principle he developed a theory of the centres of gravity of plane and solid figures. He was also the first to state and prove the principle of buoyancy—that floating bodies displace their equal in weight—and to use it for proving the conditions of stability of segments of spheres and

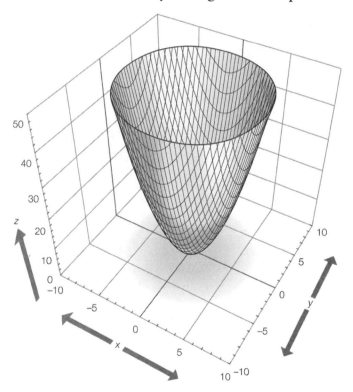

The figure shows part of the elliptic paraboloid $z = x^2 + y^2$, which can be generated by rotating the parabola $z = x^2$ (or $z = y^2$) about the z-axis. Note that cross sections of the surface parallel to the xy plane, as shown by the cutoff at the top of the figure, are ellipses. Encyclopædia Britannica, Inc.

paraboloids, solids formed by rotating a parabolic segment about its axis. Archimedes proved the conditions under which these solids will return to their initial position if tipped, in particular for the positions now called "stable I" and "stable II," where the vertex faces up and down, respectively.

In his work *Method Concerning Mechanical Theorems*, Archimedes also set out a special "mechanical method" that he used for the discovery of results on volumes and centres of gravity. He employed the bold notion of constituting solids from the plane figures formed as their sections (e.g., the circles that are the plane sections of

hyperbolic paraboloid

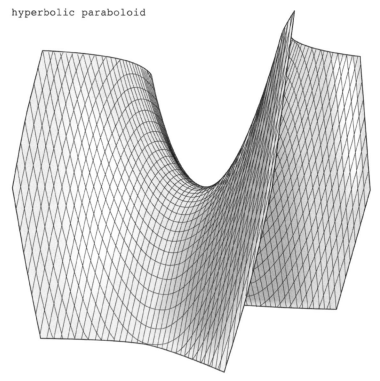

The figure shows part of the hyperbolic paraboloid $x^2 a^2 - y^2 b^2 = 2cz$. Note that cross sections of the surface parallel to the xz- and yz-plane are parabolas, while cross sections parallel to the xy-plane are hyperbolas. Encyclopædia Britannica, Inc.

spheres, cones, cylinders, and other solids of revolution), assigning to such figures a weight proportional to their area. For example, to measure the volume of a sphere, he imagined a balance beam, one of whose arms is a diameter of the sphere with the fulcrum at one endpoint of this diameter and the other arm an extension of the diameter to the other side of the fulcrum by a length equal to the diameter. Archimedes showed that the three circular cross sections made by a plane cutting the sphere and the associated cone and cylinder will be in balance (the circle in the cylinder with the circles in the sphere and cone) if the circle in the cylinder is kept in its original place while the circles in the sphere and cone are placed with their centres of gravity at the opposite end of the balance. Doing this for all the sets of circles formed as cross sections of these solids by planes, he concluded that the solids themselves are in balance—the cylinder with the sphere and the cone together—if the cylinder is left where it is, while the sphere and cone are placed with their centres of gravity at the opposite end of the balance. Since the centre of

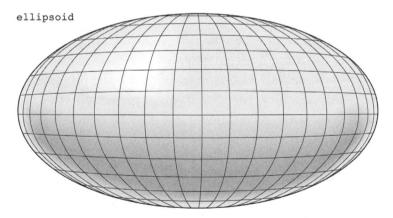

ellipsoid

An ellipsoid is a closed surface such that its intersection with any plane will produce an ellipse or a circle. The formula for an ellipsoid is $x^2 a^2 + y^2 b^2 + z^2 c^2 = 1$. A spheroid, or ellipsoid of revolution, is an ellipsoid generated by rotating an ellipse about one of its axes. Encyclopædia Britannica, Inc.

gravity of the cylinder is the midpoint of its axis, it follows that (sphere + cone):cylinder = 1:2 (by the inverse proportion of weights and distances). Since the volume of the cone is one-third that of the cylinder, however, the volume of the sphere is found to be one-sixth that of the cylinder. In similar manner, Archimedes worked out the volumes and centres of gravity of spherical segments and segments of the solids of revolution of conic sections—paraboloids, ellipsoids, and hyperboloids. The critical notions—constituting solids out of their plane sections and assigning weights to geometric figures—were not formally valid within the standard conceptions of Greek geometry, and Archimedes admitted this. But he maintained that, although his arguments were not "demonstrations" (i.e., proofs), they had value for the discovery of results about these figures.

The geometric study of astronomy has pre-Euclidean roots, Eudoxus having developed a model for planetary motions around a stationary Earth. Accepting the principle—which, according to Eudemus, was first proposed by Plato—that only combinations of uniform circular motions are to be used, Eudoxus represented the path of a planet as the result of superimposing rotations of three or more concentric spheres whose axes are set at different angles. Although the fit with the phenomena was unsatisfactory, the curves thus generated (the *hippopede*, or "horse-fetter") continued to be of interest for their geometric properties, as is known through remarks by Proclus. Later geometers continued the search for geometric patterns satisfying the Platonic conditions. The simplest model, a scheme of circular orbits centred on the Sun, was introduced by Aristarchus of Samos (3rd century BCE), but this was rejected by others, since a moving Earth was judged to be impossible on physical grounds. But Aristarchus's scheme could have suggested use of an "eccentric" model, in which the planets rotate about the Sun and the Sun in turn rotates about the Earth. Apollonius introduced an alternative "epicyclic" model, in which the planet turns about a point that itself orbits in a circle (the "deferent") centred at or near the Earth. As Apollonius knew, his epicyclic model is geometrically equivalent to an eccentric. These models were well adapted for explaining

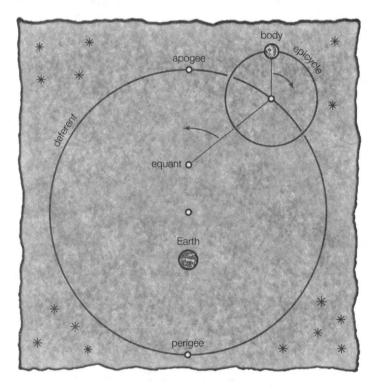

In Ptolemy's geocentric model of the universe, the Sun, Moon, and each planet orbit a stationary Earth. For the Greeks, heavenly bodies must move in the most perfect possible fashion, hence in perfect circles. In order to retain such motion and still explain the erratic apparent paths of the bodies, Ptolemy shifted the centre of each body's orbit (deferent) from the Earth—accounting for the body's apogee and perigee—and added a second orbital motion (epicycle) to explain retrograde motion. The equant is the point from which each body sweeps out equal angles along the deferent in equal times. The centre of the deferent is midway between the equant and the Earth. Encyclopædia Britannica, Inc.

other phenomena of planetary motion. For instance, if the Earth is displaced from the centre of a circular orbit (as in the eccentric scheme), the orbiting body will appear to vary in speed (appearing faster when nearer the observer, slower when farther away), as is in fact observed for the Sun, Moon, and planets. By varying the relative sizes and rotation rates of the epicycle and deferent, in combination with the eccentric, a flexible device may be obtained for representing planetary motion.

LATER TRENDS IN GEOMETRY AND ARITHMETIC

After the 3rd century BCE, mathematical research shifted increasingly away from the pure forms of constructive geometry toward areas related to the applied disciplines, in particular to astronomy. The necessary theorems on the geometry of the sphere (called spherics) were compiled into textbooks, such as the one by Theodosius (3rd or 2nd century BCE) that consolidated the earlier work by Euclid and the work of Autolycus of Pitane (fl. *c.* 300 BCE) on spherical astronomy. More significant, in the 2nd century BCE, the Greeks first came into contact with the fully developed Mesopotamian astronomical systems and took from them many of their observations and parameters (for example, values for the average periods of astronomical phenomena). While retaining their own commitment to geometric models rather than adopting the arithmetic schemes of the Mesopotamians, the Greeks nevertheless followed the Mesopotamians' lead in seeking a predictive astronomy based on a combination of mathematical theory and observational parameters. They thus made it their goal not merely to describe but to calculate the angular positions of the planets on the basis of the numerical and geometric content of the theory. This major restructuring of Greek astronomy, in both its theoretical and practical respects, was primarily due to Hipparchus (2nd century BCE), whose work was consolidated and further advanced by Ptolemy.

GREEK TRIGONOMETRY AND MENSURATION

To facilitate their astronomical researches, the Greeks developed techniques for the numerical measurement of angles, a precursor of trigonometry, and produced tables suitable for practical computation. Early efforts to measure the numerical ratios in triangles were made by Archimedes and Aristarchus. Their results were soon extended, and comprehensive treatises on the measurement of chords (in effect, a construction of a table of values equivalent to the trigonometric sine) were produced by Hipparchus and by Menelaus of Alexandria (1st century CE). These works are now lost, but the essential theorems and tables are preserved in Ptolemy's *Almagest* (Book I, chapter 10). For computing with angles, the Greeks adopted the Mesopotamian sexagesimal method in arithmetic, whence it survives in the standard units for angles and time employed to this day.

NUMBER THEORY

Although Euclid handed down a precedent for number theory in Books VII–IX of the *Elements*, later writers made no further effort to extend the field of theoretical arithmetic in his demonstrative manner. Beginning with Nicomachus of Gerasa (fl. *c.* 100 CE), several writers produced collections expounding a much simpler form of number theory. A favourite result is the representation of arithmetic progressions in the form of "polygonal numbers." For instance, if the numbers 1, 2, 3, 4,...are added successively, the "triangular" numbers 1, 3, 6, 10,...are obtained. Similarly, the odd numbers 1, 3, 5, 7,...sum to the "square" numbers 1, 4, 9, 16,..., while the sequence 1, 4, 7, 10,..., with a constant difference of 3, sums to the "pentagonal" numbers 1, 5, 12, 22,.... In general, these results can be expressed in the form of geometric shapes formed by lining up dots in the appropriate two-dimensional configurations. In the ancient arithmetics such results are invariably presented as particular cases, without any general notational method or general proof. The writers in this tradition are called neo-Pythagoreans, since they viewed themselves as continuing the Pythagorean school of the 5th century BCE, and, in the spirit of ancient Pythagoreanism, they

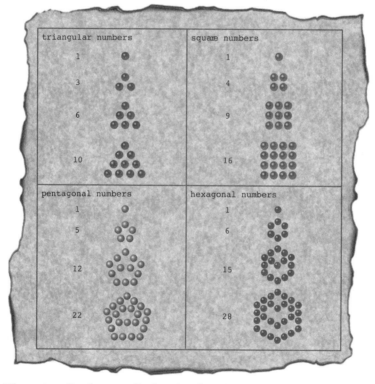

The ancient Greeks generally thought of numbers in concrete terms, particularly as measurements and geometric dimensions. Thus, they often arranged pebbles in various patterns to discern arithmetical, as well as mystical, relationships between numbers. A few such patterns are indicated in the figure. Encyclopædia Britannica, Inc.

tied their numerical interests to a philosophical theory that was an amalgam of Platonic metaphysical and theological doctrines. With its exponent Iamblichus of Chalcis (4th century CE), neo-Pythagoreans became a prominent part of the revival of pagan religion in opposition to Christianity in late antiquity.

An interesting concept of this school of thought, which Iamblichus attributes to Pythagoras himself, is that of "amicable numbers": two numbers are amicable if each is equal to the sum of the proper divisors of the other (for example, 220 and 284). Attributing virtues such as friendship and justice to numbers was characteristic of the Pythagoreans at all times.

Of much greater mathematical significance is the arithmetic work of Diophantus of Alexandria (c. 3rd century CE). His writing, the *Arithmetica*, originally in 13 books (six survive in Greek, another four in medieval Arabic translation), sets out hundreds of arithmetic problems with their solutions. For example, Book II, problem 8, seeks to express a given square number as the sum of two square numbers (here and throughout, the "numbers" are rational). Like those of the neo-Pythagoreans, his treatments are always of particular cases rather than general solutions. Thus, in this problem the given number is taken to be 16, and the solutions worked out are 256/25 and 144/25. In this example, as is often the case, the solutions are not unique. Indeed, in the very next problem Diophantus shows how a number given as the sum of two squares (e.g., 13 = 4 + 9) can be expressed differently as the sum of two other squares (for example, 13 = 324/25 + 1/25).

To find his solutions, Diophantus adopted an arithmetic form of the method of analysis. He first reformulated the problem in terms of one of the unknowns, and he then manipulated it as if it were known until an explicit value for the unknown emerged. He even adopted an abbreviated notational scheme to facilitate such operations, where, for example, the unknown is symbolized by a figure somewhat resembling the Roman letter S. (This is a standard abbreviation for the word *number* in ancient Greek manuscripts.) Thus, in the first problem discussed above, if S is one of the unknown solutions, then $16 - S^2$ is a square. Supposing the other unknown to be $2S - 4$ (where the 2 is arbitrary but the 4 chosen because it is the square root of the given number 16), Diophantus found from summing the two unknowns ($[2S - 4]^2$ and S^2) that $4S^2 - 16S + 16 + S^2 = 16$, or $5S^2 = 16S$; that is, $S = 16/5$. So one solution is $S^2 = 256/25$, while the other solution is $16 - S^2$, or $144/25$.

SURVIVAL AND INFLUENCE OF GREEK MATHEMATICS

Notable in the closing phase of Greek mathematics were Pappus (early 4th century CE), Theon (late 4th century), and Theon's daughter Hypatia. All were active in Alexandria as professors of mathematics and astronomy, and they produced extensive commentaries on the major authorities—Pappus and Theon on Ptolemy, Hypatia on Diophantus and Apollonius. Later, Eutocius of Ascalon (early 6th century) produced commentaries on Archimedes and Apollonius. While much of their output has since been lost, much survives. They proved themselves reasonably competent in technical matters but little inclined toward significant insights (their aim was usually to fill in minor steps assumed in the proofs, to append alternative proofs, and the like), and their level of originality was very low. But these scholars frequently preserved fragments of older works that are now lost, and their teaching and editorial efforts assured the survival of the works of Euclid, Archimedes, Apollonius, Diophantus,

Ptolemy, and others that now do exist, either in Greek manuscripts or in medieval translations (Arabic, Hebrew, and Latin) derived from them.

The legacy of Greek mathematics, particularly in the fields of geometry and geometric science, was enormous. From an early period the Greeks formulated the objectives of mathematics not in terms of practical procedures but as a theoretical discipline committed to the development of general propositions and formal demonstrations. The range and diversity of their findings, especially those of the masters of the 3rd century BCE, supplied geometers with subject matter for centuries thereafter, even though the tradition that was transmitted into the Middle Ages and Renaissance was incomplete and defective.

The rapid rise of mathematics in the 17th century was based in part on the conscious imitation of the ancient classics and on competition with them. In the geometric mechanics of Galileo and the infinitesimal researches of Johannes Kepler and Bonaventura Cavalieri, it is possible to perceive a direct inspiration from Archimedes. The study of the advanced geometry of Apollonius and Pappus stimulated new approaches in geometry—for example, the analytic methods of René Descartes and the projective theory of Girard Desargues. Purists like Christiaan Huygens and Isaac Newton insisted on the Greek geometric style as a model of rigour, just as others sought to escape its forbidding demands of completely worked-out proofs. The full impact of Diophantus's work is evident particularly with Pierre de Fermat in his researches in algebra and number theory. Although mathematics has today gone far beyond the ancient achievements, the leading figures of antiquity, like Archimedes, Apollonius, and Ptolemy, can still be rewarding reading for the ingenuity of their insights.

MATHEMATICS IN THE ISLAMIC WORLD (8TH–15TH CENTURY)

The legacy of the mathematics practiced in the Islamic world hundreds of years ago continues to live with us today. For example, the basic mathematical terms of *algebra* and *algorithm* are descended from Arabic words.

ORIGINS

In Hellenistic times and in late antiquity, scientific learning in the eastern part of the Roman world was spread over a variety of centres, and Justinian's closing of the pagan academies in Athens in 529 gave further impetus to this diffusion. An additional factor was the translation and study of Greek scientific and philosophical texts sponsored both by monastic centres of the various Christian churches in the Levant, Egypt, and Mesopotamia and by enlightened rulers of the Sāsānian dynasty in places like the medical school at Gondeshapur.

Also important were developments in India in the first few centuries CE. Although the decimal system for whole numbers was apparently not known to the Indian astronomer Aryabhata I (born 476), it was used by his pupil Bhaskara I in 620, and by 670 the system had reached northern Mesopotamia, where the Nestorian bishop Severus Sebokht praised its Hindu inventors as discoverers of things more ingenious than those of the Greeks. Earlier, in the late 4th or early 5th century, the anonymous Hindu author of an astronomical handbook, the *Surya Siddhanta*, had tabulated the sine function (unknown in Greece) for every 3 ¾° of arc from 3 ¾° to 90°.

Within this intellectual context the rapid expansion of Islam took place between the time of Muhammad's return to Mecca in 630 from his exile in Medina and the Muslim

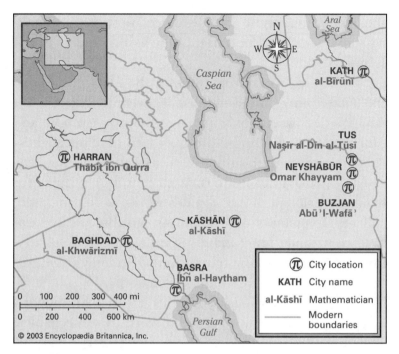

This map spans more than 600 years of prominent Islamic mathematicians, from al-Khwārizmī (c. 800 CE) to al-Kāshī (c. 1400 CE). Their names are located on the map under their cities of birth.

conquest of lands extending from Spain to the borders of China by 715. Not long afterward, Muslims began the acquisition of foreign learning, and, by the time of the caliph al-Mansur (died 775), such Indian and Persian astronomical material as the *Brahma-sphuta-siddhanta* and the *Shah's Tables* had been translated into Arabic. The subsequent acquisition of Greek material was greatly advanced when the caliph al-Ma'mun constructed a translation and research centre, the House of Wisdom, in Baghdad during his reign (813–833). Most of the translations were done from Greek and Syriac by Christian scholars, but the impetus and support for this activity came from Muslim patrons. These included not only the caliph but also wealthy individuals such as the three brothers known as

73

the Banu Musa, whose treatises on geometry and mechanics formed an important part of the works studied in the Islamic world.

Of Euclid's works the *Elements*, the *Data*, the *Optics*, the *Phaenomena*, and *On Divisions* were translated. Of Archimedes' works only two—*Sphere and Cylinder* and *Measurement of the Circle*—are known to have been translated, but these were sufficient to stimulate independent researches from the 9th to the 15th century. On the other hand, virtually all of Apollonius's works were translated, and of Diophantus and Menelaus one book each, the *Arithmetica* and the *Sphaerica*, respectively, were translated into Arabic. Finally, the translation of Ptolemy's *Almagest* furnished important astronomical material.

Of the minor writings, Diocles' treatise on mirrors, Theodosius's *Spherics*, Pappus's work on mechanics, Ptolemy's *Planisphaerium*, and Hypsicles' treatises on regular polyhedra (the so-called Books XIV and XV of Euclid's *Elements*) were among those translated.

MATHEMATICS IN THE 9TH CENTURY

Thābit ibn Qurrah (836–901), a Sabian from Harran in northern Mesopotamia, was an important translator and reviser of these Greek works. In addition to translating works of the major Greek mathematicians (for the Banu Musa, among others), he was a court physician. He also translated Nicomachus of Gerasa's *Arithmetic* and discovered a beautiful rule for finding amicable numbers, a pair of numbers such that each number is the sum of the set of proper divisors of the other number. The investigation of such numbers formed a continuing tradition in Islam. Kamal al-Dīn al-Farisi (died *c.* 1320) gave the pair 17,926 and 18,416 as an example of Thābit's rule, and in the 17th century, Muhammad Baqir Yazdi gave the pair 9,363,584 and 9,437,056.

One scientist typical of the 9th century was Muhammad ibn Musa al-Khwārizmī. Working in the House of Wisdom, he introduced Indian material in his astronomical works and also wrote an early book explaining Hindu arithmetic, the *Book of Addition and Subtraction According to the Hindu Calculation*. In another work, the *Book of Restoring and Balancing*, he provided a systematic introduction to algebra, including a theory of quadratic equations. Both works had important consequences for Islamic mathematics. *Hindu Calculation* began a tradition of arithmetic books that, by the middle of the next century, led to the invention of decimal fractions (complete with a decimal point), and *Restoring and Balancing* became the point of departure and model for later writers such as the Egyptian Abu Kamil. Both books were translated into Latin, and *Restoring and Balancing* was the origin of the word *algebra*, from the Arabic word for "restoring" in its title (*al-jabr*). The *Hindu Calculation*, from a Latin form of the author's name, *algorismi*, yielded the word *algorithm*.

Al-Khwārizmī's algebra also served as a model for later writers in its application of arithmetic and algebra to the distribution of inheritances according to the complex requirements of Muslim religious law. This tradition of service to the Islamic faith was an enduring feature of mathematical work in Islam and one that, in the eyes of many, justified the study of secular learning. In the same category are al-Khwārizmī's method of calculating the time of visibility of the new moon (which signals the beginning of the Muslim month) and the expositions by astronomers of methods for finding the direction to Mecca for the five daily prayers.

Mathematics in the 10th Century

Islamic scientists in the 10th century were involved in three major mathematical projects: the completion of arithmetic algorithms, the development of algebra, and the extension of geometry.

The first of these projects led to the appearance of three complete numeration systems, one of which was the finger arithmetic used by the scribes and treasury officials. This ancient arithmetic system, which became known throughout the East and Europe, employed mental arithmetic and a system of storing intermediate results on the fingers as an aid to memory. (Its use of unit fractions recalls the Egyptian system.) During the 10th and 11th centuries, capable mathematicians, such as Abū'l-Wafā' (940–997/998), wrote on this system, but it was eventually replaced by the decimal system.

A second common system was the base-60 numeration inherited from the Babylonians via the Greeks and known as the arithmetic of the astronomers. Although astronomers used this system for their tables, they usually converted numbers to the decimal system for complicated calculations and then converted the answer back to sexagesimals.

The third system was Indian arithmetic, whose basic numeral forms, complete with the zero, eastern Islam took over from the Hindus. (Different forms of the numerals, whose origins are not entirely clear, were used in western Islam.) The basic algorithms also came from India, but these were adapted by al-Uqlidisi (c. 950) to pen and paper instead of the traditional dust board, a move that helped to popularize this system. Also, the arithmetic algorithms were completed in two ways: by the extension of root-extraction procedures, known to Hindus and Greeks only for square and cube roots, to roots of higher degree and by the extension of the Hindu decimal system for whole numbers to include decimal fractions. These fractions appear simply as computational devices in the work of both al-Uqlidisi and al-Baghdadi (*c.* 1000), but in subsequent centuries they received systematic treatment as a general method. As for extraction of roots, Abū'l-Wafā' wrote a treatise (now lost) on the topic, and Omar Khayyam (1048–1131) solved the general problem of extracting roots of any desired degree. Omar's treatise too is lost, but the method is known from other writers, and it appears that a major step in its development was al-Karaji's 10th-century derivation by means of mathematical induction of the binomial theorem for whole-number exponents—i.e., his discovery that

$$(a+b)^n = a^n + na^{n-1}b + \frac{n(n-1)}{2}a^{n-2}b^2 + \frac{n(n-1)(n-2)}{2 \cdot 3}a^{n-3}b^3 + \text{L} + nab^{n-1} + b^n.$$

During the 10th century, Islamic algebraists progressed from al-Khwārizmī's quadratic polynomials to the mastery of the algebra of expressions involving arbitrary positive or negative integral powers of the unknown. Several algebraists explicitly stressed the analogy between the rules for working with powers of the unknown in algebra and those for working with powers of 10 in arithmetic, and there was interaction between the development of arithmetic and algebra from the 10th to the 12th century. A 12th-century student of al-Karaji's works, al-Samaw'al, was able to approximate the quotient $(20x^2 + 30x)/(6x^2 + 12)$ as

$$3\frac{1}{3} + 5\left(\frac{1}{x}\right) - 6\frac{2}{3}\left(\frac{1}{x^2}\right) - 10\left(\frac{1}{x^3}\right) + \text{L} - 40\left(\frac{1}{x^7}\right)$$

and also gave a rule for finding the coefficients of the successive powers of $1/x$. Although none of this employed symbolic algebra, algebraic symbolism was in use by the 14th century in the western part of the Islamic world. The context for this well-developed symbolism was, it seems, commentaries that were destined for teaching purposes, such as that of Ibn Qunfudh (1330–1407) of Algeria on the algebra of Ibn al-Banna' (1256–1321) of Morocco.

Other parts of algebra developed as well. Both Greeks and Hindus had studied indeterminate equations, and the translation of this material and the application of the newly developed algebra led to the investigation of Diophantine equations by writers like Abu Kamil, al-Karaji, and Abu Ja'far al-Khazin (first half of 10th century), as well as to attempts to prove a special case of what is now known as Fermat's last theorem—namely, that there are no rational solutions to $x^3 + y^3 = z^3$. The great scientist Ibn al-Haytham (965–1040) solved problems involving congruences by what is now called Wilson's theorem, which states that, if p is a prime, then p divides $(p - 1) \times (p - 2) \cdots \times 2 \times 1 + 1$, and al-Baghdadi gave a variant of the idea of amicable numbers by defining two numbers to "balance" if the sums of their divisors are equal.

However, not only arithmetic and algebra but geometry too underwent extensive development. Thābit ibn Qurrah, his grandson Ibrahim ibn Sinan (909–946), Abu Sahl al-Kuhi (died *c.* 995), and Ibn al-Haytham solved problems involving the pure geometry of conic sections, including the areas and volumes of plane and solid figures formed from them, and also investigated the optical properties of mirrors made from conic sections. Ibrahim ibn Sinan, Abu Sahl al-Kuhi, and Ibn al-Haytham used the ancient technique of analysis to reduce the solution of problems to constructions involving conic sections. (Ibn al-Haytham, for example, used this method to find the point on a convex spherical mirror at which a given object is seen by a given observer.) Thābit and Ibrahim showed how to design the curves needed for sundials. Abu'l-Wafa', whose book on the arithmetic of the scribes is mentioned above, also wrote on geometric methods needed by artisans.

In addition, in the late 10th century, Abū'l-Wafā' and the prince Abu Nasr Mansur stated and proved theorems of plane and spherical geometry that could be applied by astronomers and geographers, including the laws of sines and tangents. Abu Nasr's pupil al-Bīrūnī (973–1048), who produced a vast amount of high-quality work, was one of the masters in applying these theorems to astronomy and to such problems in mathematical geography as the determination of latitudes and longitudes, the distances between cities, and the direction from one city to another.

OMAR KHAYYAM

The mathematician and poet Omar Khayyam was born in Neyshabur (in Iran) only a few years before al-Bīrūnī's death. He later lived in Samarkand and Esfahan, and his brilliant work there continued many of the main lines of development in 10th-century mathematics. Not only did he discover a general method of extracting roots of arbitrary high degree, but his *Algebra* contains the first complete treatment of the solution of cubic equations. Omar did this by means of conic sections, but he declared his hope that his successors would succeed where he had failed in finding an algebraic formula for the roots.

Omar was also a part of an Islamic tradition, which included Thābit and Ibn al-Haytham, of investigating Euclid's parallel postulate. To this tradition Omar contributed the idea of a quadrilateral with two congruent sides perpendicular to the base. The parallel postulate would be proved, Omar recognized, if he could show that the remaining two angles were right angles. In this he failed, but his question about the quadrilateral became the standard way of discussing the parallel postulate.

That postulate, however, was only one of the questions on the foundations of mathematics that interested Islamic scientists. Another was the definition of ratios. Omar Khayyam, along with others before him, felt that

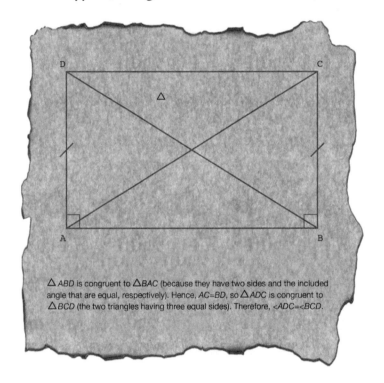

△ *ABD* is congruent to △*BAC* (because they have two sides and the included angle that are equal, respectively). Hence, *AC=BD*, so △*ADC* is congruent to △*BCD* (the two triangles having three equal sides). Therefore, <*ADC*=<*BCD*.

Omar Khayyam constructed the quadrilateral shown in the figure in an effort to prove that Euclid's fifth postulate, concerning parallel lines, is superfluous. He began by constructing line segments AD and BC of equal length perpendicular to the line segment AB. Omar recognized that if he could prove that the internal angles at the top of the quadrilateral, formed by connecting C and D, are right angles, then he would have proved that DC is parallel to AB. Although Omar showed that the internal angles at the top are equal (as shown by the proof demonstrated in the figure), he could not prove that they are right angles. Encyclopædia Britannica, Inc.

the theory in Book V of Euclid's *Elements* was logically satisfactory but intuitively unappealing, so he proved that a definition known to Aristotle was equivalent to that given in Euclid. In fact, Omar argued that ratios should be regarded as "ideal numbers," and so he conceived of a much broader system of numbers than that used since Greek antiquity, that of the positive real numbers.

ISLAMIC MATHEMATICS TO THE 15TH CENTURY

In the 12th century, the physician al-Samaw'al continued and completed the work of al-Karaji in algebra and also provided a systematic treatment of decimal fractions as a means of approximating irrational quantities. In his method of finding roots of pure equations, $x^n = N$, he used what is now known as Horner's method to expand the binomial $(a + y)^n$. His contemporary Sharaf al-Dīn al-Tūsī late in the 12th century provided a method of approximating the positive roots of arbitrary equations, based on an approach virtually identical to that discovered by François Viète in 16th-century France. The important step here was less the general idea than the development of the numerical algorithms necessary to effect it.

Sharaf al-Dīn was the discoverer of a device, called the linear astrolabe, that places him in another important Islamic mathematical tradition, one that centred on the design of new forms of the ancient astronomical instrument known as the astrolabe. The astrolabe, whose mathematical theory is based on the stereographic projection of the sphere, was invented in late antiquity, but its extensive development in Islam made it the pocket watch of the medievals. In its original form, it required a different plate of horizon coordinates for each latitude, but in the 11th century, the Spanish Muslim astronomer al-Zarqallu invented a single plate that worked for all latitudes. Slightly earlier, astronomers in the East had experimented with plane projections of the sphere, and al-Bīrūnī invented such a projection that could be used to produce a map of a hemisphere. The culminating masterpiece was the astrolabe of the Syrian Ibn al-Shatir (1305–75), a mathematical tool that could be used to solve all the standard problems of spherical astronomy in five different ways.

On the other hand, Muslim astronomers had developed other methods for solving these problems using the highly accurate trigonometry tables and the new trigonometry theorems they had developed. Out of these developments came the creation of trigonometry as a mathematical discipline, separate from its astronomical applications, by Nasīr al-Dīn al-Tūsī at his observatory in Maragheh in the 13th century. (It was there too that al-Tūsī's pupil Qutb al-Dīn al-Shirazi [1236–1311] and his pupil Kamal al-Dīn Farisi, using Ibn al-Haytham's great work, the *Optics*, were able to give the first mathematically satisfactory explanation of the rainbow.)

Al-Tūsī's observatory was supported by a grandson of Genghis Khan, Hülegü, who sacked Baghdad in 1258. Ulugh Beg, the grandson of the Mongol conqueror Timur, founded an observatory at Samarkand in the early years of the 15th century. Ulugh Beg was himself a good astronomer, and his tables of sines and tangents for every minute of arc (accurate to five sexagesimal places) were one of the great achievements in numerical mathematics up to his time. He was also the patron of Jamshid al-Kāshī (died 1429), whose work *The Reckoners' Key* summarizes most of the arithmetic of his time and includes sections on algebra and practical geometry as well. Among al-Kāshī's works is a masterful computation of the value of 2π, which, when expressed in decimal fractions, is accurate to 16 places, as well as the application of a numerical method, now known as fixed-point iteration, for solving the cubic equation with sin 1° as a root. His work was indeed of a quality deserving Ulugh Beg's description as "known among the famous of the world."

Al-Kāshī lived almost five centuries after the first translations of Arabic material into Latin, and by his time the Islamic mathematical tradition had given the West not only its first versions of many of the Greek classics but also a complete set of algorithms for Hindu-Arabic arithmetic, plane and spherical trigonometry, and the powerful tool of algebra. Although mathematical inquiry continued in Islam in the centuries after al-Kāshī's time, the mathematical centre of gravity was shifting to the West. That this was so is, of course, in no small measure due to what the Western mathematicians had learned from their Islamic predecessors during the preceding centuries.

B eginning in the Middle Ages, mathematics emerged from the fallow period that had begun with the fall of the Roman Empire. Such mathematicians as Leonardo of Pisa and Nicholas Oresme were able to apply and extend the knowledge that had been preserved in the Islamic world.

EUROPEAN MATHEMATICS DURING THE MIDDLE AGES AND RENAISSANCE

Until the 11th century, only a small part of the Greek mathematical corpus was known in the West. Because almost no one could read Greek, what little was available came from the poor texts written in Latin in the Roman Empire, together with the very few Latin translations of Greek works. Of these the most important were the treatises by Boethius, who about 500 CE made Latin redactions of a number of Greek scientific and logical writings. His *Arithmetic*, which was based on Nicomachus, was well known and was the means by which medieval scholars learned of Pythagorean number theory. Boethius and Cassiodorus provided the material for the part of the monastic education called the quadrivium: arithmetic, geometry, astronomy, and music theory. Together with the trivium (grammar, logic, rhetoric), these subjects formed the seven liberal arts, which were taught in the monasteries, cathedral schools, and, from the 12th century on, universities and which constituted the principal university instruction until modern times.

For monastic life it sufficed to know how to calculate with Roman numerals. The principal application of arithmetic was a method for determining the date of Easter, the computus, that was based on the lunar cycle of 19 solar years (i.e., 235 lunar revolutions) and the 28-year solar cycle. Between the time of Bede (died 735), when the system was fully developed, and about 1500, the computus was reduced to a series of verses that were learned by rote.

Boethius. Hulton Archive/Getty Images

Until the 12th century, geometry was largely concerned with approximate formulas for measuring areas and volumes in the tradition of the Roman surveyors. About 1000 CE the French scholar Gerbert of Aurillac, later Pope Sylvester II, introduced a type of abacus in which numbers were represented by stones bearing Arabic numerals. Such novelties were known to very few.

THE TRANSMISSION OF GREEK AND ARABIC LEARNING

In the 11th century, a new phase of mathematics began with the translations from Arabic. Scholars throughout Europe went to Toledo, Córdoba, and elsewhere in Spain to translate into Latin the accumulated learning of the Muslims. Along with philosophy, astronomy, astrology, and medicine, important mathematical achievements of the Greek, Indian, and Islamic civilizations became available in the West. Particularly important were Euclid's *Elements*, the works of Archimedes, and al-Khwārizmī's treatises on arithmetic and algebra. Western texts called *algorismus* (a Latin form of the name al-Khwārizmī) introduced the Hindu-Arabic numerals and applied them in calculations. Thus, modern numerals first came into use in universities and then became common among merchants and other laymen. It should be noted that, up to the 15th century, calculations were often performed with board and counters. Reckoning with Hindu-Arabic numerals was used by merchants at least from the time of Leonardo of Pisa (beginning of the 13th century), first in Italy and then in the trading cities of southern Germany and France, where *maestri d'abbaco* or *Rechenmeister* taught commercial arithmetic in the various vernaculars. Some schools were private, while others were run by the community.

THE UNIVERSITIES

Mathematics was studied from a theoretical standpoint in the universities. The Universities of Paris and Oxford, which were founded relatively early (*c.* 1200), were centres for mathematics and philosophy. Of particular importance in these universities were the Arabic-based versions of Euclid, of which there were at least four by the 12th century. Of the numerous redactions and compendia which were made, that of Johannes Campanus (*c.* 1250; first printed in 1482) was easily the most popular, serving as a textbook for many generations. Such redactions of the *Elements* were made to help students not only to understand Euclid's textbook but also to handle other, particularly philosophical, questions suggested by passages in Aristotle. The ratio theory of the *Elements* provided a means of expressing the various relations of the quantities associated with moving bodies, relations that now would be expressed by formulas. Also in Euclid were to be found methods of analyzing infinity and continuity (paradoxically, because Euclid always avoided infinity).

Studies of such questions led not only to new results but also to a new approach to what is now called physics. Thomas Bradwardine, who was active in Merton College, Oxford, in the first half of the 14th century, was one of the first medieval scholars to ask whether the continuum can be divided infinitely or whether there are smallest parts (indivisibles). Among other topics, he compared different geometric shapes in terms of the multitude of points that were assumed to compose them, and from such an approach paradoxes were generated that were not to be solved for centuries. Another fertile question stemming from Euclid concerned the angle between a circle and a line tangent to it (called the horn angle): if this angle is not

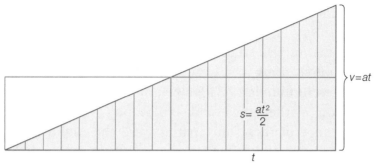

Uniformly accelerated motion; s = speed, a = acceleration, t = time, and v = velocity. Encyclopædia Britannica, Inc.

zero, a contradiction quickly ensues, but, if it is zero, then, by definition, there can be no angle. For the relation of force, resistance, and the speed of the body moved by this force, Bradwardine suggested an exponential law. Nicholas Oresme (died 1382) extended Bradwardine's ideas to fractional exponents.

Another question having to do with the quantification of qualities, the so-called latitude of forms, began to be discussed at about this time in Paris and in Merton College. Various Aristotelian qualities (e.g., heat, density, and velocity) were assigned an intensity and extension, which were sometimes represented by the height and bases (respectively) of a geometric figure. The area of the figure was then considered to represent the quantity of the quality. In the important case in which the quality is the motion of a body, the intensity its speed, and the extension its time, the area of the figure was taken to represent the distance covered by the body. Uniformly accelerated motion starting at zero velocity gives rise to a triangular figure. It was proved by the Merton school that the quantity of motion in such a case is equal to the quantity of a uniform motion at the speed achieved halfway through the accelerated motion. In modern formulation, $s = \frac{1}{2}at^2$ (Merton rule). Discussions like this certainly influenced

Galileo indirectly and may have influenced the founding of coordinate geometry in the 17th century. Another important development in the scholastic "calculations" was the summation of infinite series.

Basing his work on translated Greek sources, about 1464 the German mathematician and astronomer Regiomontanus wrote the first book (printed in 1533) in the West on plane and spherical trigonometry independent of astronomy. He also published tables of sines and tangents that were in constant use for more than two centuries.

THE RENAISSANCE

Italian artists and merchants influenced the mathematics of the late Middle Ages and the Renaissance in several ways. In the 15th century, a group of Tuscan artists — including Filippo Brunelleschi, Leon Battista Alberti, and Leonardo da Vinci — incorporated linear perspective into their practice and teaching, about a century before the subject was formally treated by mathematicians. Italian *maestri d'abbaco* tried, albeit unsuccessfully, to solve nontrivial cubic equations. In fact, the first general solution was found by Scipione del Ferro at the beginning of the 16th century and rediscovered by Niccolò Tartaglia several years later. The solution was published by Gerolamo Cardano in his *Ars magna* (*Ars Magna or the Rules of Algebra*) in 1545, together with Lodovico Ferrari's solution of the quartic equation.

By 1380 an algebraic symbolism had been developed in Italy in which letters were used for the unknown, for its square, and for constants. The symbols used today for the unknown (for example, x), the square root sign, and the signs + and - came into general use in southern Germany beginning about 1450. They were used by Regiomontanus and by Fridericus Gerhart and received an impetus about

Filippo Brunelleschi. Hulton Archive/Getty Images

1486 at the University of Leipzig from Johann Widman. The idea of distinguishing between known and unknown quantities in algebra was first consistently applied by François Viète, with vowels for unknown and consonants for known quantities. Viète found some relations between the coefficients of an equation and its roots. This was suggestive of the idea, explicitly stated by Albert Girard in 1629 and proved by Carl Friedrich Gauss in 1799, that an equation of degree *n* has *n* roots. Complex numbers, which are implicit in such ideas, were gradually accepted about the time of Rafael Bombelli (died 1572), who used them in connection with the cubic.

Apollonius's *Conics* and the investigations of areas (quadratures) and of volumes (cubatures) by Archimedes formed part of the humanistic learning of the 16th century. These studies strongly influenced the later developments of analytic geometry, the infinitesimal calculus, and the theory of functions, subjects that were developed in the 17th century.

MATHEMATICS IN THE 17TH AND 18TH CENTURIES

The 17th century, the period of the scientific revolution, witnessed the consolidation of Copernican heliocentric astronomy and the establishment of inertial physics in the work of Johannes Kepler, Galileo, René Descartes, and Isaac Newton. This period was also one of intense activity and innovation in mathematics. The methods developed then paved the way in the 18th century for new branches of mathematics such as the calculus of variations and differential geometry.

THE 17TH CENTURY

Advances in numerical calculation, the development of symbolic algebra and analytic geometry, and the invention of the differential and integral calculus resulted in a major expansion of the subject areas of mathematics. By the end of the 17th century, a program of research based in analysis had replaced classical Greek geometry at the centre of advanced mathematics. In the next century, this program would continue to develop in close association with physics, more particularly mechanics and theoretical astronomy. The extensive use of analytic methods, the incorporation of applied subjects, and the adoption of a pragmatic attitude to questions of logical rigour distinguished the new mathematics from traditional geometry.

Institutional Background

Until the middle of the 17th century, mathematicians worked alone or in small groups, publishing their work in books or communicating with other researchers by letter. At a time when people were often slow to publish, "invisible colleges," networks of scientists who corresponded privately, played an important role in coordinating and stimulating mathematical research. Marin Mersenne in Paris acted as a clearinghouse for new results, informing his many correspondents—including Pierre de Fermat, Descartes, Blaise Pascal, Gilles Personne de Roberval, and Galileo—of challenge problems and novel solutions. Later in the century, John Collins, librarian of London's Royal Society, performed a similar function among British mathematicians.

In 1660 the Royal Society of London was founded, to be followed in 1666 by the French Academy of Sciences, in 1700 by the Berlin Academy, and in 1724 by the St. Petersburg Academy. The official publications sponsored by the academies, as well as independent journals such as the *Acta Eruditorum* (founded in 1682), made possible the open and prompt communication of research findings. Although universities in the 17th century provided some support for mathematics, they became increasingly ineffective as state-supported academies assumed direction of advanced research.

Numerical Calculation

The development of new methods of numerical calculation was a response to the increased practical demands of numerical computation, particularly in trigonometry, navigation, and astronomy. New ideas spread quickly across Europe and resulted by 1630 in a major revolution in numerical practice.

Simon Stevin of Holland, in his short pamphlet *La Disme* (1585), introduced decimal fractions to Europe and showed how to extend the principles of Hindu-Arabic arithmetic to calculation with these numbers. Stevin emphasized the utility of decimal arithmetic "for all accounts that are encountered in the affairs of men," and he explained in an appendix how it could be applied to surveying, stereometry, astronomy, and mensuration. His idea was to extend the base-10 positional principle to numbers with fractional parts, with a corresponding extension of notation to cover these cases. In his system the number 237.578 was denoted

$$237 \enspace \textcircled{0} \enspace 5 \enspace \textcircled{1} \enspace 7 \enspace \textcircled{2} \enspace 8 \enspace \textcircled{3},$$

in which the digits to the left of the zero are the integral part of the number. To the right of the zero are the digits of the fractional part, with each digit succeeded by a circled number that indicates the negative power to which 10 is raised. Stevin showed how the usual arithmetic of whole numbers could be extended to decimal fractions, using rules that determined the positioning of the negative powers of 10.

In addition to its practical utility, *La Disme* was significant for the way it undermined the dominant style of classical Greek geometry in theoretical mathematics. Stevin's proposal required a rejection of the distinction in Euclidean geometry between magnitude, which is continuous, and number, which is a multitude of indivisible units. For Euclid, unity, or one, was a special sort of thing, not number but the origin, or principle, of number. The introduction of decimal fractions seemed to imply that the unit could be subdivided and that arbitrary continuous magnitude could be represented numerically. It implicitly supposed the concept of a general positive real number.

Tables of logarithms were first published in 1614 by the Scottish laird John Napier in his treatise *Description of the Marvelous Canon of Logarithms*. This work was followed (posthumously) five years later by another in which Napier set forth the principles used in the construction of his tables. The basic idea behind logarithms is that addition and subtraction are easier to perform than multiplication and division, which, as Napier observed, require a "tedious expenditure of time" and are subject to "slippery errors." By the law of exponents, $a^n a^m = a^{n+m}$; that is, in the multiplication of numbers, the exponents are related additively. By correlating the geometric sequence of numbers a, a^2, a^3,...(a is called the base) and the arithmetic sequence 1, 2, 3,...and interpolating to fractional values, it is possible to reduce the problem of multiplication and division to one of addition and subtraction. To do this Napier chose a base that was very close to 1, differing from it by only $1/10^7$. The resulting geometric sequence therefore yielded a dense set of values, suitable for constructing a table.

In his work of 1619, Napier presented an interesting kinematic model to generate the geometric and arithmetic sequences used in the construction of his tables. Assume two particles move along separate lines from given initial points. The particles begin moving at the same instant with the same velocity. The first particle continues to move with a speed that is decreasing, proportional at each instant to the distance remaining between it and some given fixed point on the line. The second particle moves with a constant speed equal to its initial velocity. Given any increment of time, the distances traveled by the first particle in successive increments form a geometrically decreasing sequence. The corresponding distances traveled by the second particle form an arithmetically increasing sequence. Napier was able to use this model to derive theorems yielding precise limits to approximate values in the two sequences.

Napier's kinematic model · indicated how skilled mathematicians had become by the early 17th century in analyzing nonuniform motion. Kinematic ideas, which appeared frequently in mathematics of the period, provided a clear and visualizable means for the generation of geometric magnitude. The conception of a curve traced by a particle moving through space later played a significant role in the development of the calculus.

Napier's ideas were taken up and revised by the English mathematician Henry Briggs, the first Savilian Professor of Geometry at Oxford. In 1624 Briggs published an extensive table of common logarithms, or logarithms to the base 10. Because the base was no longer close to 1, the table could not be obtained as simply as Napier's, and Briggs therefore devised techniques involving the calculus of finite differences to facilitate calculation of the entries. He also devised interpolation procedures of great computational efficiency to obtain intermediate values.

In Switzerland the instrument maker Joost Bürgi arrived at the idea for logarithms independently of Napier, although he did not publish his results until 1620. Four years later a table of logarithms prepared by Kepler appeared in Marburg. Both Bürgi and Kepler were astronomical observers, and Kepler included logarithmic tables in his famous *Tabulae Rudolphinae* (1627; "Rudolphine Tables"), astronomical tabulations of planetary motion derived by using the assumption of elliptical orbits about the Sun.

ANALYTIC GEOMETRY

The invention of analytic geometry was, next to the differential and integral calculus, the most important mathematical development of the 17th century. Originating in the work of the French mathematicians Viète, Fermat, and Descartes, it had by the middle of the century established itself as a major program of mathematical research.

Two tendencies in contemporary mathematics stimulated the rise of analytic geometry. The first was an increased interest in curves, resulting in part from the recovery and Latin translation of the classical treatises of Apollonius, Archimedes, and Pappus, and in part from the increasing importance of curves in such applied fields as astronomy, mechanics, optics, and stereometry. The second was the emergence a century earlier of an established algebraic practice in the work of the Italian and German algebraists and its subsequent shaping by Viète into a powerful mathematical tool at the end of the century.

Viète was a prominent representative of the humanist movement in mathematics that set itself the project of restoring and furthering the achievements of the Classical Greek geometers. In his *In artem analyticem isagoge* (1591; "Introduction to the Analytic Arts"), Viète, as part of his program of rediscovering the method of analysis used by the ancient Greek mathematicians, proposed new algebraic methods that employed variables, constants, and equations, but he saw this as an advancement over the ancient method, a view he arrived at by comparing the geometric analysis contained in Book VII of Pappus's *Collection* with the arithmetic analysis of Diophantus's *Arithmetica*. Pappus had employed an analytic method for the discovery of theorems and the construction of problems. In analysis, by contrast to synthesis, one proceeds from what is sought until one arrives at something known. In approaching an arithmetic problem by laying down an equation among known and unknown magnitudes and then solving for the unknown, one was, Viète reasoned, following an "analytic" procedure.

Viète introduced the concept of algebraic variable, which he denoted using a capital vowel (A, E, I, O, U), as well as the concept of parameter (an unspecified constant quantity), denoted by a capital consonant (B, C, D, and so on). In his system the equation $5BA^2 - 2CA + A^3 = D$ would appear as $B5$ in A quad - C plano 2 in A + A cub aequatur D solido.

Viète retained the classical principle of homogeneity, according to which terms added together must all be of the same dimension. In the above equation, for example, each of the terms has the dimension of a solid or cube. Thus, the constant C, which denotes a plane, is combined with A to form a quantity having the dimension of a solid.

It should be noted that in Viète's scheme the symbol A is part of the expression for the object obtained by operating on the magnitude denoted by A. Thus, operations on the quantities denoted by the variables are reflected in the algebraic notation itself. This innovation, considered by historians of mathematics to be a major conceptual advance in algebra, facilitated the study of the symbolic solution of algebraic equations and led to the creation of the first conscious theory of equations.

After Viète's death the analytic art was applied to the study of curves by his countrymen Fermat and Descartes. Both men were motivated by the same goal, to apply the new algebraic techniques to Apollonius's theory of loci as preserved in Pappus's *Collection*. The most celebrated of these problems consisted of finding the curve or locus traced by a point whose distances from several fixed lines satisfied a given relation.

Fermat adopted Viète's notation in his paper *Ad Locos Planos et Solidos Isagoge* (1636; "Introduction to Plane and Solid Loci"). The title of the paper refers to the ancient classification of curves as plane (straight lines, circles), solid (ellipses, parabolas, and hyperbolas), or linear (curves defined kinematically or by a locus condition). Fermat considered an equation among two variables. One of the variables represented a line measured horizontally from a given initial point, while the other represented a second line positioned at the end of the first line and inclined at a fixed angle to the horizontal. As the first variable varied in magnitude, the second took on a value determined by the equation, and the endpoint of the second line traced out a curve in space. By means of this construction Fermat was able to formulate the fundamental principle of analytic geometry:

> *Whenever two unknown quantities are found in final equality, there results a locus fixed in place, and the endpoint of one of these unknown quantities describes a straight line or a curve.*

The principle implied a correspondence between two different classes of mathematical objects: geometric curves and algebraic equations. In the paper of 1636, Fermat showed that, if the equation is a quadratic, then the curve is a conic section—that is, an ellipse, parabola, or hyperbola. He also showed that the determination of the curve given by an equation is simplified by a transformation involving a change of variables to an equation in standard form.

Descartes's *La Géométrie* appeared in 1637 as an appendix to his famous *Discourse on Method*, the treatise that presented the foundation of his philosophical system. Although supposedly an example from mathematics of his rational method, *La Géométrie* was a technical treatise understandable independently of philosophy. It was destined to become one of the most influential books in the history of mathematics.

In the opening sections of *La Géométrie*, Descartes introduced two innovations. In place of Viète's notation he initiated the modern practice of denoting variables by letters at the end of the alphabet (x, y, z) and parameters by letters at the beginning of the alphabet (a, b, c) and of using exponential notation to indicate powers of x (x^2, x^3,...). More significant conceptually, he set aside Viète's principle of homogeneity, showing by means of a simple construction how to represent multiplication and division of lines by lines. Thus, all magnitudes (lines, areas, and volumes) could be represented independently of their dimension in the same way.

Descartes's goal in *La Géométrie* was to achieve the construction of solutions to geometric problems by means of instruments that were acceptable generalizations of ruler and compass. Algebra was a tool to be used in this program:

> *If, then, we wish to solve any problem, we first suppose the solution already effected, and give names to all the lines that seem necessary for its construction—to those that are unknown as well as to those that are known. Then, making no distinction in any way between known and unknown lines, we must unravel the difficulty in any way that shows most naturally the relations between these lines, until we find it possible to express a single quantity in two ways. This will constitute an equation, since the terms of one of these two expressions are together equal to the terms of the other.*

In the problem of Apollonius, for example, one sought to find the locus of points whose distances from a collection of fixed lines satisfied a given relation. One used this relation to derive an equation, and then, using a geometric procedure involving acceptable instruments of construction, one obtained points on the curve given by the roots of the equation.

Descartes described instruments more general than the compass for drawing "geometric" curves. He stipulated that the parts of the instrument be linked together so that the ratio of the motions of the parts could be knowable. This restriction excluded "mechanical" curves generated by kinematic processes. The Archimedean spiral, for example, was generated by a point moving on a line as the line rotated uniformly about the origin. The ratio of the circumference to the diameter did not permit exact determination:

> *the ratios between straight and curved lines are not known, and I even believe cannot be discovered by men, and therefore no conclusion based upon such ratios can be accepted as rigorous and exact.*

Descartes concluded that a geometric or nonmechanical curve was one whose equation $f(x, y) = 0$ was a polynomial of finite degree in two variables. He wished to restrict mathematics to the consideration of such curves.

Descartes's emphasis on construction reflected his classical orientation. His conservatism with respect to what curves were acceptable in mathematics further distinguished him as a traditional thinker. At the time of his death, in 1650, he had been overtaken by events, as research moved away from questions of construction to problems of finding areas (then called problems of quadrature) and tangents. The geometric objects that were then of growing interest were precisely the mechanical curves that Descartes had wished to banish from mathematics.

Following the important results achieved in the 16th century by Gerolamo Cardano and the Italian algebraists, the theory of algebraic equations reached an impasse. The ideas needed to investigate equations of degree higher than four were slow to develop. The immediate historical influence of Viète, Fermat, and Descartes was to furnish algebraic methods for the investigation of curves. A vigorous school of research became established in Leiden around Frans van Schooten, a Dutch mathematician who edited and published in 1649 a Latin translation of *La Géométrie*. Van Schooten published a second two-volume translation of the same work in 1659–1661 that also contained mathematical appendixes by three of his disciples, Johan de Witt, Johan Hudde, and Hendrick van Heuraet. The Leiden group of mathematicians, which also included Christiaan Huygens, was in large part responsible for the rapid development of Cartesian geometry in the middle of the century.

THE CALCULUS

The historian Carl Boyer called the calculus "the most effective instrument for scientific investigation that mathematics has ever produced." As the mathematics of variability and change, the calculus was the characteristic product of the scientific revolution. The subject was properly the invention of two mathematicians, the German Gottfried Wilhelm Leibniz and the Englishman Isaac Newton. Both men published their researches in the 1680s, Leibniz in 1684 in the recently founded journal *Acta Eruditorum* and Newton in 1687 in his great treatise, the *Principia*. Although a bitter dispute over priority developed later between followers of the two men, it is now clear that they each arrived at the calculus independently.

The calculus developed from techniques to solve two types of problems, the determination of areas and volumes and the calculation of tangents to curves. In classical geometry Archimedes had advanced farthest in this part of mathematics, having used the method of exhaustion to establish rigorously various results on areas and volumes and having derived for some curves (e.g., the spiral) significant results concerning tangents. In the early 17th century, there was a sharp revival of interest in both classes of problems. The decades between 1610 and 1670, referred to in the history of mathematics as "the precalculus period," were a time of remarkable activity in which researchers throughout Europe contributed novel solutions and competed with each other to arrive at important new methods.

The Precalculus Period

In his treatise *Geometria Indivisibilibus Continuorum* (1635; "Geometry of Continuous Indivisibles"), Bonaventura Cavalieri, a professor of mathematics at the University of Bologna, formulated a systematic method for the determination of areas and volumes. As had Archimedes, Cavalieri regarded a plane figure as being composed of a collection of indivisible lines, "all the lines" of the plane figure. The collection was generated by a fixed line moving through space parallel to itself. Cavalieri showed that these collections could be interpreted as magnitudes obeying the rules of Euclidean ratio theory. In proposition 4 of Book II, he derived the result that is written today as

$$\int_0^1 x^2 dx = \frac{1}{3}:$$

Let there be given a parallelogram in which a diagonal is drawn; then "all the squares" of the parallelogram will be triple "all the squares" of each of the triangles determined by the diagonal.

Cavalieri showed that this proposition could be interpreted in different ways—as asserting, for example, that the volume of a cone is one-third the volume of the circumscribed cylinder or that the area under a segment of a

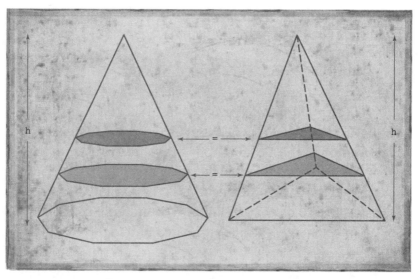

Bonaventura Cavalieri observed that figures (solids) of equal height and in which all corresponding cross sections match in length (area) are of equal area (volume). For example, take a regular polygon equal in area to an equilateral triangle; erect a pyramid on the triangle and a conelike figure of the same height on the polygon; cross sections of both figures taken at the same height above the bases are equal; therefore, by Cavalieri's theorem, so are the volumes of the solids. Encyclopædia Britannica, Inc.

parabola is one-third the area of the associated rectangle. In a later treatise, he generalized the result by proving

$$\int_0^1 x^n dx = \frac{1}{(n+1)}$$

for $n = 3$ to $n = 9$. To establish these results, he introduced transformations among the variables of the problem, using a result equivalent to the binomial theorem for integral exponents. The ideas involved went beyond anything that had appeared in the classical Archimedean theory of content.

Although Cavalieri was successful in formulating a systematic method based on general concepts, his ideas were not easy to apply. The derivation of very simple results required intricate geometric considerations, and the turgid style of the *Geometria Indivisibilibus* was a barrier to its reception.

John Wallis presented a quite different approach to the theory of quadratures in his *Arithmetica Infinitorum* (1655; *The Arithmetic of Infinitesimals*). Wallis, a successor to Henry Briggs as the Savilian Professor of Geometry at Oxford, was a champion of the new methods of arithmetic algebra that he had learned from his teacher William Oughtred. Wallis expressed the area under a curve as the sum of an infinite series and used clever and unrigorous inductions to determine its value. To calculate the area under the parabola,

$$\int_0^1 x^2 \, dx,$$

he considered the successive sums

$$\frac{0+1}{1+1} = \frac{1}{3} + \frac{1}{6}, \frac{0+1+4}{4+4+4} = \frac{1}{3} + \frac{1}{12}, \frac{0+1+4+9}{9+9+9+9} = \frac{1}{3} + \frac{1}{18}$$

and inferred by "induction" the general relation

$$\frac{0^2 + 1^2 + 2^2 + \cdots + n^2}{n^2 + n^2 + n^2 + \cdots + n^2} = \frac{1}{3} + \frac{1}{6n}.$$

By letting the number of terms be infinite, he obtained 1/3 as the limiting value of the expression. With more complicated curves, he achieved very impressive results, including the infinite expression now known as Wallis's product:

$$\frac{4}{\pi} = \frac{3}{2} \cdot \frac{3}{4} \cdot \frac{5}{4} \cdot \frac{5}{6} \cdot \frac{7}{6} \cdots.$$

Research on the determination of tangents, the other subject leading to the calculus, proceeded along different lines. In *La Géométrie* Descartes had presented a method that could in principle be applied to any algebraic or "geometric" curve—i.e., any curve whose equation was a polynomial of finite degree in two variables. The method depended upon finding the normal, the line perpendicular to the tangent, using the algebraic condition that it be the unique radius to intersect the curve in only one point. Descartes's method was simplified by Hudde, a member of the Leiden group of mathematicians, and was published in 1659 in van Schooten's edition of *La Géométrie*

A class of curves of growing interest in the 17th century comprised those generated kinematically by a point moving through space. The famous cycloidal curve, for example, was traced by a point on the perimeter of a wheel that rolled on a line without slipping or sliding. These curves were nonalgebraic and hence could not be treated by Descartes's method. Gilles Personne de Roberval, professor at the Collège Royale in Paris, devised a method borrowed from dynamics to determine their tangents. In his analysis of projectile motion, Galileo had shown that the instantaneous velocity of a particle is compounded of two separate motions: a constant horizontal motion and an increasing vertical motion due to gravity. If the motion of the generating point of a kinematic curve is likewise

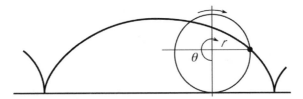

A cycloid is produced by a point on the circumference of a circle as the circle rolls along a straight line. Encyclopædia Britannica, Inc.

regarded as the sum of two velocities, then the tangent will lie in the direction of their sum. Roberval applied this idea to several different kinematic curves, obtaining results that were often ingenious and elegant.

In an essay of 1636 circulated among French mathematicians, Fermat presented a method of tangents adapted from a procedure he had devised to determine maxima and minima and used it to find tangents to several algebraic curves of the form $y = x^n$. His account was short and contained no explanation of the mathematical basis of the new method. It is possible to see in his procedure an argument involving infinitesimals, and Fermat has sometimes been proclaimed the discoverer of the differential

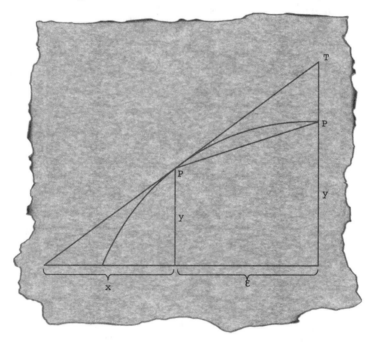

Pierre de Fermat anticipated the calculus with his approach to finding the tangent line to a given curve. To find the tangent to a point P (x, y), he began by drawing a secant line to a nearby point P1 (x + ε, y1). For small ε, the secant line PP1 is approximately equal to the angle PAB at which the tangent meets the x-axis. Finally, Fermat allowed ε to shrink to zero, thus obtaining a mathematical expression for the true tangent line. Encyclopædia Britannica, Inc.

calculus. Modern historical study, however, suggests that he was working with concepts introduced by Viète and that his method was based on finite algebraic ideas.

Isaac Barrow, the Lucasian Professor of Mathematics at the University of Cambridge, published in 1670 his *Geometrical Lectures*, a treatise that more than any other anticipated the unifying ideas of the calculus. In it he adopted a purely geometric form of exposition to show how the determinations of areas and tangents are inverse problems. He began with a curve and considered the slope of its tangent corresponding to each value of the abscissa. He then defined an auxiliary curve by the condition that its ordinate be equal to this slope and showed that the area

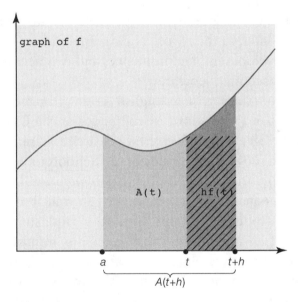

Graphical illustration of the fundamental theorem of calculus: $\frac{d}{dt}\left(\int_a^t f(u)\,du\right)$ *= f(t). By definition, the derivative of A(t) is equal to [A(t + h) - A(t)]/h as h tends to zero. Note that the triangle in the illustration is equal to the numerator of the preceding quotient and that the striped region, whose area is equal to its base h times its height f(t), tends to the same value for small h. By replacing the numerator, A(t + h) - A(t), by hf(t) and dividing by h, f(t) is obtained. Taking the limit as h tends to zero completes the proof of the fundamental theorem of calculus.* Encyclopædia Britannica, Inc.

under the auxiliary curve corresponding to a given abscissa is equal to the rectangle whose sides are unity and the ordinate of the original curve. When reformulated analytically, this result expresses the inverse character of differentiation and integration, the fundamental theorem of the calculus. Although Barrow's decision to proceed geometrically prevented him from taking the final step to a true calculus, his lectures influenced both Newton and Leibniz.

Newton and Leibniz

The essential insight of Newton and Leibniz was to use Cartesian algebra to synthesize the earlier results and to develop algorithms that could be applied uniformly to a wide class of problems. The formative period of Newton's researches was from 1665 to 1670, while Leibniz worked a few years later, in the 1670s. Their contributions differ in origin, development, and influence, and it is necessary to consider each man separately.

Newton, the son of an English farmer, became in 1669 the Lucasian Professor of Mathematics at the University of Cambridge. Newton's earliest researches in mathematics grew in 1665 from his study of van Schooten's edition of *La Géométrie* and Wallis's *Arithmetica Infinitorum*. Using the Cartesian equation of the curve, he reformulated Wallis's results, introducing for this purpose infinite sums in the powers of an unknown x, now known as infinite series. Possibly under the influence of Barrow, he used infinitesimals to establish for various curves the inverse relationship of tangents and areas. The operations of differentiation and integration emerged in his work as analytic processes that could be applied generally to investigate curves.

Unusually sensitive to questions of rigour, Newton at a fairly early stage tried to establish his new method on a sound foundation using ideas from kinematics. A variable was regarded as a "fluent," a magnitude that flows with time. Its derivative or rate of change with respect to time was called a "fluxion," denoted by the given variable with a dot above it. The basic problem of the calculus was to investigate relations among fluents and their fluxions. Newton finished a treatise on the method of fluxions as early as 1671, although it was not published until 1736. In the 18th century, this method became the preferred approach to the calculus among British mathematicians, especially after the appearance in 1742 of Colin Maclaurin's influential *Treatise of Fluxions*.

Newton first published the calculus in Book I of his great *Philosophiae Naturalis Principia Mathematica* (1687; *Mathematical Principles of Natural Philosophy*). Originating as a treatise on the dynamics of particles, the *Principia* presented an inertial physics that combined Galileo's mechanics and Kepler's planetary astronomy. It was written in the early 1680s at a time when Newton was reacting against Descartes's science and mathematics. Setting aside the analytic method of fluxions, Newton introduced in 11 introductory lemmas his calculus of first and last ratios, a geometric theory of limits that provided the mathematical basis of his dynamics.

Newton's use of the calculus in the *Principia* is illustrated by proposition 11 of Book I: if the orbit of a particle moving under a centripetal force is an ellipse with the centre of force at one focus, then the force is inversely proportional to the square of the distance from the centre. Because the planets were known by Kepler's laws to move in ellipses with the Sun at one focus, this result supported his inverse square law of gravitation. To establish the proposition, Newton derived an approximate measure for the force by using small lines defined in terms of the radius (the line from the force centre to the particle) and the tangent to the curve at a point. This result expressed geometrically the proportionality of force to vector acceleration. Using properties of the ellipse known from classical geometry, Newton calculated the limit of this measure and showed that it was equal to a constant times 1 over the square of the radius.

Newton avoided analytic processes in the *Principia* by expressing magnitudes and ratios directly in terms of geometric quantities, both finite and infinitesimal. His decision to eschew analysis constituted a striking rejection of the algebraic methods that had been important in his own early researches on the calculus. Although the *Principia* was of inestimable value for later mechanics, it would be reworked by researchers on the Continent and expressed in the mathematical idiom of the Leibnizian calculus.

Leibniz's interest in mathematics was aroused in 1672 during a visit to Paris, where the Dutch mathematician Christiaan Huygens introduced him to his work on the theory of curves. Under Huygens's tutelage Leibniz immersed himself for the next several years in the study of mathematics. He investigated relationships between the summing and differencing of finite and infinite sequences of numbers. Having read Barrow's geometric lectures, he devised a transformation rule to calculate quadratures, obtaining the famous infinite series for $\pi/4$:

$$\frac{\pi}{4} = \frac{1}{1} - \frac{1}{3} + \frac{1}{5} - \frac{1}{7} + \cdots$$

Leibniz was interested in questions of logic and notation, of how to construct a *characteristica universalis* for rational investigation. After considerable experimentation he arrived by the late 1670s at an algorithm based on the symbols d and $\int$. He first published his research on differential calculus in 1684 in an article in the *Acta Eruditorum*,

Nova Methodus pro Maximis et Minimis, Itemque Tangentibus, qua nec Fractas nec Irrationales Quantitates Moratur, et Singulare pro illi Calculi Genus ("A New Method for Maxima and Minima as Well as Tangents, Which Is Impeded Neither by Fractional nor by Irrational Quantities, and a Remarkable Type of Calculus for This"). In this article he introduced the differential dx satisfying the rules $d(x + y) = dx + dy$ and $d(xy) = xdy + ydx$ and illustrated his calculus with a few examples. Two years later he published a second article, *On a Deeply Hidden Geometry,* in which he introduced and explained the symbol $\int$ for integration. He stressed the power of his calculus to investigate transcendental curves, the very class of "mechanical" objects Descartes had believed lay beyond the power of analysis, and derived a simple analytic formula for the cycloid.

Leibniz continued to publish results on the new calculus in the *Acta Eruditorum* and began to explore his ideas in extensive correspondence with other scholars. Within a few years, he had attracted a group of researchers to promulgate his methods, including the brothers Johann Bernoulli and Jakob Bernoulli in Basel and the priest Pierre Varignon and Guillaume-François-Antoine de L'Hospital in Paris. In 1700 he persuaded Frederick William I of Prussia to establish the Brandenburg Society of Sciences (later renamed the Berlin Academy of Sciences), with himself appointed president for life.

Leibniz's vigorous espousal of the new calculus, the didactic spirit of his writings, and his ability to attract a community of researchers contributed to his enormous influence on subsequent mathematics. In contrast, Newton's slowness to publish and his personal reticence resulted in a reduced presence within European mathematics. Although the British school in the 18th century included capable researchers, Abraham de Moivre, James Stirling, Brook Taylor, and Maclaurin among them, they failed to establish a program of research comparable to that established by Leibniz's followers on the Continent. There is a certain tragedy in Newton's isolation and his reluctance to acknowledge the superiority of continental analysis. As the historian Michael Mahoney observed:

> *Whatever the revolutionary influence of the* Principia, *mathematics would have looked much the same if Newton had never existed. In that endeavour he belonged to a community, and he was far from indispensable to it.*

The 18th Century

Institutional Background

After 1700 a movement to found learned societies on the model of Paris and London spread throughout Europe and the American colonies. The academy was the predominant institution of science until it was displaced by the university in the 19th century. The leading mathematicians of the period, such as Leonhard Euler, Jean Le Rond d'Alembert, and Joseph-Louis Lagrange, pursued academic careers at St. Petersburg, Paris, and London.

The French Academy of Sciences (Paris) provides an informative study of the 18th-century learned society. The academy was divided into six sections, three for the mathematical and three for the physical sciences. The mathematical sections were for geometry, astronomy, and mechanics, the physical sections for chemistry, anatomy, and botany. Membership in the academy was divided by section, with each section contributing three *pensionnaires*, two associates, and two adjuncts. There was also a group of free associates, distinguished men of science from the provinces, and foreign associates, eminent international figures in the field. A larger group of 70 corresponding

Jean le Rond d'Alembert. SSPL via Getty Images

members had partial privileges, including the right to communicate reports to the academy. The administrative core consisted of a permanent secretary, treasurer, president, and vice president. In a given year, the average total membership in the academy was 153.

Prominent characteristics of the academy included its small and elite membership, made up heavily of men from the middle class, and its emphasis on the mathematical sciences. In addition to holding regular meetings and publishing memoirs, the academy organized scientific expeditions and administered prize competitions on important mathematical and scientific questions.

The historian Roger Hahn noted that the academy in the 18th century allowed "the coupling of relative doctrinal freedom on scientific questions with rigorous evaluations by peers," an important characteristic of modern professional science. Academic mathematics and science did, however, foster a stronger individualistic ethos than is usual today. A determined individual such as Euler or Lagrange could emphasize a given program of research through his own work, the publications of the academy, and the setting of the prize competitions. The academy as an institution may have been more conducive to the solitary patterns of research in a theoretical subject like mathematics than it was to the experimental sciences. The separation of research from teaching is perhaps the most striking characteristic that distinguished the academy from the model of university-based science that developed in the 19th century.

Analysis and Mechanics

The scientific revolution had bequeathed to mathematics a major program of research in analysis and mechanics. The period from 1700 to 1800, "the century of analysis," witnessed the consolidation of the calculus and its extensive application to mechanics. With expansion came specialization as different parts of the subject acquired their own identity: ordinary and partial differential equations, calculus of variations, infinite series, and differential geometry. The applications of analysis were also varied, including the theory of the vibrating string, particle dynamics, the theory of rigid bodies, the mechanics of flexible and elastic media, and the theory of compressible and incompressible

fluids. Analysis and mechanics developed in close association, with problems in one giving rise to concepts and
techniques in the other, and all the leading mathematicians
of the period made important contributions to mechanics.

The close relationship between mathematics and
mechanics in the 18th century had roots extending deep
into Enlightenment thought. In the organizational chart
of knowledge at the beginning of the preliminary discourse
to the *Encyclopédie*, Jean Le Rond d'Alembert distinguished
between "pure" mathematics (geometry, arithmetic, algebra,
calculus) and "mixed" mathematics (mechanics, geometric
astronomy, optics, art of conjecturing). Mathematics generally was classified as a "science of nature" and separated
from logic, a "science of man." The modern disciplinary
division between physics and mathematics and the association of the latter with logic had not yet developed.

Mathematical mechanics itself as it was practiced in
the 18th century differed in important respects from later
physics. The goal of modern physics is to explore the
ultimate particulate structure of matter and to arrive at
fundamental laws of nature to explain physical phenomena. The character of applied investigation in the 18th
century was rather different. The material parts of a given
system and their interrelationship were idealized for the
purposes of analysis. A material object could be treated as
a point-mass (a mathematical point at which it is assumed
all the mass of the object is concentrated), as a rigid body,
as a continuously deformable medium, and so on. The
intent was to obtain a mathematical description of the
macroscopic behaviour of the system rather than to ascertain the ultimate physical basis of the phenomena. In this
respect the 18th-century viewpoint is closer to modern
mathematical engineering than it is to physics.

Mathematical research in the 18th century was coordi-
nated by the Paris, Berlin, and St. Petersburg academies,

as well as by several smaller provincial scientific academies and societies. Although England and Scotland were important centres early in the century, with Maclaurin's death in 1746 the British flame was all but extinguished.

HISTORY OF ANALYSIS

The history of analysis in the 18th century can be followed in the official memoirs of the academies and in independently published expository treatises. In the first decades of the century, the calculus was cultivated in an atmosphere of intellectual excitement as mathematicians applied the new methods to a range of problems in the geometry of curves. The brothers Johann and Jakob Bernoulli showed that the shape of a smooth wire along which a particle descends in the least time is the cycloid, a transcendental curve much studied in the previous century. Working in a spirit of keen rivalry, the two brothers arrived at ideas that would later develop into the calculus of variations. In his study of the rectification of the lemniscate, a ribbon-shaped curve discovered by Jakob Bernoulli in 1694, Giulio Carlo Fagnano (1682–1766) introduced ingenious analytic transformations that laid the foundation for the theory of elliptic integrals. Nikolaus I Bernoulli (1687–1759), the nephew of Johann and Jakob, proved the equality of mixed second-order partial derivatives and made important contributions to differential equations by the construction of orthogonal trajectories to families of curves. Pierre Varignon (1654–1722), Johann Bernoulli, and Jakob Hermann (1678–1733) continued to develop analytic dynamics as they adapted Leibniz's calculus to the inertial mechanics of Newton's *Principia*.

Geometric conceptions and problems predominated in the early calculus. This emphasis on the curve as the object of study provided coherence to what was otherwise a disparate collection of analytic techniques. With its continued

the occasion to develop his ideas for an algebraic foundation of the subject. The lectures were published in 1797 under the title *Théorie des fonctions analytiques* ("Theory of Analytical Functions"), a treatise whose contents were summarized in its longer title, "Containing the Principles of the Differential Calculus Disengaged from All Consideration of Infinitesimals, Vanishing Limits, or Fluxions and Reduced to the Algebraic Analysis of Finite Quantities." Lagrange published a second treatise on the subject in 1801, a work that appeared in a revised and expanded form in 1806.

The range of subjects presented and the consistency of style distinguished Lagrange's didactic writings from other contemporary expositions of the calculus. He began with Euler's notion of a function as an analytic expression composed of variables and constants. He defined the "derived function," or derivative $f'(x)$ of $f(x)$, to be the coefficient of i in the Taylor expansion of $f(x + i)$. Assuming the general possibility of such expansions, he attempted a rather complete theory of the differential and integral calculus, including extensive applications to geometry and mechanics. Lagrange's lectures represented the most advanced development of the 18th-century analytic conception of the calculus.

Beginning with Baron Cauchy in the 1820s, later mathematicians used the concept of limit to establish the calculus on an arithmetic basis. The algebraic viewpoint of Euler and Lagrange was rejected. To arrive at a proper historical appreciation of their work, it is necessary to reflect on the meaning of analysis in the 18th century. Since Viète, analysis had referred generally to mathematical methods that employed equations, variables, and constants. With the extensive development of the calculus by Leibniz and his school, analysis became identified with all calculus-related subjects. In addition to this historical association, there was a deeper sense in which analytic methods were fundamental to the new mathematics. An analytic equation implied the existence of a relation that remained valid as the variables changed continuously in magnitude. Analytic algorithms and transformations presupposed a correspondence between local and global change, the basic concern of the calculus. It is this aspect of analysis that fascinated Euler and Lagrange and caused them to see in it the "true metaphysics" of the calculus.

Other Developments

During the period 1600–1800, significant advances occurred in the theory of equations, foundations of Euclidean geometry, number theory, projective geometry, and probability theory. These subjects, which became mature branches of mathematics only in the 19th century, never rivaled analysis and mechanics as programs of research.

Theory of Equations

After the dramatic successes of Niccolò Fontana Tartaglia and Lodovico Ferrari in the 16th century, the theory of equations developed slowly, as problems resisted solution by known techniques. In the later 18th century, the subject experienced an infusion of new ideas. Interest was concentrated on two problems. The first was to establish the existence of a root of the general polynomial equation of degree n. The second was to express the roots as algebraic functions of the coefficients or to show why it was not, in general, possible to do so.

The proposition that the general polynomial with real coefficients has a root of the form $a + b\sqrt{-1}$ became known later as the fundamental theorem of algebra. By 1742 Euler had recognized that roots appear in conjugate pairs. If $a + b\sqrt{-1}$ is a root, then so is $a - b\sqrt{-1}$. Thus, if $a + b\sqrt{-1}$ is a root of $f(x) = 0$, then $f(x) = (x^2 - 2ax - a^2 - b^2)g(x)$. The fundamental theorem was therefore equivalent to asserting that a polynomial may be decomposed into linear and quadratic factors. This result was of considerable importance for the theory of integration, since by the method of partial fractions it ensured that a rational function, the quotient of two polynomials, could always be integrated in terms of algebraic and elementary transcendental functions.

Although d'Alembert, Euler, and Lagrange worked on the fundamental theorem, the first successful proof was developed by Carl Friedrich Gauss in his doctoral dissertation of 1799. Earlier researchers had investigated special cases or had concentrated on showing that all possible roots were of the form $a \pm b\sqrt{-1}$. Gauss tackled the problem of existence directly. Expressing the unknown in terms of the polar coordinate variables r and θ, he showed that a solution of the polynomial would lie at the intersection of two curves of the form $T(r, \theta) = 0$ and $U(r, \theta) = 0$. By a careful and rigorous investigation he proved that the two curves intersect.

Gauss's demonstration of the fundamental theorem initiated a new approach to the question of mathematical existence. In the 18th century, mathematicians were interested in the nature of particular analytic processes or the form that given solutions should take. Mathematical entities were regarded as things that were given, not as things whose existence needed to be established. Because analysis was applied in geometry and mechanics, the formalism seemed to possess a clear interpretation that obviated any need to consider questions of existence. Gauss's demonstration was the beginning of a change of attitude in mathematics, of a shift to the rigorous, internal development of the subject.

The problem of expressing the roots of a polynomial as functions of the coefficients was addressed by several mathematicians independently about 1770. The Cambridge mathematician Edward Waring published treatises in 1762 and 1770 on the theory of equations. In 1770 Lagrange presented a long expository memoir on the subject to the Berlin Academy, and in 1771 Alexandre Vandermonde submitted a paper to the French Academy of Sciences. Although the ideas of the three men were related, Lagrange's memoir was the most extensive and most influential historically.

Lagrange presented a detailed analysis of the solution by radicals of second-, third-, and fourth-degree equations and investigated why these solutions failed when the degree was greater than or equal to five. He introduced the novel idea of considering functions of the roots and examining the values they assumed as the roots were permuted. He was able to show that the solution of an equation depends on the construction of a second resolvent equation, but he was unable to provide a general procedure for solving the resolvent when the degree of the original equation was greater than four. Although his theory left the subject in an unfinished condition, it provided a solid basis for future work. The search for a general solution to the polynomial equation would provide the greatest single impetus for the transformation of algebra in the 19th century.

The efforts of Lagrange, Vandermonde, and Waring illustrate how difficult it was to develop new concepts in algebra. The history of the theory of equations belies the view that mathematics is subject to almost automatic technical development. Much of the later algebraic work would be devoted to devising terminology, concepts, and methods necessary to advance the subject.

Foundations of Geometry

Although the emphasis of mathematics after 1650 was increasingly on analysis, foundational questions in classical geometry continued to arouse interest. Attention centred on the fifth postulate of Book I of the *Elements*, which Euclid had used to prove the existence of a unique parallel through a point to a given line. Since antiquity, Greek, Islamic, and European geometers had attempted unsuccessfully to show that the parallel postulate need not be a postulate but could instead be deduced from the other postulates of Euclidean geometry. During the period 1600–1800, mathematicians continued these efforts by trying to show that the postulate was equivalent to some result that was considered self-evident. Although the decisive breakthrough to non-Euclidean geometry would not occur until the 19th century, researchers did achieve a deeper and more systematic understanding of the classical properties of space.

Interest in the parallel postulate developed in the 16th century after the recovery and Latin translation of Proclus's commentary on Euclid's *Elements*. The Italian researchers Christopher Clavius in 1574 and Giordano Vitale in 1680 showed that the postulate is equivalent to asserting that the line equidistant from a straight line is a straight line. In 1693 John Wallis, Savilian Professor of Geometry at Oxford, attempted a different demonstration, proving that the axiom follows from the assumption that to every figure there exists a similar figure of arbitrary magnitude.

In 1733 the Italian Girolamo Saccheri published his *Euclides ab Omni Naevo Vindicatus* ("Euclid Cleared of Every Flaw"). This was an important work of synthesis in which he provided a complete analysis of the problem of parallels in terms of Omar Khayyam's quadrilateral. Using the Euclidean assumption that straight lines do not enclose an area, he was able to exclude geometries that contain no parallels. It remained to prove the existence of a unique parallel through a point to a given line. To do this, Saccheri adopted the procedure of reductio ad absurdum. He assumed the existence of more than one parallel and attempted to derive a contradiction. After a long and detailed investigation, he was able to convince himself (mistakenly) that he had found the desired contradiction.

In 1766 Johann Heinrich Lambert of the Berlin Academy composed *Die Theorie der Parallellinien* ("The Theory of Parallel Lines"; published 1786), a penetrating study of the fifth postulate in Euclidean geometry. Among other theorems Lambert proved is that the parallel axiom is equivalent to the assertion that the sum of the angles of a triangle is equal to two right angles. He combined this fact with Wallis's result to arrive at an unexpected characterization of classical space. According to Lambert, if the parallel postulate is rejected, it follows that for every angle θ less than $2R/3$ (R is a right angle) an equilateral triangle can be constructed with corner angle θ. By Wallis's result any triangle similar to this triangle must be congruent to it. It is therefore possible to associate with every angle a definite length, the side of the corresponding equilateral triangle. Since the measurement of angles is absolute, independent of any convention concerning the selection of units, it follows that an absolute unit of length exists. Hence, to accept the parallel postulate is to deny the possibility of an absolute concept of length.

The final 18th-century contribution to the theory of parallels was Adrien-Marie Legendre's textbook *Éléments de géométrie* (*Elements of Geometry and Trigonometry*), the first edition of which appeared in 1794. Legendre presented an elegant demonstration that purported to show that the sum of the angles of a triangle is equal to two right angles. He believed that he had conclusively established the validity of the parallel postulate. His work attracted a large audience and was influential in informing readers of the new ideas in geometry.

The 18th-century failure to develop a non-Euclidean geometry was rooted in deeply held philosophical beliefs. In his *Critique of Pure Reason* (1781), Immanuel Kant had emphasized the synthetic a priori character of mathematical judgments. From this standpoint, statements of geometry and arithmetic were necessarily true propositions with definite empirical content. The existence of similar figures of different size, or the conventional character of units of length, appeared self-evident to mathematicians of the period. As late as 1824 Pierre-Simon, marquis de Laplace, wrote:

> *Thus the notion of space includes a special property, self-evident, without which the properties of parallels cannot be rigorously established. The idea of a bounded region, e.g., the circle, contains nothing which depends on its absolute magnitude. But if we imagine its radius to diminish, we are brought without fail to the diminution in the same ratio of its circumference and the sides of all the inscribed figures. This proportionality appears to me a more natural postulate than that of Euclid, and it is worthy of note that it is discovered afresh in the results of the theory of universal gravitation.*

MATHEMATICS IN THE 19TH AND 20TH CENTURIES

Most of the powerful abstract mathematical theories in use today originated in the 19th century, so any historical account of the period should be supplemented by reference to detailed treatments of these topics. Yet mathematics grew so much during this period that any account must necessarily be selective. Nonetheless, some broad features stand out. The growth of mathematics as a profession was accompanied by a sharpening division between mathematics and the physical sciences, and contact between the two subjects takes place today across a clear professional boundary. One result of this separation has been that mathematics, no longer able to rely on its scientific import for its validity, developed markedly higher standards of rigour. It was also freed to develop in directions that had little to do with applicability. Some of these pure creations have turned out to be surprisingly applicable, while the attention to rigour has led to a wholly novel conception of the nature of mathematics and logic. Moreover, many outstanding questions in mathematics yielded to the more conceptual approaches that came into vogue.

PROJECTIVE GEOMETRY

The French Revolution provoked a radical rethinking of education in France, and mathematics was given a prominent role. The École Polytechnique was established in 1794 with the ambitious task of preparing all candidates for the specialist civil and military engineering schools of the republic. Mathematicians of the highest calibre were involved. The result was a rapid and sustained development of the subject. The inspiration for the École was that of Gaspard Monge, who believed strongly that mathematics should serve the scientific and technical needs of the state. To that end he devised a syllabus that promoted his own descriptive geometry, which was useful in the design of forts, gun emplacements, and machines and which was employed to great effect in the Napoleonic survey of Egyptian historical sites.

In Monge's descriptive geometry, three-dimensional objects are described by their orthogonal projections onto a horizontal and a vertical plane, the plan and elevation of the object. A pupil of Monge, Jean-Victor Poncelet, was taken prisoner during Napoleon's retreat from Moscow and sought to keep up his spirits while in jail in Saratov by thinking over the geometry he had learned. He dispensed with the restriction to orthogonal projections and decided to investigate what properties figures have in common with their shadows. There are several of these properties: a straight line casts a straight shadow, and a tangent to a curve casts a shadow that is tangent to the shadow of the curve. But some properties are lost: the lengths and angles of a figure bear no relation to the lengths and angles of its shadow. Poncelet felt that the properties that survive are worthy of study, and, by considering only those properties that a figure shares with all its shadows, Poncelet hoped to put truly geometric reasoning on a par with algebraic geometry.

In 1822 Poncelet published the *Traité des propriétés projectives des figures* ("Treatise on the Projective Properties of Figures"). From his standpoint every conic section is equivalent to a circle, so his treatise contained a unified treatment of the theory of conic sections. It also established several new results. Geometers who took up his work divided into two groups: those who accepted his terms and those who, finding them obscure, reformulated his ideas in the spirit of algebraic geometry. On the algebraic side, it was taken up in Germany by August Ferdinand Möbius, who seems to have come to his ideas independently of Poncelet, and then by Julius Plücker. They showed how rich was the projective geometry of curves defined by algebraic equations and thereby gave an enormous boost to the algebraic study of curves, comparable to the original impetus provided by Descartes. Germany also produced synthetic projective geometers, notably Jakob Steiner (born in Switzerland but educated in Germany) and Karl Georg Christian von Staudt, who emphasized what can be understood about a figure from a careful consideration of all its transformations.

Within the debates about projective geometry emerged one of the few synthetic ideas to be discovered since the days of Euclid, that of duality. This associates with each point a line and with each line a point, in such a way that (1) three points lying in a line give rise to three lines meeting in a point and, conversely, three lines meeting in a point give rise to three points lying on a line and (2) if one starts with a point (or a line) and passes to the associated line (point) and then repeats the process, one returns to the original point (line). One way of using duality (presented by Poncelet) is to pick an arbitrary conic and then to associate with a point P lying outside the conic the line that joins the points R and S at which the tangents through P to the conic touch the conic. A second method is needed for points on or inside the conic. The feature of duality that makes it so exciting is that one can apply it mechanically to every proof in geometry, interchanging "point" and line" and "collinear" and "concurrent" throughout, and so obtain a new result. Sometimes a result turns out to be equivalent to the original, sometimes to its converse, but at a single stroke the number of theorems was more or less doubled.

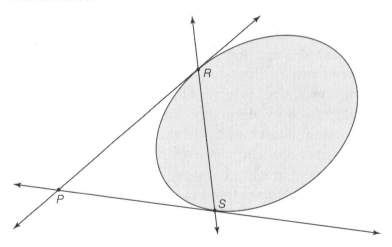

Duality associates with the point P the line RS, and vice versa. Encyclopædia Britannica, Inc.

MAKING THE CALCULUS RIGOROUS

Monge's educational ideas were opposed by Lagrange, who favoured a more traditional and theoretical diet of advanced calculus and rational mechanics (the application of the calculus to the study of the motion of solids and liquids). Eventually Lagrange won, and the vision of mathematics that was presented to the world was that of an autonomous subject that was also applicable to a broad range of phenomena by virtue of its great generality, a view that has persisted to the present day.

During the 1820s Augustin-Louis, Baron Cauchy, lectured at the École Polytechnique on the foundations of the calculus. Since its invention it had been generally agreed that the calculus gave correct answers, but no one had been able to give a satisfactory explanation of why this was so. Cauchy rejected Lagrange's algebraic approach and proved that Lagrange's basic assumption that every function has a power series expansion is in fact false. Newton had suggested a geometric or dynamic basis for calculus, but this ran the risk of introducing a vicious circle when the calculus was applied to mechanical or geometric problems. Cauchy proposed basing the calculus on a sophisticated and difficult interpretation of the idea of two points

Augustin-Louis, Baron Cauchy. SSPL via Getty Images

or numbers being arbitrarily close together. Although his students disliked the new approach, and Cauchy was ordered to teach material that the students could actually understand and use, his methods gradually became established and refined to form the core of the modern rigorous calculus, a subject now called mathematical analysis.

Traditionally, the calculus had been concerned with the two processes of differentiation and integration and the reciprocal relation that exists between them. Cauchy provided a novel underpinning by stressing the importance of the concept of continuity, which is more basic than either. He showed that, once the concepts of a continuous function and limit are defined, the concepts of a differentiable function and an integrable function can be defined in terms of them. Unfortunately, neither of these concepts is easy to grasp, and the much-needed degree of precision they bring to mathematics has proved difficult to appreciate. Roughly speaking, a function is continuous at a point in its domain if small changes in the input around the specified value produce only small changes in the output.

Thus, the familiar graph of a parabola $y = x^2$ is continuous around the point $x = 0$; as x varies by small amounts, so necessarily does y. On the other hand, the graph of the function that takes the value 0 when x is negative or zero, and the value 1 when x is positive, plainly has a discontinuous graph at the point $x = 0$, and it is indeed discontinuous there according to the definition. If x varies from 0 by any small positive amount, the value of the function jumps by the fixed amount 1, which is not an arbitrarily small amount.

Cauchy said that a function $f(x)$ tends to a limiting value l as x tends to the value a whenever the value of the difference $f(x) - f(a)$ becomes arbitrarily small as the difference $x - a$ itself becomes arbitrarily small. He then showed

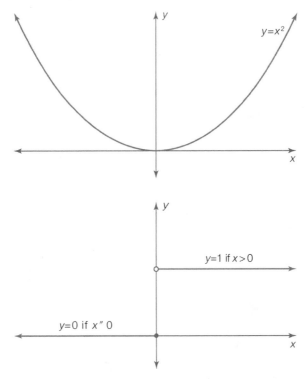

Continuous and discontinuous functions. Encyclopædia Britannica, Inc.

that, if $f(x)$ is continuous at a, the limiting value of the function as x tended to a was indeed $f(a)$. The crucial feature of this definition is that it defines what it means for a variable quantity to tend to something entirely without reference to ideas of motion.

Cauchy then said a function $f(x)$ is differentiable at the point a if, as x tends to a (which it is never allowed to reach), the value of the quotient $[f(x) - f(a)]/(x - a)$ tends to a limiting value, called the derivative of the function $f(x)$ at a. To define the integral of a function $f(x)$ between the values a and b, Cauchy went back to the primitive idea of the integral as the measure of the area under the graph of the function. He approximated this area by rectangles

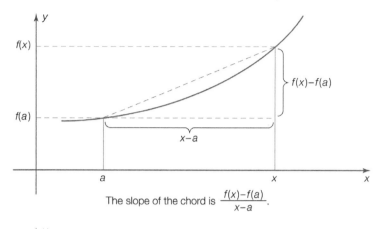

The slope of the chord is $\dfrac{f(x)-f(a)}{x-a}$.

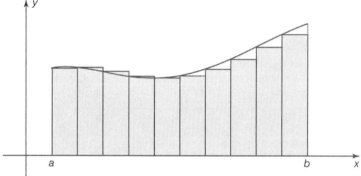

The area under $y=f(x)$ between $x=a$ and $x=b$ is approximately the area of the rectangles, as the number of rectangles increases indefinitely.

Differentiation and integration. Encyclopædia Britannica, Inc.

and said that, if the sum of the areas of the rectangles tends to a limit as their number increases indefinitely and if this limiting value is the same however the rectangles are obtained, then the function is integrable. Its integral is the common limiting value. After he had defined the integral independently of the differential calculus, Cauchy had to prove that the processes of integrating and differentiating are mutually inverse. This he did, giving for the first time a rigorous foundation to all the elementary calculus of his day.

FOURIER SERIES

The other crucial figure of the time in France was Joseph, Baron Fourier. His major contribution, presented in *The Analytical Theory of Heat* (1822), was to the theory of heat diffusion in solid bodies. He proposed that any function could be written as an infinite sum of the trigonometric functions cosine and sine; for example,

$$f(x) = a_0 + a_1 \sin x + a_2 \sin 2x + \ldots.$$

Expressions of this kind had been written down earlier, but Fourier's treatment was new in the degree of attention given to their convergence. He investigated the question "Given the function $f(x)$, for what range of values of x does the expression above sum to a finite number?" It turned out that the answer depends on the coefficients a_n, and Fourier gave rules for obtaining them of the form

$$a_n = \int_{-\pi}^{\pi} f(x) \sin(nx)dx.$$

Had Fourier's work been entirely correct, it would have brought all functions into the calculus, making possible the solution of many kinds of differential equations and greatly extending the theory of mathematical physics. But his arguments were unduly naive: after Cauchy it was not clear that the function $f(x) \sin(nx)$ was necessarily integrable. When Fourier's ideas were finally published, they were eagerly taken up, but the more cautious mathematicians, notably the influential German Peter Gustav Lejeune Dirichlet, wanted to rederive Fourier's conclusions in a more rigorous way. Fourier's methodology was widely accepted, but questions about its validity in detail were to occupy mathematicians for the rest of the century.

Elliptic Functions

The theory of functions of a complex variable was also being decisively reformulated. At the start of the 19th century, complex numbers were discussed from a quasi-philosophical standpoint by several French writers, notably Jean-Robert Argand. A consensus emerged that complex numbers should be thought of as pairs of real numbers, with suitable rules for their addition and multiplication so that the pair (0, 1) was a square root of -1. The underlying meaning of such a number pair was given by its geometric interpretation either as a point in a plane or as a directed segment joining the coordinate origin to the point in question. (This representation is sometimes called the Argand diagram.) In 1827, while revising an earlier manuscript for publication, Cauchy showed how the problem of integrating functions of two variables can be illuminated by a theory of functions of a single complex variable, which he was then developing. But the decisive influence on the growth of the subject came from the theory of elliptic functions.

The study of elliptic functions originated in the 18th century, when many authors studied integrals of the form

$$\int_0^x \frac{p(t)dt}{\sqrt{q(t)}},$$

where $p(t)$ and $q(t)$ are polynomials in t and $q(t)$ is of degree 3 or 4 in t. Such integrals arise naturally, for example, as an expression for the length of an arc of an ellipse (whence the name). These integrals cannot be evaluated explicitly. They do not define a function that can be obtained from the rational and trigonometric functions, a difficulty that added to their interest. Elliptic integrals were intensively studied for many years by the French mathematician Legendre, who was able to calculate tables of values for such expressions as functions of their upper endpoint, x. But the topic was completely transformed in the late 1820s by the independent but closely overlapping discoveries of two young mathematicians, the Norwegian Niels Henrik Abel and the German Carl Jacobi. These men showed that, if one allowed the variable x to be complex and the problem was inverted, so that the object of study became

$$u = \int_0^x \frac{p(t)dt}{\sqrt{q(t)}},$$

considered as defining a function x of a variable u, then a remarkable new theory became apparent. The new function, for example, possessed a property that generalized the basic property of periodicity of the trigonometric functions sine and cosine: $\sin(x) = \sin(x + 2\pi)$. Any function of the kind just described has two distinct periods, ω_1 and ω_2:

$$x(u) = x(u + \omega_1) = x(u + \omega_2).$$

These new functions, the elliptic functions, aroused a considerable degree of interest. The analogy with trigonometric functions ran very deep (indeed the trigonometric functions turned out to be special cases of elliptic functions), but their greatest influence was on the burgeoning general study of functions of a complex variable. The theory of elliptic functions became the paradigm of what could be discovered by allowing variables to be complex instead of real. But their natural generalization to functions defined by more complicated integrands, although it yielded partial results, resisted analysis until the second half of the 19th century.

THE THEORY OF NUMBERS

While the theory of elliptic functions typifies the 19th century's enthusiasm for pure mathematics, some contemporary mathematicians said that the simultaneous developments in number theory carried that enthusiasm to excess. Nonetheless, during the 19th century, the algebraic theory of numbers grew from being a minority interest to its present central importance in pure mathematics. The earlier investigations of Fermat had eventually drawn the attention of Euler and Lagrange. Euler proved some of Fermat's unproven claims and discovered many new and surprising facts. Lagrange not only supplied proofs of many remarks that Euler had merely conjectured but also worked them into something like a coherent theory. For example, it was known to Fermat that the numbers that can be written as the sum of two squares are the number 2, squares themselves, primes of the form $4n + 1$, and products of these numbers. Thus, 29, which is $4 \times 7 + 1$, is $5^2 + 2^2$, but 35, which is not of this form, cannot be written as the sum of two squares. Euler had proved this result and had gone on to consider similar cases, such as primes of the form $x^2 + 2y^2$ or $x^2 + 3y^2$. But it was left to Lagrange to provide a general theory covering all expressions of the form $ax^2 + bxy + cy^2$, quadratic forms, as they are called.

Lagrange's theory of quadratic forms had made considerable use of the idea that a given quadratic form could often be simplified to another with the same properties but with smaller coefficients. To do this in practice, it was often necessary to consider whether a given integer left a remainder that was a square when it was divided by another given integer. (For example, 48 leaves a remainder of 4 upon division by 11, and 4 is a square.) Legendre discovered a remarkable connection between the question "Does the integer p leave a square remainder on division by q?" and the seemingly unrelated question "Does the integer q leave a square remainder upon division by p?" He saw, in fact, that, when p and q are primes, both questions have the same answer unless both primes are of the form $4n - 1$. Because this observation connects two questions in which the integers p and q play mutually opposite roles, it became known as the law of quadratic reciprocity. Legendre also gave an effective way of extending his law to cases when p and q are not prime.

All this work set the scene for the emergence of Carl Friedrich Gauss, whose *Disquisitiones Arithmeticae* (1801) not only consummated what had gone before but also directed number theorists in new and deeper directions. He rightly showed that Legendre's proof of the law of quadratic reciprocity was fundamentally flawed and gave the first rigorous proof. His work suggested that there were profound connections between the original question and other branches of number theory, a fact that he perceived to be of signal importance for the subject. He extended Lagrange's theory of quadratic forms by showing how two quadratic forms can be "multiplied" to obtain a third. Later mathematicians were to rework this into an important example of the theory of finite commutative groups. And in the long final section of his book, Gauss gave the theory that lay behind his first discovery as a mathematician: that a regular 17-sided figure can be constructed by circle and straightedge alone.

The discovery that the regular "17-gon" is so constructible was the first such discovery since the Greeks—who had known only of the equilateral triangle, the square, the regular pentagon, the regular 15-sided figure, and the figures that can be obtained from these by successively bisecting all the sides. But what was of much greater significance than the discovery was the theory that underpinned it, the theory of what are now called algebraic numbers. It may be thought of as an analysis of how complicated a number may be while yet being amenable to an exact treatment.

The simplest numbers to understand and use are the integers and the rational numbers. The irrational numbers seem to pose problems. Famous among these is $\sqrt{2}$. It cannot be written as a finite or repeating decimal (because it is not rational), but it can be manipulated algebraically very easily. It is necessary only to replace every occurrence of $(\sqrt{2})^2$ by 2. In this way expressions of the form $m + n\sqrt{2}$, where m and n are integers, can be handled arithmetically. These expressions have many properties akin to those of whole numbers, and mathematicians have even defined prime numbers of this form; therefore, they are called algebraic integers. In this case they are obtained by grafting onto the rational numbers a solution of the polynomial equation $x^2 - 2 = 0$. In general an algebraic integer is any solution, real or complex, of a polynomial equation with integer coefficients in which the coefficient of the highest power of the unknown is 1.

Gauss's theory of algebraic integers led to the question of determining when a polynomial of degree n with integer coefficients can be solved given the solvability of polynomial equations of lower degree but with coefficients that are algebraic integers. For example, Gauss regarded the coordinates of the 17 vertices of a regular 17-sided figure as complex numbers satisfying the equation $x^{17} - 1 = 0$ and thus as algebraic integers. One such integer is 1. He showed that the rest are obtained by solving a succession of four quadratic equations. Because solving a quadratic equation is equivalent to performing a construction with a ruler and compass, as Descartes had shown long before, Gauss had shown how to construct the regular 17-gon.

Inspired by Gauss's works on the theory of numbers, a growing school of mathematicians was drawn to the subject. Like Gauss, the German mathematician Ernst Eduard Kummer sought to generalize the law of quadratic reciprocity to deal with questions about third, fourth, and higher powers of numbers. He found that his work led him in an unexpected direction, toward a partial resolution of Fermat's last theorem. In 1637 Fermat wrote in the margin of his copy of Diophantus's *Arithmetica* the claim to have a proof that there are no solutions in positive integers to the equation $x^n + y^n = z^n$ if $n > 2$. However, no proof was ever discovered among his notebooks.

Kummer's approach was to develop the theory of algebraic integers. If it could be shown that the equation had no solution in suitable algebraic integers, then a fortiori there could be no solution in ordinary integers. He was eventually able to establish the truth of Fermat's last theorem for a large class of prime exponents n (those satisfying some technical conditions needed to make the proof work). This was the first significant breakthrough in the study of the theorem. Together with the earlier work of the French mathematician Sophie Germain, it enabled mathematicians to establish Fermat's last theorem for every value of n from 3 to 4,000,000. However, Kummer's way around the difficulties he encountered further propelled the theory of algebraic integers into the realm of abstraction. It amounted to the suggestion that there should be yet other types of integers, but many found these ideas obscure.

In Germany Richard Dedekind patiently created a new approach, in which each new number (called an ideal) was defined by means of a suitable set of algebraic integers in such a way that it was the common divisor of the set of algebraic integers used to define it. Dedekind's work was slow to gain approval, yet it illustrates several of the most profound features of modern mathematics. It was clear to Dedekind that the ideal algebraic integers were the work of the human mind. Their existence can be neither based on nor deduced from the existence of physical objects, analogies with natural processes, or some process of abstraction from more familiar things. A second feature of Dedekind's work was its reliance on the idea of sets of objects, such as sets of numbers, even sets of sets. Dedekind's work showed how basic the naive conception of a set could be. The third crucial feature of his work was its emphasis on the structural aspects of algebra. The presentation of number theory as a theory about objects that can be manipulated (in this case, added and multiplied) according to certain rules akin to those governing ordinary numbers was to be a paradigm of the more formal theories of the 20th century.

THE THEORY OF EQUATIONS

Another subject that was transformed in the 19th century was the theory of equations. Ever since Tartaglia and Ferrari in the 16th century had found rules giving the solutions of cubic and quartic equations in terms of the coefficients of the equations, formulas had unsuccessfully been sought for equations of the fifth and higher degrees. At stake was the existence of a formula that expresses the roots of a quintic equation in terms of the coefficients. This formula, moreover, must involve only the operations of addition, subtraction, multiplication, and division, together with the extraction of roots, since that was all that had been required for the solution of quadratic, cubic, and quartic equations. If such a formula were to exist, the quintic would accordingly be said to be solvable by radicals.

In 1770 Lagrange had analyzed all the successful methods he knew for second-, third-, and fourth-degree equations in an attempt to see why they worked and how they could be generalized. His analysis of the problem in terms of permutations of the roots was promising, but he became more and more doubtful as the years went by that his complicated line of attack could be carried through. The first valid proof that the general quintic is not solvable by radicals was offered only after his death, in a startlingly short paper by Niels Henrik Abel, written in 1824.

Abel also showed by example that some quintic equations were solvable by radicals and that some equations could be solved unexpectedly easily. For example, the equation $x^5 - 1 = 0$ has one root $x = 1$, but the remaining four roots can be found just by extracting square roots, not fourth roots as might be expected. He therefore raised the question "What equations of degree higher than four are solvable by radicals?"

Abel died in 1829 at the age of 26 and did not resolve the problem he had posed. Almost at once, however, the astonishing prodigy Évariste Galois burst upon the Parisian mathematical scene. He submitted an account of his novel theory of equations to the Academy of Sciences in 1829, but the manuscript was lost. A second version was also lost and was not found among Fourier's papers when Fourier, the secretary of the academy, died in 1830. Galois was killed in a duel in 1832, at the age of 20, and it was not until his papers were published in Joseph Liouville's *Journal de mathématiques* in 1846 that his work began to receive the attention it deserved. His theory eventually made the theory of equations into a mere part of the theory of groups. Galois emphasized the group (as he called it) of permutations of the roots of an equation. This move took him away from the equations themselves and turned him instead toward the markedly more tractable study of permutations. To any given equation there corresponds a definite group, with a definite collection of subgroups. To explain which equations were solvable by radicals and which were not, Galois analyzed the ways in which these subgroups were related to one another: solvable equations gave rise to what are now called a chain of normal subgroups with cyclic quotients. This technical condition makes it clear how far mathematicians had gone from the familiar questions of 18th-century mathematics, and it marks a transition characteristic of modern mathematics: the replacement of formal calculation by conceptual analysis. This is a luxury available to the pure mathematician that the applied mathematician faced with a concrete problem cannot always afford.

According to this theory, a group is a set of objects that one can combine in pairs in such a way that the resulting object is also in the set. Moreover, this way of combination has to obey the following rules (here objects in the group are denoted a, b, etc., and the combination of a and b is written $a * b$):

- There is an element e such that $a * e = a = e * a$ for every element a in the group. This element is called the identity element of the group.
- For every element a there is an element, written a^{-1}, with the property that $a * a^{-1} = e = a^{-1} * a$. The elment a^{-1} is called the inverse of a.
- For every a, b, and c in the group the associative law holds: $(a * b) * c = a * (b * c)$.

Examples of groups include the integers with * interpreted as addition and the positive rational numbers with * interpreted as multiplication. An important property shared by some groups but not all is commutativity: for every element a and b, $a * b = b * a$. The rotations of an object in the plane around a fixed point form a commutative group, but the rotations of a three-dimensional object around a fixed point form a noncommutative group.

GAUSS

A convenient way to assess the situation in mathematics in the mid-19th century is to look at the career of its greatest exponent, Carl Friedrich Gauss, the last man to be called the "Prince of Mathematics." In 1801, the same year in which he published his *Disquisitiones Arithmeticae*, he rediscovered the asteroid Ceres (which had disappeared behind the Sun not long after it was first discovered and before its orbit was precisely known). He was the first to give a sound analysis of the method of least squares in the analysis of statistical data. Gauss did important work in potential theory and, with the German physicist Wilhelm Weber, built the first electric telegraph. He helped conduct the first survey of the Earth's magnetic field and did both theoretical and field work in cartography and surveying. He was a polymath who almost single-handedly embraced what elsewhere was being put asunder: the world of science and the world of mathematics. It is his purely mathematical work, however, that in its day was— and ever since has been—regarded as the best evidence of his genius.

Gauss's writings transformed the theory of numbers. His theory of algebraic integers lay close to the theory of equations as Galois was to redefine it. More remarkable are his extensive writings, dating from 1797 to the 1820s but unpublished at his death, on the theory of elliptic functions. In 1827 he published his crucial discovery that the curvature of a surface can be defined intrinsically—that is, solely in terms of properties defined within the surface and without reference to the surrounding Euclidean space. This result was to be decisive in the acceptance of non-Euclidean geometry. All of Gauss's work displays a sharp concern for rigour and a refusal to rely on intuition or physical analogy, which was to serve as an inspiration

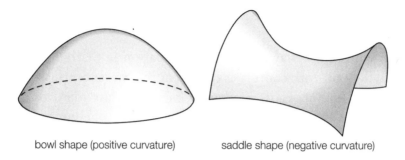

bowl shape (positive curvature)   saddle shape (negative curvature)

Intrinsic curvature of a surface. Encyclopædia Britannica, Inc.

to his successors. His emphasis on achieving full conceptual understanding, which may have led to his dislike of publication, was by no means the least influential of his achievements.

NON-EUCLIDEAN GEOMETRY

Perhaps it was this desire for conceptual understanding that made Gauss reluctant to publish the fact that he was led more and more "to doubt the truth of geometry," as he put it. For if there was a logically consistent geometry differing from Euclid's only because it made a different assumption about the behaviour of parallel lines, it too could apply to physical space, and so the truth of (Euclidean) geometry could no longer be assured a priori, as Kant had thought.

Gauss's investigations into the new geometry went further than any one else's before him, but he did not publish them. The honour of being the first to proclaim the existence of a new geometry belongs to two others, who did so in the late 1820s: Nicolay Ivanovich Lobachevsky in Russia and János Bolyai in Hungary. Because the similarities in the work of these two men far exceed the differences, it is convenient to describe their work together.

Both men made an assumption about parallel lines that differed from Euclid's and proceeded to draw out its consequences. This way of working cannot guarantee the consistency of one's findings, so, strictly speaking, they could not prove the existence of a new geometry in this way. Both men described a three-dimensional space different from Euclidean space by couching their findings in the language of trigonometry. The formulas they obtained were exact analogs of the formulas that describe triangles drawn on the surface of a sphere, with the usual trigonometric functions replaced by those of hyperbolic trigonometry. The functions hyperbolic cosine, written cosh, and hyperbolic sine, written sinh, are defined as follows: $\cosh x = (e^x + e^{-x})/2$, and $\sinh x = (e^x - e^{-x})/2$. They are called hyperbolic because of their use in describing the hyperbola. Their names derive from the evident analogy with the trigonometric functions, which Euler showed satisfy these equations: $\cos x = (e^{ix} + e^{-ix})/2$, and $\sin x = (e^{ix} - e^{-ix})/2i$. The formulas were what gave the work of Lobachevsky and of Bolyai the precision needed to give

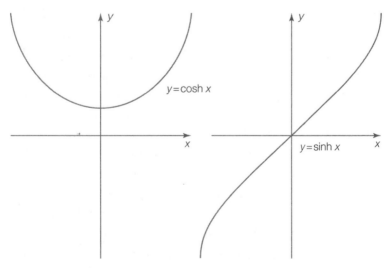

The hyperbolic functions cosh x and sinh x. Encyclopædia Britannica, Inc.

conviction in the absence of a sound logical structure. Both men observed that it had become an empirical matter to determine the nature of space, Lobachevsky even going so far as to conduct astronomical observations, although these proved inconclusive.

The work of Bolyai and of Lobachevsky was poorly received. Gauss endorsed what they had done, but so discreetly that most mathematicians did not find out his true opinion on the subject until he was dead. The main obstacle each man faced was surely the shocking nature of their discovery. It was easier, and in keeping with 2,000 years of tradition, to continue to believe that Euclidean geometry was correct and that Bolyai and Lobachevsky had somewhere gone astray, like many an investigator before them.

The turn toward acceptance came in the 1860s, after Bolyai and Lobachevsky had died. The Italian mathematician Eugenio Beltrami decided to investigate Lobachevsky's work and to place it, if possible, within the context of differential geometry as redefined by Gauss. He therefore moved independently in the direction already taken by Bernhard Riemann. Beltrami investigated the surface of constant negative curvature and found that on such a surface triangles obeyed the formulas of hyperbolic trigonometry that Lobachevsky had discovered were appropriate to his form of non-Euclidean geometry. Thus, Beltrami gave the first rigorous description of a geometry other than Euclid's. Beltrami's account of the surface of constant negative curvature was ingenious. He said it was an abstract surface that he could describe by drawing maps of it, much as one might describe a sphere by means of the pages of a geographic atlas. He did not claim to have constructed the surface embedded in Euclidean two-dimensional space; David Hilbert later showed that it cannot be done.

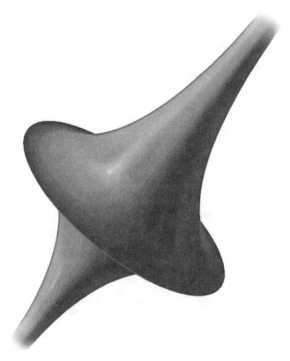

The pseudosphere has constant negative curvature; i.e., it maintains a constant concavity over its entire surface. Unable to be shown in its entirety in an illustration, the pseudosphere tapers to infinity in both directions away from the central disk. The pseudosphere was one of the first models for a non-Euclidean space. Encyclopædia Britannica, Inc.

RIEMANN

When Gauss died in 1855, his post at Göttingen was taken by Peter Gustav Lejeune Dirichlet. One mathematician who found the presence of Dirichlet a stimulus to research was Bernhard Riemann, and his few short contributions to mathematics were among the most influential of the century. Riemann's first paper, his doctoral thesis (1851) on the theory of complex functions, provided the foundations for a geometric treatment of functions of a complex variable. His main result guaranteed the existence of a wide class of complex functions satisfying only

Bernhard Riemann. SSPL via Getty Images

modest general requirements and so made it clear that complex functions could be expected to occur widely in mathematics. More important, Riemann achieved this result by yoking together the theory of complex functions with the theory of harmonic functions and with potential theory. The theories of complex and harmonic functions were henceforth inseparable.

Riemann then wrote on the theory of Fourier series and their integrability. His paper was directly in the tradition that ran from Cauchy and Fourier to Dirichlet, and it marked a considerable step forward in the precision with which the concept of integral can be defined. In 1854 he took up a subject that much interested Gauss, the hypotheses lying at the basis of geometry.

The study of geometry has always been one of the central concerns of mathematicians. It was the language, and the principal subject matter, of Greek mathematics, was the mainstay of elementary education in the subject, and has an obvious visual appeal. It seems easy to apply, for one can proceed from a base of naively intelligible concepts. In keeping with the general trends of the century, however, it was just the naive concepts that Riemann chose to refine. What he proposed as the basis of geometry was far more radical and fundamental than anything that had gone before.

Riemann took his inspiration from Gauss's discovery that the curvature of a surface is intrinsic, and he argued that one should therefore ignore Euclidean space and treat each surface by itself. A geometric property, he argued, was one that was intrinsic to the surface. To do geometry, it was enough to be given a set of points and a way of measuring lengths along curves in the surface. For this, traditional ways of applying the calculus to the study of curves could be made to suffice. But Riemann did not stop with surfaces. He proposed that geometers study spaces of any dimension in this spirit—even, he said, spaces of infinite dimension.

Several profound consequences followed from this view. It dethroned Euclidean geometry, which now became just one of many geometries. It allowed the geometry of Bolyai and Lobachevsky to be recognized as the geometry of a surface of constant negative curvature, thus resolving doubts about the logical consistency of their work. It highlighted the importance of intrinsic concepts in geometry. It helped open the way to the study of spaces of many dimensions. Last but not least, Riemann's work ensured that any investigation of the geometric nature of physical space would thereafter have to be partly empirical. One could no longer say that physical space is Euclidean because there is no geometry but Euclid's. This realization finally destroyed any hope that questions about the world could be answered by a priori reasoning.

In 1857 Riemann published several papers applying his very general methods for the study of complex functions to various parts of mathematics. One of these papers solved the outstanding problem of extending the theory of elliptic functions to the integration of any algebraic function. It opened up the theory of complex functions of several variables and showed how Riemann's novel topological ideas were essential in the study of complex functions. (In subsequent lectures Riemann showed how the special case of the theory of elliptic functions could be regarded as the study of complex functions on a torus.)

In another paper Riemann dealt with the question of how many prime numbers are less than any given number x. The answer is a function of x, and Gauss had conjectured on the basis of extensive numerical evidence that this function was approximately $x/\ln(x)$. This turned out to be true, but it was not proved until 1896, when both Charles-Jean de la Vallée Poussin of Belgium and Jacques-Salomon Hadamard of France independently proved it. It is remarkable that a question about integers led to a discussion of functions of a complex variable, but similar connections had previously been made by Dirichlet. Riemann took the expression $\Pi(1 - p^{-s})^{-1} = \Sigma n^{-s}$, introduced by Euler the century before, where the infinite product is taken over all prime numbers p and the sum over all whole numbers n, and treated it as a function of s. The infinite sum makes sense whenever s is real and greater than 1. Riemann proceeded to study this function when s is complex (now called the Riemann zeta function), and he thereby not only helped clarify the question of the distribution of primes but also was led to several other remarks that later mathematicians were to find of exceptional interest. One remark has continued to elude proof and remains one of the greatest conjectures in mathematics: the claim that the nonreal zeros of the zeta function are complex numbers whose real part is always equal to 1/2.

Riemann's Influence

In 1859 Dirichlet died and Riemann became a full professor, but he was already ill with tuberculosis, and in 1862 his health broke. He died in 1866. His work, however, exercised a growing influence on his successors. His work on trigonometric series, for example, led to a deepening investigation of the question of when a function is integrable. Attention was concentrated on the nature of the sets of points at which functions and their integrals (when these existed) had unexpected properties. The conclusions that emerged were at first obscure, but it became clear that some properties of point sets were important in the theory of integration, while others were not. (These other properties proved to be a vital part of the emerging subject of topology.) The properties of point sets that matter in integration have to do with the size of the set. If one can change the values of a function on a set of points without changing its integral, it is said that the set is of negligible size. The naive idea is that integrating is a generalization of counting: negligible sets do not need to be counted. About the turn of the century, the French mathematician Henri-Léon Lebesgue managed to systematize this naive idea into a new theory about the size of sets, which included integration as a special case. In this theory, called measure theory, there are sets that can be measured, and they either have positive measure or are negligible (they have zero measure), and there are sets that cannot be measured at all.

The first success for Lebesgue's theory was that, unlike the Cauchy-Riemann integral, it obeyed the rule that, if

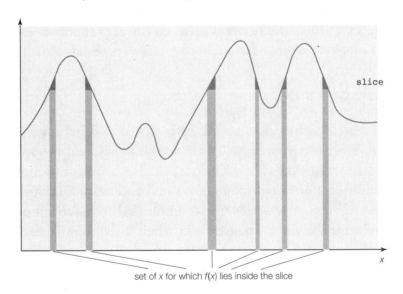

In this diagram of the Lebesgue integral, note that the areas, or slices, to be summed are horizontal rather than vertical. One such slice, the grey horizontal band, indicates the (disjoint) set, at the base of the vertical bars, that corresponds to that slice's range of values. Encyclopædia Britannica, Inc.

a sequence of functions $f_n(x)$ tends suitably to a function $f(x)$, then the sequence of integrals $\int f_n(x)dx$ tends to the integral $\int f(x)dx$. This has made it the natural theory of the integral when dealing with questions about trigonometric series. Another advantage is that it is very general. For example, in probability theory it is desirable to estimate the likelihood of certain outcomes of an experiment. By imposing a measure on the space of all possible outcomes, the Russian mathematician Andrey Kolmogorov was the first to put probability theory on a rigorous mathematical footing.

Another example is provided by a remarkable result discovered by the 20th-century American mathematician Norbert Wiener: within the set of all continuous functions on an interval, the set of differentiable functions has measure zero. In probabilistic terms, therefore, the chance that a function taken at random is differentiable has probability zero. In physical terms, this means that, for example, a particle moving under Brownian motion almost certainly is moving on a nondifferentiable path. This discovery clarified Albert Einstein's fundamental ideas about Brownian motion (displayed by the continual motion of specks of dust in a fluid under the constant bombardment of surrounding molecules). The hope of physicists is that Richard Feynman's theory of quantum electrodynamics will yield to a similar measure-theoretic treatment, for it has the disturbing aspect of a theory that has not been made rigorous mathematically but that accords excellently with observation.

Yet another setting for Lebesgue's ideas was to be the theory of Lie groups. The Hungarian mathematician Alfréd Haar showed how to define the concept of measure so that functions defined on Lie groups could be integrated. This became a crucial part of Hermann Weyl's way of representing a Lie group as acting linearly on the space of all (suitable) functions on the group (for technical reasons, *suitable* means that the square of the function is integrable with respect to a Haar measure on the group).

DIFFERENTIAL EQUATIONS

Another field that developed considerably in the 19th century was the theory of differential equations. The pioneer in this direction once again was Cauchy. Above all, he insisted that one should prove that solutions do indeed exist. It is not a priori obvious that every ordinary differential equation has solutions. The methods that Cauchy proposed for these problems fitted naturally into his program of providing rigorous foundations for all the calculus. The solution method he preferred, although the less-general of his two approaches, worked equally well in the real and complex cases. It established the existence of a solution equal to the one obtainable by traditional power series methods using newly developed techniques in his theory of functions of a complex variable.

The harder part of the theory of differential equations concerns partial differential equations, those for which the unknown function is a function of several variables. In the early 19th century, there was no known method of proving that a given second- or higher-order partial differential equation had a solution, and there was not even a method of writing down a plausible candidate. In this case progress was to be much less marked. Cauchy found new and more rigorous methods for first-order partial differential equations, but the general case eluded treatment.

An important special case was successfully prosecuted, that of dynamics. Dynamics is the study of the motion of a physical system under the action of forces.

Working independently of each other, William Rowan Hamilton in Ireland and Carl Jacobi in Germany showed how problems in dynamics could be reduced to systems of first-order partial differential equations. From this base grew an extensive study of certain partial differential operators. These are straightforward generalizations of a single partial differentiation $(\partial/\partial x)$ to a sum of the form

$$a_1 \frac{\partial}{\partial x_1} + \ldots + a_n \frac{\partial}{\partial x_n},$$

where the a's are functions of the x's. The effect of performing several of these in succession can be complicated, but Jacobi and the other pioneers in this field found that there are formal rules which such operators tend to satisfy. This enabled them to shift attention to these formal rules, and gradually an algebraic analysis of this branch of mathematics began to emerge.

The most influential worker in this direction was the Norwegian Sophus Lie. Lie, and independently Wilhelm Killing in Germany, came to suspect that the systems of partial differential operators they were studying came in a limited variety of types. Once the number of independent variables was specified (which fixed the dimension of the system), a large class of examples, including many of considerable geometric significance, seemed to fall into a small number of patterns. This suggested that the systems could be classified, and such a prospect naturally excited mathematicians. After much work by Lie and by Killing and later by the French mathematician Élie-Joseph Cartan, they were classified. Initially, this discovery aroused interest because it produced order where previously the complexity had threatened chaos and because it could be made to make sense geometrically. The realization that there were to be major implications of this work for the study of physics lay well in the future.

LINEAR ALGEBRA

Differential equations, whether ordinary or partial, may profitably be classified as linear or nonlinear. Linear differential equations are those for which the sum of two solutions is again a solution. The equation giving the shape of a vibrating string is linear, which provides the mathematical reason why a string may simultaneously emit more than one frequency. The linearity of an equation makes it easy to find all its solutions, so in general linear problems have been tackled successfully, while nonlinear equations continue to be difficult. Indeed, in many linear problems there can be found a finite family of solutions with the property that any solution is a sum of them (suitably multiplied by arbitrary constants). Obtaining such a family, called a basis, and putting them into their simplest and most useful form, was an important source of many techniques in the field of linear algebra.

Consider, for example, the system of linear differential equations

$$\frac{dy_1}{dx} = a y_1 + b y_2, \quad \frac{dy_2}{dx} = c y_1 + d y_2.$$

It is evidently much more difficult to study than the system $dy_1/dx = \alpha y_1$, $dy_2/dx = \beta y_2$, whose solutions are (constant multiples of) $y_1 = \exp(\alpha x)$ and $y_2 = \exp(\beta x)$. But if a suitable linear combination of y_1 and y_2 can be found so that the first system reduces to the second, then it is enough to solve the second system. The existence of such a reduction is determined by an array (called a matrix) of the four numbers. In 1858 the English mathematician Arthur Cayley began the study of matrices in their own right when he noticed that they satisfy polynomial equations. The matrix

$$A = \begin{bmatrix} a & b \\ c & d \end{bmatrix},$$

for example, satisfies the equation $A^2 - (a + d)A + (ad - bc) = 0$. Moreover, if this equation has two distinct roots—say, α and β—then the sought-for reduction will exist, and the coefficients of the simpler system will indeed be those roots α and β. If the equation has a repeated root, then the reduction usually cannot be carried out. In either case the difficult part of solving the original differential equation has been reduced to elementary algebra.

The study of linear algebra begun by Cayley and continued by Leopold Kronecker includes a powerful theory of vector spaces. These are sets whose elements can be added together and multiplied by arbitrary numbers, such as the family of solutions of a linear differential equation. A more familiar example is that of three-dimensional space. If one picks an origin, then every point in space can be labeled by the line segment (called a vector) joining it to the origin. Matrices appear as ways of representing linear transformations of a vector space—i.e., transformations that preserve sums and multiplication by numbers: the transformation T is linear if, for any vectors u, v, $T(u + v) = T(u) + T(v)$ and, for any scalar λ, $T(\lambda v) = \lambda T(v)$. When the vector space is finite-dimensional, linear algebra and geometry form a potent combination. Vector spaces of infinite dimensions also are studied.

The theory of vector spaces is useful in other ways. Vectors in three-dimensional space represent such physically important concepts as velocities and forces. Such an assignment of vector to point is called a vector field. Examples include electric and magnetic fields. Scientists such as James Clerk Maxwell and J. Willard Gibbs took up vector analysis and were able to extend vector methods to the calculus. They introduced in this way measures of how a vector field varies infinitesimally, which, under the names div, grad, and curl, have become the standard tools in the study of electromagnetism and potential theory. To the modern mathematician, div, grad, and curl form part of a theory to which Stokes's law (a special case of which is Green's theorem) is central. The Gauss-Green-Stokes theorem, named after Gauss and two leading English applied mathematicians of the 19th century (George Green and George Stokes), generalizes the fundamental theorem of the calculus to functions of several variables. The fundamental theorem of calculus asserts that

$$\int_a^b f'(x) = f(b) - f(a),$$

which can be read as saying that the integral of the derivative of some function in an interval is equal to the difference in the values of the function at the endpoints of the interval. Generalized to a part of a surface or space, this asserts that the integral of the derivative of some function over a region is equal to the integral of the function over the boundary of the region. In symbols this says that $\int d\omega = \int \omega$, where the first integral is taken over the region in question and the second integral over its boundary, while $d\omega$ is the derivative of ω.

THE FOUNDATIONS OF GEOMETRY

By the late 19th century, the hegemony of Euclidean geometry had been challenged by non-Euclidean geometry and projective geometry. The first notable attempt to reorganize the study of geometry was made by the German mathematician Felix Klein and published at Erlangen in 1872. In his *Erlanger Programm* Klein proposed that Euclidean and non-Euclidean geometry be regarded as special cases of projective geometry. In each case the common features that, in Klein's opinion, made them geometries were that there were a set of points, called a "space," and a group of transformations by means of which figures could be moved around in the space without altering their essential properties. For example, in Euclidean plane geometry the space is the familiar plane, and the transformations are rotations, reflections, translations, and their composites, none of which change either length or angle, the basic properties of figures in Euclidean geometry. Different geometries would have different spaces and different groups, and the figures would have different basic properties.

Klein produced an account that unified a large class of geometries—roughly speaking, all those that were homogeneous in the sense that every piece of the space looked like every other piece of the space. This excluded, for example, geometries on surfaces of variable curvature, but it produced an attractive package for the rest and gratified the intuition of those who felt that somehow projective geometry was basic. It continued to look like the right approach when Lie's ideas appeared, and there seemed to be a good connection between Lie's classification and the types of geometry organized by Klein.

Mathematicians could now ask why they had believed Euclidean geometry to be the only one when, in fact, many different geometries existed. The first to take up this question successfully was the German mathematician Moritz Pasch, who argued in 1882 that the mistake had been to rely too heavily on physical intuition. In his view an argument in mathematics should depend for its validity not on the physical interpretation of the terms involved but upon purely formal criteria. Indeed, the principle of duality did violence to the sense of geometry as a formalization of what one believed about (physical) points and lines. One did not believe that these terms were interchangeable.

The ideas of Pasch caught the attention of the German mathematician David Hilbert, who, with the French mathematician Henri Poincaré, came to dominate mathematics at the beginning of the 20th century. In wondering why it was that mathematics—and in particular geometry— produced correct results, he came to feel increasingly that it was not because of the lucidity of its definitions. Rather, mathematics worked because its (elementary) terms were meaningless. What kept it heading in the right direction was its rules of inference. Proofs were valid because they were constructed through the application of the rules of inference, according to which new assertions could be declared to be true simply because they could be derived, by means of these rules, from the axioms or previously proven theorems. The theorems and axioms were viewed as formal statements that expressed the relationships between these terms.

The rules governing the use of mathematical terms were arbitrary, Hilbert argued, and each mathematician could choose them at will, provided only that the choices made were self-consistent. A mathematician produced abstract systems unconstrained by the needs of science, and, if scientists found an abstract system that fit one of their concerns, they could apply the system secure in the knowledge that it was logically consistent.

Hilbert first became excited about this point of view (presented in his *Grundlagen der Geometrie* [1899; *Foundations of Geometry*]) when he saw that it led not merely to a clear way of sorting out the geometries in Klein's hierarchy according to the different axiom systems they obeyed but to new geometries as well. For the first time, there was a way of discussing geometry that lay beyond even the very general terms proposed by Riemann. Not all of these geometries have continued to be of interest, but the general moral that Hilbert first drew for geometry he was shortly to draw for the whole of mathematics.

The Foundations of Mathematics

By the late 19th century, the debates about the foundations of geometry had become the focus for a running debate about the nature of the branches of mathematics. Cauchy's work on the foundations of the calculus, completed by the German mathematician Karl Weierstrass in the late 1870s, left an edifice that rested on concepts such as that of the natural numbers (the integers 1, 2, 3, and so on) and on certain constructions involving them. The algebraic theory of numbers and the transformed theory of equations had focused attention on abstract structures in mathematics. Questions that had been raised about numbers since Babylonian times turned out to be best cast theoretically in terms of entirely modern creations whose independence from the physical world was beyond dispute. Finally, geometry, far from being a kind of abstract physics, was now seen as dealing with meaningless terms obeying arbitrary systems of rules. Although there had been no conscious plan leading in that direction, the stage was set for a consideration of questions about the fundamental nature of mathematics.

Similar currents were at work in the study of logic, which had also enjoyed a revival during the 19th century. The work of the English mathematician George Boole and the American Charles Sanders Peirce had contributed to the development of a symbolism adequate to explore all elementary logical deductions. Significantly, Boole's book on the subject was called *An Investigation of the Laws of Thought, on Which Are Founded the Mathematical Theories of Logic and Probabilities* (1854). In Germany the logician Gottlob Frege had directed keen attention to such fundamental questions as what it means to define something and what sorts of purported definitions actually do define.

CANTOR

All of these debates came together through the pioneering work of the German mathematician Georg Cantor on the concept of a set. Cantor had begun work in this area because of his interest in Riemann's theory of trigonometric series, but the problem of what characterized the set of all real numbers came to occupy him more and more. He began to discover unexpected properties of sets. For example, he could show that the set of all algebraic numbers, and a fortiori the set of all rational numbers, is countable in the sense that there is a one-to-one correspondence between the integers and the members of each of these sets by means of which for any member of the set of algebraic numbers (or rationals), no matter how large, there is always a unique integer it may be placed in correspondence with. But, more surprisingly, he could also show that the set of all real numbers is not countable. So, although the set of all integers and the set of all real numbers are both infinite, the set of all real numbers is a strictly larger infinity. This was in complete contrast to the prevailing orthodoxy, which proclaimed that infinite could mean only "larger than any finite amount."

Here the concept of number was being extended and undermined at the same time. The concept was extended because it was now possible to count and order sets that the set of integers was too small to measure, and it was undermined because even the integers ceased to be basic undefined objects. Cantor himself had given a way of defining real numbers as certain infinite sets of rational numbers. Rational numbers were easy to define in terms of the integers, but now integers could be defined by means of sets. One way was given by Frege in *Die Grundlagen der Arithmetik* (1884; *The Foundations of Arithmetic*). He regarded two sets as the same if they contained the same elements. So in his opinion there was only one empty set (today symbolized by Ø), the set with no members. A second set could be defined as having only one element by letting that element be the empty set itself (symbolized by {Ø}), a set with two elements by letting them be the two sets just defined (i.e., {Ø, {Ø}}), and so on. Having thus defined the integers in terms of the primitive concepts "set" and "element of," Frege agreed with Cantor that there was no logical reason to stop, and he went on to define infinite sets in the same way Cantor had. Indeed, Frege was clearer than Cantor about what sets and their elements actually were.

Frege's proposals went in the direction of a reduction of all mathematics to logic. He hoped that every mathematical term could be defined precisely and manipulated according to agreed, logical rules of inference. This, the "logicist" program, was dealt an unexpected blow in 1902 by the English mathematician and philosopher Bertrand Russell, who pointed out unexpected complications with the naive concept of a set. Nothing seemed to preclude the possibility that some sets were elements of themselves while others were not, but, asked Russell, "What then of the set of all sets that were not elements of themselves?" If it is an element of itself, then it is not (an element of itself), but, if it is not, then it is. Russell had identified a fundamental problem in set theory with his paradox. Either the idea of a set as an arbitrary collection of already defined objects was flawed, or else the idea that one could legitimately form the set of all sets of a given kind was incorrect. Frege's program never recovered from this blow, and Russell's similar approach of defining mathematics in terms of logic, which he developed together with Alfred

North Whitehead in their *Principia Mathematica* (1910–13), never found lasting appeal with mathematicians.

Greater interest attached to the ideas that Hilbert and his school began to advance. It seemed to them that what had worked once for geometry could work again for all of mathematics. Rather than attempt to define things so that problems could not arise, they suggested that it was possible to dispense with definitions and cast all of mathematics in an axiomatic structure using the ideas of set theory. Indeed, the hope was that the study of logic could be embraced in this spirit, thus making logic a branch of mathematics, the opposite of Frege's intention. There was considerable progress in this direction, and there emerged both a powerful school of mathematical logicians (notably in Poland) and an axiomatic theory of sets that avoided Russell's paradoxes and the others that had sprung up.

In the 1920s Hilbert put forward his most detailed proposal for establishing the validity of mathematics. According to his theory of proofs, everything was to be put into an axiomatic form, allowing the rules of inference to be only those of elementary logic, and only those conclusions that could be reached from this finite set of axioms and rules of inference were to be admitted. He proposed that a satisfactory system would be one that was consistent, complete, and decidable. By "consistent" Hilbert meant that it should be impossible to derive both a statement and its negation; by "complete," that every properly written statement should be such that either it or its negation was derivable from the axioms; by "decidable," that one should have an algorithm that determines of any given statement whether it or its negation is provable. Such systems did exist—for example, the first-order predicate calculus—but none had been found capable of allowing mathematicians to do interesting mathematics.

Hilbert's program, however, did not last long. In 1931 the Austrian-born American mathematician and logician Kurt Gödel showed that there was no system of Hilbert's type within which the integers could be defined and that was both consistent and complete. Gödel and, independently, the English mathematician Alan Turing later showed that decidability was also unattainable. Perhaps paradoxically, the effect of this dramatic discovery was to alienate mathematicians from the whole debate. Instead, mathematicians, who may not have been too unhappy with the idea that there is no way of deciding the truth of a proposition automatically, learned to live with the idea that not even mathematics rests on rigorous foundations. Progress since has been in other directions. An alternative axiom system for set theory was later put forward by the Hungarian-born American mathematician John von Neumann, which he hoped would help resolve contemporary problems in quantum mechanics. There was also a renewal of interest in statements that are both interesting mathematically and independent of the axiom system in use. The first of these was the American mathematician Paul Cohen's surprising resolution in 1963 of the continuum hypothesis, which was Cantor's conjecture that the set of all subsets of the rational numbers was of the same size as the set of all real numbers. This turns out to be independent of the usual axioms for set theory, so there are set theories (and therefore types of mathematics) in which it is true and others in which it is false.

MATHEMATICAL PHYSICS

At the same time that mathematicians were attempting to put their own house in order, they were also looking with renewed interest at contemporary work in physics.

Jules Henri Poincaré. Popperfoto/Getty Images

The man who did the most to rekindle their interest was Poincaré. Poincaré showed that dynamic systems described by quite simple differential equations, such as the solar system, can nonetheless yield the most random-looking, chaotic behaviour. He went on to explore ways in which mathematicians can nonetheless say things about this chaotic behaviour and so pioneered the way in which probabilistic statements about dynamic systems can be found to describe what otherwise defies intelligence.

Poincaré later turned to problems of electrodynamics. After many years' work, the Dutch physicist Hendrik Antoon Lorentz had been led to an apparent dependence of length and time on motion, and Poincaré was pleased to notice that the transformations that Lorentz proposed as a way of converting one observer's data into another's formed a group. This appealed to Poincaré and strengthened his belief that there was no sense in a concept of absolute motion; all motion was relative. Poincaré thereupon gave an elegant mathematical formulation of Lorentz's ideas, which fitted them into a theory in which the motion of the electron is governed by Maxwell's equations. Poincaré, however, stopped short of denying the reality of the ether or of proclaiming that the velocity of light is the same for all observers, so credit for the first truly relativistic theory of the motion of the electron rests with Einstein and his special theory of relativity (1905).

Einstein's special theory is so called because it treats only the special case of uniform relative motion. The much more important case of accelerated motion and motion in a gravitational field was to take a further decade and to require a far more substantial dose of mathematics. Einstein changed his estimate of the value of pure mathematics, which he had hitherto disdained, only when he discovered that many of the questions he was led to had already been formulated mathematically and had been solved. He was most struck by theories derived from the study of geometry in the sense in which Riemann had formulated it.

By 1915 a number of mathematicians were interested in reapplying their discoveries to physics. The leading institution in this respect was the University of Göttingen, where Hilbert had unsuccessfully attempted to produce a general theory of relativity before Einstein, and it was there that many of the leaders of the coming revolution in quantum mechanics were to study. There too went many of the leading mathematicians of their generation, notably John von Neumann and Hermann Weyl, to study with Hilbert. In 1904 Hilbert had turned to the study of integral equations. These arise in many problems where the unknown is itself a function of some variable, and especially in those parts of physics that are expressed in terms of extremal principles (such as the principle of least action). The extremal principle usually yields information about an integral involving the sought-for function, hence the name *integral equation*. Hilbert's contribution was to bring together many different strands of contemporary work and to show how they could be elucidated if cast in the form of arguments about objects in certain infinite-dimensional vector spaces.

The extension to infinite dimensions was not a trivial task, but it brought with it the opportunity to use geometric intuition and geometric concepts to analyze problems about integral equations. Hilbert left it to his students to provide the best abstract setting for his work, and thus was born the concept of a Hilbert space. Roughly, this is an infinite-dimensional vector space in which it makes sense to speak of the lengths of vectors and the angles between them. Useful examples include certain spaces of sequences and certain spaces of functions. Operators defined on these spaces are also of great interest; their study forms part of the field of functional analysis.

When in the 1920s mathematicians and physicists were seeking ways to formulate the new quantum mechanics, von Neumann proposed that the subject be written in the language of functional analysis. The quantum mechanical world of states and observables, with its mysterious wave packets that were sometimes like particles and sometimes like waves depending on how they were observed, went very neatly into the theory of Hilbert spaces. Functional analysis has ever since grown with the fortunes of particle physics.

ALGEBRAIC TOPOLOGY

The early 20th century saw the emergence of a number of theories whose power and utility reside in large part in their generality. Typically, they are marked by an attention to the set or space of all examples of a particular kind. (Functional analysis is such an endeavour.) One of the most energetic of these general theories was that of algebraic topology. In this subject a variety of ways are developed for replacing a space by a group and a map between spaces by a map between groups. It is like using X-rays: information is lost, but the shadowy image of the original space may turn out to contain, in an accessible form, enough information to solve the question at hand.

Interest in this kind of research came from various directions. Galois's theory of equations was an example of what could be achieved by transforming a problem in one branch of mathematics into a problem in another, more abstract branch. Another impetus came from Riemann's theory of complex functions. He had studied algebraic functions—that is, loci defined by equations of the form $f(x, y) = 0$, where f is a polynomial in x whose coefficients are polynomials in y. When x and y are complex variables, the

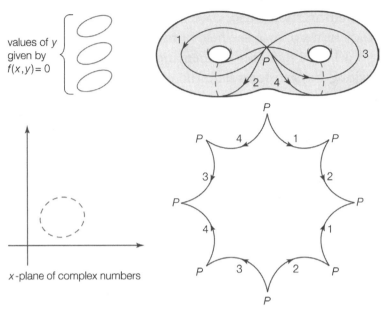

(Left) *Pieces of a surface given by f(x, y) = 0.* (Right) *If the surface is cut along the curves, an octagon is obtained.* Encyclopædia Britannica, Inc.

locus can be thought of as a real surface spread out over the x plane of complex numbers (today called a Riemann surface). To each value of x there correspond a finite number of values of y. Such surfaces are not easy to comprehend, and Riemann had proposed to draw curves along them in such a way that, if the surface was cut open along them, it could be opened out into a polygonal disk. He was able to establish a profound connection between the minimum number of curves needed to do this for a given surface and the number of functions (becoming infinite at specified points) that the surface could then support.

The natural problem was to see how far Riemann's ideas could be applied to the study of spaces of higher dimension. Here two lines of inquiry developed. One emphasized what could be obtained from looking at the projective geometry involved. This point of view was fruitfully applied by the Italian school of algebraic geometers. It ran into problems, which it was not wholly able to solve, having to do with the singularities a surface can possess. Whereas a locus given by $f(x, y) = 0$ may intersect itself only at isolated points, a locus given by an equation of the form $f(x, y, z) = 0$ may intersect itself along curves, a problem that caused considerable difficulties. The second approach emphasized what can be learned from the study of integrals along paths on the surface. This approach, pursued by Charles-Émile Picard and by Poincaré, provided a rich generalization of Riemann's original ideas.

On this base, conjectures were made and a general theory produced, first by Poincaré and then by the American engineer-turned-mathematician Solomon Lefschetz, concerning the nature of manifolds of arbitrary dimension. Roughly speaking, a manifold is the n-dimensional generalization of the idea of a surface. It is a space any small piece of which looks like a piece of n-dimensional space. Such an object is often given by a single algebraic equation in $n + 1$ variables. At first the work of Poincaré and of Lefschetz was concerned with how these manifolds may be decomposed into pieces, counting the number of pieces and decomposing them in their turn. The result was a list of numbers, called Betti numbers in honour of the Italian mathematician Enrico Betti, who had taken the first steps of this kind to extend Riemann's work. It was only in the late 1920s that the German mathematician Emmy Noether suggested how the Betti numbers might be thought of as measuring the size of certain groups. At her instigation a number of people then produced a theory of these groups, the so-called homology and cohomology groups of a space.

Two objects that can be deformed into one another will have the same homology and cohomology groups.

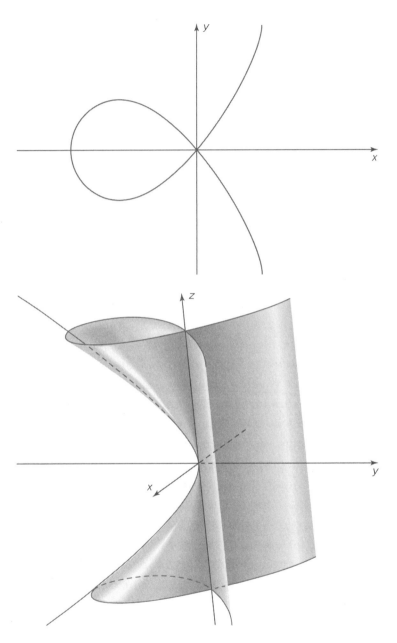

(Top) $f(x, y) = x2(x + 1) - y2 = 0$ *intersects itself at* $(x, y) = (0, 0)$. (Bottom) $E(x, y, z) = 0 = y2(y + z2) - x2$ *intersects itself along the z-axis, but the origin is a triple self-intersection.* Encyclopædia Britannica, Inc.

To assess how much information is lost when a space is replaced by its algebraic topological picture, Poincaré asked the crucial converse question "According to what algebraic conditions is it possible to say that a space is topologically equivalent to a sphere?" He showed by an ingenious example that having the same homology is not enough and proposed a more delicate index, which has since grown into the branch of topology called homotopy theory. Being more delicate, it is both more basic and more difficult. There are usually standard methods for computing homology and cohomology groups, and they are completely known for many spaces. In contrast, there is scarcely an interesting class of spaces for which all the homotopy groups are known. Poincaré's conjecture that a space with the homotopy of a sphere actually is a sphere was shown to be true in the 1960s in dimensions five and above, and in the 1980s it was shown to be true for four-dimensional spaces. In 2006 Grigori Perelman was awarded a Fields Medal for proving Poincaré's conjecture true in three dimensions, the only dimension in which Poincaré had studied it.

DEVELOPMENTS IN PURE MATHEMATICS

The interest in axiomatic systems at the turn of the century led to axiom systems for the known algebraic structures, that for the theory of fields, for example, being developed by the German mathematician Ernst Steinitz in 1910. The theory of rings (structures in which it is possible to add, subtract, and multiply but not necessarily divide) was much harder to formalize. It is important for two reasons: the theory of algebraic integers forms part of it, because algebraic integers naturally form into rings; and (as Kronecker and Hilbert had argued) algebraic geometry forms another part. The rings that arise there are rings of functions definable on the curve, surface, or manifold or are definable on specific pieces of it.

Problems in number theory and algebraic geometry are often very difficult, and it was the hope of mathematicians such as Noether, who laboured to produce a formal, axiomatic theory of rings, that, by working at a more rarefied level, the essence of the concrete problems would remain while the distracting special features of any given case would fall away. This would make the formal theory both more general and easier, and to a surprising extent these mathematicians were successful.

A further twist to the development came with the work of the American mathematician Oscar Zariski, who had studied with the Italian school of algebraic geometers but came to feel that their method of working was imprecise. He worked out a detailed program whereby every kind of geometric configuration could be redescribed in algebraic terms. His work succeeded in producing a rigorous theory, although some, notably Lefschetz, felt that the geometry had been lost sight of in the process.

The study of algebraic geometry was amenable to the topological methods of Poincaré and Lefschetz so long as the manifolds were defined by equations whose coefficients were complex numbers. But, with the creation of an abstract theory of fields, it was natural to want a theory of varieties defined by equations with coefficients in an arbitrary field. This was provided for the first time by the French mathematician André Weil, in his *Foundations of Algebraic Geometry* (1946), in a way that drew on Zariski's work without suppressing the intuitive appeal of geometric concepts. Weil's theory of polynomial equations is the proper setting for any investigation that seeks to determine what properties of a geometric object can be derived solely by algebraic means. But it falls tantalizingly short of one topic of importance: the solution of polynomial equations in integers. This was the topic that Weil took up next.

The central difficulty is that in a field it is possible to divide but in a ring it is not. The integers form a ring but not a field (dividing 1 by 2 does not yield an integer). But Weil showed that simplified versions (posed over a field) of any question about integer solutions to polynomials could be profitably asked. This transferred the questions to the domain of algebraic geometry. To count the number of solutions, Weil proposed that, since the questions were now geometric, they should be amenable to the techniques of algebraic topology. This was an audacious move, since there was no suitable theory of algebraic topology available, but Weil conjectured what results it should yield. The difficulty of Weil's conjectures may be judged by the fact that the last of them was a generalization to this setting of the famous Riemann hypothesis about the zeta function, and they rapidly became the focus of international attention.

Weil, along with Claude Chevalley, Henri Cartan, Jean Dieudonné, and others, created a group of young French mathematicians who began to publish virtually an encyclopaedia of mathematics under the name Nicolas Bourbaki, taken by Weil from an obscure general of the Franco-German War. Bourbaki became a self-selecting group of young mathematicians who were strong on algebra, and the individual Bourbaki members were interested in the Weil conjectures. In the end they succeeded completely. A new kind of algebraic topology was developed, and the Weil conjectures were proved. The generalized Riemann hypothesis was the last to surrender, being established by the Belgian Pierre Deligne in the early 1970s. Strangely, its resolution still leaves the original Riemann hypothesis unsolved.

Bourbaki was a key figure in the rethinking of structural mathematics. Algebraic topology was axiomatized by

Samuel Eilenberg, a Polish-born American mathematician and Bourbaki member, and the American mathematician Norman Steenrod. Saunders Mac Lane, also of the United States, and Eilenberg extended this axiomatic approach until many types of mathematical structures were presented in families, called categories. Hence there was a category consisting of all groups and all maps between them that preserve multiplication, and there was another category of all topological spaces and all continuous maps between them. To do algebraic topology was to transfer a problem posed in one category (that of topological spaces) to another (usually that of commutative groups or rings). When he created the right algebraic topology for the Weil conjectures, the German-born French mathematician Alexandre Grothendieck, a Bourbaki of enormous energy, produced a new description of algebraic geometry. In his hands it became infused with the language of category theory. The route to algebraic geometry became the steepest ever, but the views from the summit have a naturalness and a profundity that have brought many experts to prefer it to the earlier formulations, including Weil's.

Grothendieck's formulation makes algebraic geometry the study of equations defined over rings rather than fields. Accordingly, it raises the possibility that questions about the integers can be answered directly. Building on the work of like-minded mathematicians in the United States, France, and Russia, the German Gerd Faltings triumphantly vindicated this approach when he solved the Englishman Louis Mordell's conjecture in 1983. This conjecture states that almost all polynomial equations that define curves have at most finitely many rational solutions. The cases excluded from the conjecture are the simple ones that are much better understood.

Meanwhile, Gerhard Frey of Germany had pointed out that, if Fermat's last theorem is false, so that there are integers u, v, w such that $u^p + v^p = w^p$ (p greater than 5), then for these values of u, v, and p the curve $y^2 = x(x - u^p)(x + v^p)$ has properties that contradict major conjectures of the Japanese mathematicians Taniyama Yutaka and Shimura Goro about elliptic curves. Frey's observation, refined by Jean-Pierre Serre of France and proved by the American Ken Ribet, meant that by 1990 Taniyama's unproven conjectures were known to imply Fermat's last theorem.

In 1993 the English mathematician Andrew Wiles established the Shimura-Taniyama conjectures in a large range of cases that included Frey's curve and therefore Fermat's last theorem—a major feat even without the connection to Fermat. It soon became clear that the argument had a serious flaw. But in May 1995 Wiles, assisted by another English mathematician, Richard Taylor, published a different and valid approach. In so doing, Wiles not only solved the most famous outstanding conjecture in mathematics but also triumphantly vindicated the sophisticated and difficult methods of modern number theory.

MATHEMATICAL PHYSICS AND THE THEORY OF GROUPS

In the 1910s the ideas of Lie and Killing were taken up by the French mathematician Élie-Joseph Cartan, who simplified their theory and rederived the classification of what came to be called the classical complex Lie algebras. The simple Lie algebras, out of which all the others in the classification are made, were all representable as algebras of matrices, and, in a sense, Lie algebra is the abstract setting for matrix algebra. Connected to each Lie algebra there were a small number of Lie groups, and there was a canonical simplest one to choose in each case. The groups had an even simpler geometric interpretation than the corresponding algebras, for they turned out to describe motions that leave certain properties of figures unaltered. For example, in Euclidean three-dimensional space, rotations leave unaltered the distances between points; the set of all rotations about a fixed point turns out to form a Lie group, and it is one of the Lie groups in the classification. The theory of Lie algebras and Lie groups shows that there are only a few sensible ways to measure properties of figures in a linear space and that these methods yield groups of motions leaving the figures, which are (more or less) groups of matrices, unaltered. The result is a powerful theory that could be expected to apply to a wide range of problems in geometry and physics.

The leader in the endeavours to make Cartan's theory, which was confined to Lie algebras, yield results for a corresponding class of Lie groups was the German American Hermann Weyl. He produced a rich and satisfying theory for the pure mathematician and wrote extensively on differential geometry and group theory and its applications to physics. Weyl attempted to produce a theory that would unify gravitation and electromagnetism. His theory met with criticism from Einstein and was generally regarded as unsuccessful. Only in the last quarter of the 20th century did similar unified field theories meet with any acceptance. Nonetheless, Weyl's approach demonstrates how the theory of Lie groups can enter into physics in a substantial way.

In any physical theory the endeavour is to make sense of observations. Different observers make different observations. If they differ in choice and direction of their coordinate axes, they give different coordinates to the same points, and so on. Yet the observers agree on certain consequences of their observations: in Newtonian physics and Euclidean geometry they agree on the distance between points. Special relativity explains how observers in a state of uniform relative motion differ about lengths and times but agree on a quantity called the interval. In each case they are able to do so because the relevant theory presents them with a group of transformations that converts one observer's measurements into another's and leaves the appropriate basic quantities invariant. What Weyl proposed was a group that would permit observers in nonuniform relative motion, and whose measurements of the same moving electron would differ, to convert their measurements and thus permit the (general) relativistic study of moving electric charges.

In the 1950s the American physicists Chen Ning Yang and Robert L. Mills gave a successful treatment of the so-called strong interaction in particle physics from the Lie group point of view. Twenty years later mathematicians took up their work, and a dramatic resurgence of interest in Weyl's theory began. These new developments, which had the incidental effect of enabling mathematicians to escape the problems in Weyl's original approach, were the outcome of lines of research that had originally been conducted with little regard for physical questions. Not for the first time, mathematics was to prove surprisingly effective—or, as the Hungarian-born American physicist Eugene Wigner said, "unreasonably effective"—in science.

Cartan had investigated how much may be accomplished in differential geometry by using the idea of moving frames of reference. This work, which was partly inspired by Einstein's theory of general relativity, was also a development of the ideas of Riemannian geometry that had originally so excited Einstein. In the modern theory, one imagines a space (usually a manifold) made up of overlapping coordinatized pieces. On each piece one supposes some functions to be defined, which might in applications be the values of certain physical quantities. Rules are given for interpreting these quantities where the pieces overlap. The data are thought of as a bundle of information

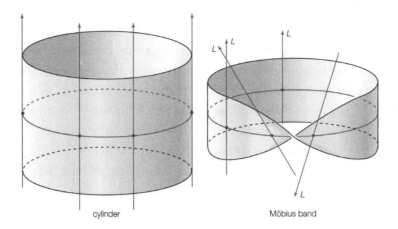

cylinder · Möbius band

As the circle is followed clockwise around the Möbius band, the line L twists through the half a turn, so the lines cannot be consistently made to point in the same direction. Encyclopædia Britannica, Inc.

provided at each point. For each function defined on each patch, it is supposed that at each point a vector space is available as mathematical storage space for all its possible values. Because a vector space is attached at each point, the theory is called the theory of vector bundles. Other kinds of space may be attached, thus entering the more general theory of fibre bundles. The subtle and vital point is that it is possible to create quite different bundles which nonetheless look similar in small patches. The cylinder and the Möbius band look alike in small pieces but are topologically distinct, since it is possible to give a standard sense of direction to all the lines in the cylinder but not to those in the Möbius band. Both spaces can be thought of as one-dimensional vector bundles over the circle, but they are very different. The cylinder is regarded as a "trivial" bundle, the Möbius band as a twisted one.

In the 1940s and '50s, a vigorous branch of algebraic topology established the main features of the theory of bundles. Then, in the 1960s, work chiefly by

Grothendieck and the English mathematician Michael Atiyah showed how the study of vector bundles on spaces could be regarded as the study of cohomology theory (called K theory). More significantly still, in the 1960s Atiyah, the American Isadore Singer, and others found ways of connecting this work to the study of a wide variety of questions involving partial differentiation, culminating in the celebrated Atiyah-Singer theorem for elliptic operators. (*Elliptic* is a technical term for the type of operator studied in potential theory.) There are remarkable implications for the study of pure geometry, and much attention has been directed to the problem of how the theory of bundles embraces the theory of Yang and Mills, which it does precisely because there are nontrivial bundles, and to the question of how it can be made to pay off in large areas of theoretical physics. These include the theories of superspace and supergravity and the string theory of fundamental particles, which involves the theory of Riemann surfaces in novel and unexpected ways.

CHAPTER 3
SOUTH AND EAST
ASIAN MATHEMATICS

From ancient times mathematics was practiced at an extremely high level in South Asia (modern India, Pakistan, Nepal, Sri Lanka, Afghanistan, and Bangladesh) and East Asia (China, Japan, Korea, and Vietnam). During and after the 19th century, South and East Asian mathematics merged with the modern Western stream of mathematics.

ANCIENT TRACES

The mathematics of classical Indian civilization is an intriguing blend of the familiar and the strange. For the modern individual, Indian decimal place-value numerals may seem familiar—and, in fact, they are the ancestors of the modern decimal number system. Familiar too are many of the arithmetic and algebraic techniques involving Indian numerals. On the other hand, Indian mathematical treatises were written in verse form, and they generally do not share modern mathematics' concern for rigorously structured formal proofs. Some historians of mathematics have deplored these aspects of the Indian tradition, seeing in them merely a habit of rote memorization and an inability to distinguish between true and false results. In fact, explanations and demonstrations were frequently added by later commentators, but these were sometimes described as "for the slow-witted." For the traditional Indian teacher of mathematics, a demonstration was perhaps not so much a solid foundation for the student's understanding as a crutch for the weak student's lack of understanding. The Indian concept of *ganita* (Sanskrit:

"computation") was a form of knowledge whose mastery implied varied talents: a good memory, swift and accurate mental arithmetic, enough logical power to understand rules without requiring minute explanations, and a sort of numerical intuition that aided in the construction of new methods and approximations.

VEDIC NUMBER WORDS AND GEOMETRY

Sanskrit, the classical language of India and the chief medium for its premodern mathematical texts, maintained a strictly oral literary tradition for many centuries. Even after writing was introduced, the traditional writing materials, such as palm leaves, birch bark, and (later) paper, did not last long in the South Asian climate. The earliest surviving Sanskrit references to mathematical subjects are some number words in the Vedas, ancient sacred texts that were passed down by recitation and memorization. (The oldest surviving Veda manuscript dates from the 16th century.) For example, an invocation in the Yajurveda ("Veda of Sacrifice") includes names for successive powers of 10 up to about 10^{12} — well beyond the thousands and ten thousands familiar to other ancient cultures. Although the Indian number system seems always to have been decimal, in the *Satapatha Brahmana* (c. 1000 BCE; "Vedic Exegesis of a Hundred Paths"), there is an interesting sequence of divisions of 720 bricks into groups of successively smaller quantities, with the explicit exclusion of all divisors that are multiples of numbers which are relatively prime to 60 (i.e., their only common divisor is 1). This is reminiscent of the structure of ancient Babylonian sexagesimal division tables and may indicate (as do some later astronomical texts) the influence of the base-60 mathematics of Mesopotamia.

The people who left these traces of their thinking about numbers were members of the Brahman class, priestly functionaries employed in the preparation and celebration of the various ritual sacrifices. The richest evidence of their mathematical activity is found in the several 1st-millennium-BCE *Sulbasutras* ("Cord-Rules"), collections of brief prose sentences prescribing techniques for constructing the brick fire altars where the sacrifices were to be carried out. Using simple tools of ropes and stakes, the altar builders could produce quite sophisticated geometric constructions, such as transforming one plane figure into a different one of equal area. The recorded rules also indicate knowledge of geometric fundamentals such as the Pythagorean theorem, values for the ratio of the circumference of a circle to its diameter (i.e., π), and values for the ratio of the diagonal of a square to its side ($\sqrt{2}$). Different shapes and sizes of sacrificial altars were described as conferring different benefits—such as wealth, sons, and attainment of heaven—upon the sponsor of the sacrifice. Perhaps these ritual associations originally inspired the development of this geometric knowledge, or perhaps it was the other way around: the beauty and harmony of the geometric discoveries were sacralized by integrating them into ritual.

THE POST-VEDIC CONTEXT

During the rise of Buddhism and Jainism after 500 BCE, the connection between mathematical and religious thought persisted. But instead of altar constructions for animal sacrifices, which Buddhist and Jain principles rejected, mathematics supplied a framework for cosmological and philosophical schemes. Jain authors in particular employed immense numbers (even infinity) in elaborate and vast models of the universe. These new religions, as well as the older Vedic religion—by this time mostly shorn of ritual animal slaughter and more akin to modern

Hinduism—also required mathematical techniques for astronomical models in order to maintain their calendars. Some of these techniques, such as the use of sexagesimal units and employing linear "zigzag" functions to represent seasonal changes in the duration of daylight, seem to have been inspired by Mesopotamian sources that reached northwest India via the Achaemenian dynasty.

Other applications of mathematics, such as in commerce and administration, must also have flourished at this time, although only occasional brief allusions survive. For instance, a Buddhist text (*c.* 1st century BCE) by Vasumitra mentions merchants' "counting pits," where tokens in a row of shallow depressions kept track of units, hundreds, and thousands (a tens pit may have been included but is not specified). Using these as a simile for the changeable aspects of unchanging realities, Vasumitra says, "When [the same] clay counting-piece is in the place of units, it is denoted as one, when in hundreds, one hundred."

INDIAN NUMERALS AND THE DECIMAL PLACE-VALUE SYSTEM

These centuries around the turn of the millennium also left some physical evidence concerning the forms of written numerals. The above-mentioned allusion to interchangeable tokens in counting pits suggests a form of decimal place value. However, inscriptions on monuments and deed plates reveal that early Indian numeral systems (e.g., the Brahmi numerals) were not place-valued. Rather, they used different symbols for the same multiple of different powers of 10. Because epigraphical styles tend to be conservative and the number of known examples is not large, it is hard to tell exactly when and how the transition was made to a purely place-value system—indeed, different systems must have coexisted for many years. But decimal place-value

Evolution of Hindu-Arabic numerals

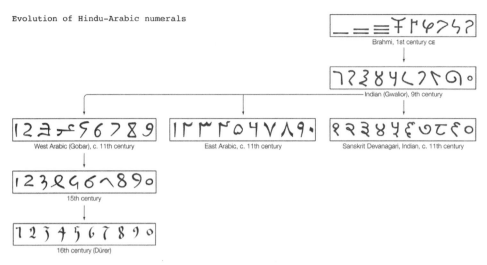

Encyclopædia Britannica, Inc.

must have been in use (at least among mathematical professionals) no later than the early 1st millennium CE. This is illustrated, for example, in a 3rd-century-CE Sanskrit adaptation of a Greek astrological text that uses the Indian "concrete number" system, where names of things stand in for numbers associated with them—e.g., "moon" for 1, "eye" for 2, "Veda" for 4, "tooth" for 32, and so on. In this way, the compound "moon-Veda-eye-moon" would be read as 1,241, implying that the reader automatically assumed a strictly decimal place-value representation.

THE "CLASSICAL" PERIOD

The founding of the Gupta dynasty in 320 CE is sometimes used as a convenient marker for the start of "classical" Indian civilization. For a while, considerable political consolidation and expansion took place within the subcontinent and beyond its shores to Southeast Asia, while direct contact with the West lessened after the heyday of trade with Rome. An increasing number of complete treatises on mathematical subjects survived from this period, beginning about the middle of the 1st millennium, in contrast to the scattered allusions and fragments of the ancient period.

THE ROLE OF ASTRONOMY AND ASTROLOGY

Greek mathematical models in astronomy and astrology appeared in India following the invasion of Alexander the Great. These models were integrated with existing Indian material to produce an extremely fruitful system of Sanskrit mathematical astronomy and astrology, known as *jyotisa*. The intellectual place of *ganita*, according to the canons of Sanskrit literature, was located within *jyotisa*, which in turn was identified as one of the six *Vedanga*s ("limbs of the Veda"), whose purpose was to support the proper performance of Vedic rituals. As a result, much of our knowledge of classical Indian mathematics is supplied by astronomical texts. Of course, there were many nonastronomical applications of *ganita* as well. Buddhists, Jains, and Hindus all valued mathematical astronomy for practical uses such as timekeeping, calendrics, and astrology and also ascribed to it intellectual and spiritual importance.

Among the earliest of these works that have been preserved are the foundational treatises of two major astronomical schools: the *Aryabhatiya* of Aryabhata (*c.* 500 CE) and the *Brahma-sphuta-siddhanta* (628; "Correctly Established Doctrine of Brahma") of Brahmagupta. Little is known of these authors. Aryabhata lived in Kusumapura (near modern Patna), and Brahmagupta is said to have been from Bhillamala (modern Bhinmal), which was the capital of the Gurjara-Pratihara dynasty. The "schools" that grew from their works were not physical institutions but rather textual lineages, built up over the subsequent centuries by the successive works of other scholars. Although members of different schools frequently criticized the astronomical parameters and techniques preferred by their rivals, their fundamental mathematical knowledge was largely the same.

The oldest surviving detailed survey of that knowledge is the first section of the *Aryabhatiya*, titled *Ganita*. Its verses are devoted to a mélange of mathematical topics ranging from extraction of square and cube roots to plane and solid geometry, simple proportions, construction of a sine table, summation of series, solution of quadratic equations, and solution of indeterminate equations of the first degree (equations of the type $ax - by = c$).

Brahmagupta collected his mathematical basics into two chapters of his treatise. Chapter 12, also called "Ganita," discusses rules for the fundamental operations on integers and fractions as well as for series, proportions, and geometry. Chapter 18 deals with indeterminate equations of the first and second degrees and with algebra techniques for linear and quadratic equations (including rules for sign manipulation and the arithmetic of zero). Trigonometric rules and tables are stated in astronomical chapters that employ them, and another chapter deals briefly with calculations relating to prosody.

Both the *Aryabhatiya* and, apparently, an early text of the *Brahma-sphuta-siddhanta* school entered the Muslim world and were translated into Arabic near the end of the 8th century, profoundly influencing the development of Islamic mathematical astronomy. The Indian decimal place-value numerals had been introduced into western Asia earlier, and the arithmetic operations involving them became widespread under the name "Indian computation." The techniques called by Arabic speakers *al-jabr* ("algebra") also may have been influenced by early Indian methods, although they do not reflect the Indian mathematicians' routine acceptance of negative numbers or their later highly developed notation.

CLASSICAL MATHEMATICAL LITERATURE

Almost all known Sanskrit mathematical texts consist mostly of concise formulas in verse. This was the standard format for many types of Sanskrit technical treatises, and the task of making sense out of its compressed formulas was aided in all its genres by prose commentaries. Verse rules about mathematics—like those in any other subject—were designed to be learned by heart, but that does not necessarily mean that nothing was expected of the student beyond rote memorization. Frequently the rules were ambiguously expressed, apparently deliberately, so that only someone who understood the underlying mathematics would be able to apply them properly. Commentaries helped by providing at least a word-by-word gloss of the meaning and usually some illustrative examples—and in some cases even detailed demonstrations.

Verse works on mathematics and astronomy faced the special challenge of verbally representing numbers (which frequently occurred in tables, constants, and examples) in strict metrical formats. "Concrete numbers" seem to have been devised for just that purpose. Another useful technique, developed somewhat later (about 500 CE), was the so-called *katapayadi* system in which each of the 10 decimal digits was assigned to a set of consonants (beginning with the letters k, t, p, and y), while vowels had no numerical significance. This meant that numbers could be represented not only by normal-sounding syllables but by actual Sanskrit words using appropriate consonants in the appropriate sequence. In fact, some astronomers constructed entire numerical tables in the form of *kata-payadi* sentences or poems.

The original physical appearance of these mathematical writings is more mysterious than their verbal content, because the treatises survive only in copies dating from much later times and reflecting later scribal conventions. There is a striking exception, however, in the Bakhshali manuscript, found in 1881 by a farmer in his field in Bakhshali (near modern Peshawar, Pakistan). Written in a variant of Buddhist Hybrid Sanskrit on birch bark, most likely about the 7th century, this manuscript is the only known Indian document on mathematics from this early period. It shows what the mathematical notation of that time and place actually looked like. The 10 decimal digits, including a dot for zero, were standard, and mathematical expressions were written without symbols, except for a square cross "+" written after negative numbers. This notation probably comes from the Indian letter for *r*, which stands for the Sanskrit word *rhna* ("negative"). Syllabic abbreviations—such as *yu* for *yuta* ("added") and *mu* for *mula* ("root")—indicated operations on quantities.

Because there are so few surviving physical representatives of mathematical works dating from earlier than the mid-2nd millennium, it is difficult to say when, where, and how some of these notational conventions changed. In later texts the writing of equations was formalized so that both sides had the same number and kinds of terms (with zero coefficients where necessary). Each unknown was designated by a different syllabic abbreviation, typically standing for the name of a colour, a word meaning "unknown," or (in word problems) the name of the commodity or other thing that the unknown represented. The practice of writing a square cross after a negative number was generally replaced by that of putting a dot over it.

THE CHANGING STRUCTURE OF MATHEMATICAL KNOWLEDGE

Conventions of classification and organization of mathematical subjects seem to have evolved rapidly in the second half of the 1st millennium. Brahmagupta's two chapters on mathematics already hint at the emerging distinction between *pati-ganita* (arithmetic; literally "board-computations" for the dust board, or sandbox, on which calculations were carried out) and *bija-ganita* (algebra; literally "seed-computations" for the manipulation of equations involving an unknown quantity, or seed). These were also called "manifest" and "unmanifest" calculation, respectively, alluding to the types of quantities that they dealt with. *Pati-ganita* comprised (besides definitions of basic weights and measures) eight "fundamental" operations of arithmetic: addition, subtraction, multiplication, division, squaring, square-root extraction, cubing, and cube-root extraction. These were supplemented by techniques for reducing fractions and solving various types of proportions. The operations were applied to problems dealing with mixtures (unequal composition of various elements), series, plane and solid geometry, and the triangular geometry of shadows. Formulas for finding areas and volumes, reckoning interest, summing series, solving quadratic equations, and solving permutations and combinations (later expanded to include magic squares) were part of the standard *pati-ganita* tool kit.

Bija-ganita was sometimes called "sixfold" because it excluded problems involving the cube root or cube of an unknown (although procedures for cubing algebraic expressions were known). It covered techniques for manipulating signs and coefficients of unknown quantities as well as surds (square roots of nonsquare integers), rules for setting up and solving equations up to second order in one or more unknowns, and rules for finding solutions to indeterminate equations of the first and second degree.

MAHAVIRA AND BHASKARA II

The *pati-ganita* and *bija-ganita* systems of arithmetic and algebra are more or less what is found in the comparatively few Sanskrit treatises that deal exclusively with mathematics (all, apparently, composed after the middle of the 1st millennium). The content and organization of the topics varies somewhat from one work to another, each author having his own ideas of what concepts should be stressed. For instance, the 9th-century *Ganita-sara-sangraha* ("Compendium of the Essence of Mathematics") by Mahavira reflects the Jain cast of his erudition in details such as the inclusion of some of the infinitesimal units of Jain cosmology in his list of weights and measures. Mahavira entirely omitted addition and subtraction from his discussion of arithmetic, instead taking multiplication as the first of the eight fundamental operations and filling the gap with summation and subtraction of series. On the other hand, the best-known of all works on Indian arithmetic and algebra, the 12th-century *Lilavati* ("The Beautiful") and the more advanced *Bijaganita*, by Bhaskara II, followed the conventional definition of the eight operations. Bhaskara asserted, however, that the "Rule of Three" (of proportionality) is the truly fundamental concept underlying both arithmetic and algebra:

> *Just as this universe is pervaded by Vishnu...with his many forms...in the same way, this whole type of computation is pervaded by the [rule of] three quantities.*

Bhaskara's two works are interesting as well for their approaches to the arithmetic of zero. Both repeat the standard (though not universal) idea that a quantity divided by zero should be defined simply as "zero-divided" and that, if such a quantity is also multiplied by zero, the zeros cancel out to restore the original quantity. But the *Bijaganita* adds:

> *In this quantity also which has zero as its divisor there is no change even when many [quantities] have entered into it or come out [of it], just as at the time of destruction and creation when throngs of creatures enter into and come out of [him, there is no change in] the infinite and unchanging [Vishnu].*

This suggests that the quantitative result of dividing by zero was considered to be an infinite amount, possibly reflecting greater sophistication of these concepts in the more advanced *Bijaganita*.

Much additional mathematical material was dealt with in Sanskrit astronomical treatises—for example, trigonometry of chords, sines, and cosines and various kinds of numerical approximation, such as interpolation and iterative rules.

TEACHERS AND LEARNERS

Almost every known mathematical author also wrote works on *jyotisa*, or astronomy and astrology. This genre was so closely linked with that of *ganita* that it was not always clear to which of them a particular text belonged. For example, Bhaskara's *Lilavati* and *Bijaganita* were often considered to be chapters of his astronomical magnum opus, *Siddhanta-siromani* ("Crest-Jewel of Astronomical Systems"). These astronomical works were primarily aimed at students and scholars pursuing astronomy, astrology, and calendrics as their hereditary occupation (generally Hindu Brahmans or scholar-monks of the heterodoxies). However, the need for more general instruction in *ganita* must certainly have affected a much broader segment of the population. Sample problems in mathematical texts (usually phrased in the second person as though addressed to a student) frequently discuss commercial transactions and often include vocatives such as "merchant" or "best of merchants," suggesting that the intended audience included members of the mercantile class.

Furthermore, some problems contain feminine vocatives such as "dear one" or "beautiful one," particularly in the *Lilavati* of Bhaskara, which later legend holds to have been named after, and written for, the author's daughter. There is a reference in a 15th-century text to certain mixture problems posed by mathematicians to ladies of the court, and many classical lists of the *kala*s, or civilized arts, include certain kinds of mathematical recreations, sometimes just mathematics in general, or even astronomy. Though the available details are very sparse, refined education for many upper-class people of both sexes was apparently expected to include some mathematics.

THE SCHOOL OF MADHAVA IN KERALA

Some of the most fascinating mathematical developments in India in the 2nd millennium—indeed, in the history of mathematics as a whole—emerged from the now-famous school of Madhava in Kerala on the Malabar Coast, a key region of the international spice trade. Madhava himself worked near the end of the 14th century, and verses attributed to him in the writings of his successors testify to his brilliant contributions on such topics as infinite series and the use of infinitesimal quantities. The work of these mathematicians anticipated several discoveries of the later European analysts, including power series for the sine, cosine, and arctangent which were also used to obtain π to 11 decimal places. Generations of Madhava's followers—in particular Jyesthadeva, Nilakantha, and Sankara—supplied ingenious geometric demonstrations of these mathematical ideas. This remarkable school also provides one of the few known examples within Indian mathematics of a continuous chain of identified direct teacher-pupil contacts extending over the course of centuries, from Madhava in the late 1300s through at least the early 1600s.

EXCHANGES WITH ISLAMIC AND WESTERN MATHEMATICS

Meanwhile, in the northern parts of India, invasion, war, and religious and caste exclusivity did not prevent a blending of Indian and Islamic mathematics in encounters between astronomers, particularly at the imperial Mughal courts. Islamic scientific works (mostly in Persian) were collaboratively translated into Sanskrit and vice versa. Concepts and results from Greco-Islamic spherical trigonometry, astronomical tables, and mathematical instruments thus found their way into Sanskrit *jyotisa*.

Similar practices at the start of Western colonization in the 16th century introduced such topics as logarithms and heliocentrism into a few Sanskrit texts. Even after the colonial policy of basing "native education" on an English curriculum was established in the 19th century, some scholars continued to recast foreign mathematics in the form of traditional Sanskrit verse treatises. However, this work was overshadowed by the rise of Indian mathematical research and mathematical societies on the lines of Western models. For the most part, by the end of the 19th century, the river of Indian *ganita* had been fully merged into the ocean of modern mathematics.

MATHEMATICS IN CHINA

The evolution of mathematical subjects within the Chinese tradition emphasized several common characteristics.

There was an interest in general algorithms. The concepts of "position" (a place-value notation involving rods or counters), a specific part devoted to configurations of numbers, and the parallelisms between procedures were also important.

THE TEXTUAL SOURCES

The most important work in the history of mathematics in Chinese is *Jiuzhang suanshu* (*The Nine Chapters on the Mathematical Art*). It contains arithmetic, algebraic, and geometric algorithms, presented in relation to problems, some of which evoke the duties of the civil administration: surveying fields (areas), levying taxes according to various types of grains (ratios), determining wages for civil servants according to their position in the hierarchy (unequal sharing), measuring planned earthworks to determine labour needs and granaries to determine storage capacity (volumes), levying fair taxes (problems combining various proportions), and so forth. This compilation from the 1st century BCE or CE (specialists disagree on the exact date of its completion) has been restored based on two main sources. The oldest extant copy, which is also the oldest existing mathematics book ever printed, dates from 1213. However, only the first five chapters survive. The complete book known today as *The Nine Chapters* is the result of an 18th-century philological work based on both the former source and exhaustive quotations in a 15th-century Chinese encyclopaedia, *Yongle dadian*, compiled under the Yongle emperor (1402–24). In any case, like Euclid's *Elements*, *The Nine Chapters* gathered and organized many mathematical achievements (including arithmetic, geometric, and algebraic algorithms) from preceding periods. And like the *Elements* in the West, *The Nine Chapters* played a preeminent role in the development of mathematics in

East Asia. Most mathematicians referred to it, and most of the subjects that they worked on stemmed from it. Its format, adopted by most subsequent authors, consists of problems for which a numerical answer and a general procedure for solution are given. As with any canonical work, many scholars wrote commentaries on *The Nine Chapters*, adding explanations and proofs, rewriting procedures, and suggesting new ones. The most important surviving commentary, attributed to Liu Hui (3rd century), contains the earliest Chinese mathematical proofs in the modern sense.

During the 7th century, certain other books were gathered together with *The Nine Chapters* and a Han astronomical treatise, *Zhoubi* ("The Gnomon of the Zhou"), by a group under the leadership of imperial mathematician and astronomer Li Chunfeng. This collection, known as *Shibu suanjing* ("Ten Classics of Mathematics"), became the manual for officials trained in the newly established office of mathematics. Although some people continued to be officially trained as mathematicians thereafter, no advancement in mathematics can be documented until the 11th century. At that time (1084) the "Ten Classics" was edited and printed, an event that seems to have been related to renewed activity in mathematics during the 11th and 12th centuries. This activity is known only through later quotations, but it probably paved the way for major achievements in the second half of the 13th century. At that time China was divided into North and South, and achievements by mathematicians in both regions are known: in the South those of Qin Jiushao and Yang Hui, and in the North those of Li Ye and Zhu Shijie. Mathematical studies in the North and South seem to have developed independently, but they attest to a common basis.

While some major works of the 13th century are recorded in the *Yongle dadian*, mathematical knowledge quickly deteriorated, as demonstrated by commentaries on these books written by the end of the 15th century that show that they were no longer understood. By the 17th century, few ancient Chinese mathematical works were available. Thereafter, as Chinese scholars became aware of European achievements, they began to look for such works throughout the country and strove to interpret them. The end of the 18th century saw a large movement of editing rediscovered texts. These critical editions are the main sources today for the history of Chinese mathematics. Discoveries of new sources are now rare, though in the 20th century a mathematical book was found in a grave sealed before the end of the 2nd century BCE, pushing back by centuries the earliest known source on the subject. It is possible that archaeology will bring to light new findings and provoke a revolution comparable to that experienced in the historiography of China in general.

THE GREAT EARLY PERIOD, 1ST–7TH CENTURIES

Books written in China from the 1st century BCE through the 7th century CE (and also in the 13th century) formed the foundation for the development of mathematics in East Asia. Most subsequent mathematical works refer to them. References found in the surviving mathematical writings from this period, as well as references made in bibliographies compiled for dynastic annals, indicate that there are many gaps in the textual record. The oldest extant works probably survived because they became official books, taught in the context of the Chinese civil examination system.

THE NINE CHAPTERS

The Nine Chapters presupposes mathematical knowledge about how to represent numbers and how to perform the four arithmetic operations of addition, subtraction, multiplication, and division. In it the numbers are written in Chinese characters, but, for most of the procedures described, the actual computations are intended to be performed on a surface, perhaps on the ground. Most probably, as can be inferred from later accounts, on this surface, or counting board, the numbers were represented by counting rods that were used according to a decimal place-value system. Numbers represented by counting rods could be

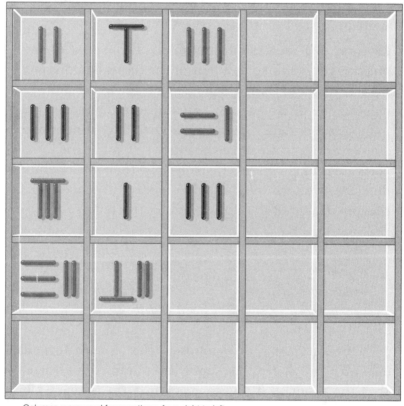

Columns were used for equations, from right to left:

$$3x + 21y - 3z = 0$$
$$-6x - 2y - z = 62$$
$$2x - 3y + 8z = 32$$

━━━━ Negative
━━━━ Positive

Counting boards and markers, or counting rods, were used in China to solve systems of linear equations. This is an example from the 1st century CE. Encyclopædia Britannica, Inc.

moved and modified within a computation. However, no written computations were recorded until much later. As will be seen, setting up the computations with counting rods greatly influenced later mathematical developments.

The Nine Chapters contains a number of mathematical achievements, already in a mature form, that were presented by most subsequent books without substantial changes. The most important achievements are described briefly in the rest of this section.

Arithmetic of Fractions

Division is a central operation in *The Nine Chapters*. Fractions are defined as a part of the result of a division, the remainder of the dividend being taken as the numerator and the divisor as the denominator. Thus, dividing 17 by 5, one obtains a quotient of 3 and a remainder of 2. This gives rise to the mixed quantity 3 + 2/5. The fractional parts are thus always less than one, and their arithmetic is described through the use of division. For instance, to get the sum of a set of fractions, one is instructed to

> *multiply the numerators by the denominators that do not correspond to them, add to get the dividend. Multiply the denominators all together to get the divisor. Perform the division. If there is a remainder, name it with the divisor.*

This algorithm corresponds to the modern formula $a/b + c/d = (ad + bc)/bd$. The sum of a set of fractions is itself thus the result of a division, of the form "integer plus proper fraction." All the arithmetic operations involving fractions are described in a similar way.

Algorithms for Areas and Volumes

The Nine Chapters gives formulas for elementary plane and solid figures, including the areas of triangles, rectangles, trapezoids, circles, and segments of circles and the volumes of prisms, cylinders, pyramids, and spheres. All these formulas are expressed as lists of operations to be performed on the data in order to get the result—i.e., as algorithms. For example, to compute the area of a circle, the following algorithm is given: "multiply the diameter by itself, triple this, divide by four." This algorithm amounts to using 3 as the value for π. Commentators added improved values for π along with some derivations. The commentary ascribed to Liu Hui computes two other approximations for π, one slightly low (157/50) and one high (3,927/1,250). *The Nine Chapters* also provides the correct formula for the area of the circle—"multiplying half the diameter and half the circumference, one gets the area"—which Liu Hui proved.

Solution of Systems of Simultaneous Linear Equations

The Nine Chapters devotes a chapter to the solution of simultaneous linear equations—that is, to collections of relations between unknowns and data (equations) where none of the unknown quantities is raised to a power higher than 1. For example, the first problem in this chapter, on the yields from three grades of grain, asks:

> *3 bundles of top-grade grain, 2 bundles of medium grade, and 1 bundle of low grade yield 39 units of grain. 2 bundles of top grade, 3 bundles of medium grade, and 1 bundle of low grade yield 34 units. 1 bundle of top grade, 2 bundles of medium grade, and 3 bundles of low grade yield 26 units. How many units does a bundle of each grade of grain yield?*

The procedure for solving a system of three equations in three unknowns involves arranging the data on the computing surface in the form of a table. The coefficients of the first equation are arranged in the first column and the coefficients of the second and third equations in the

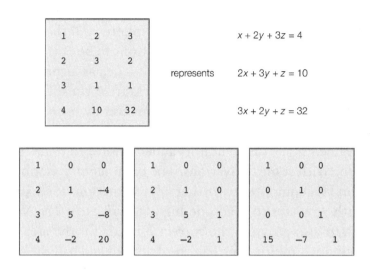

Encyclopædia Britannica, Inc.

second and third columns. Consequently, the numbers of the first row, comprising the first coefficient in each equation, correspond to the first unknown. This is an instance of a place-value notation, in which the position of a number in a numerical configuration has a mathematical meaning. The main tool for the solution is the use of column reduction (elimination of variables by reducing their coefficients to zero) to obtain an equivalent configuration. Next, the unknown of the third row is found by division, and hence the second and the first unknowns are found as well. This algorithm is known in the West as Gauss elimination.

The algorithm described above relies in an essential way on the configuration given to the set of data on the counting surface. Because the procedure implies a column-to-column subtraction, it gives rise to negative numbers. *The Nine Chapters* describes detailed methods for computing with positive and negative coefficients that enable problems involving two to seven unknowns to be solved. This seems to be the first occurrence of negative numbers in the history of mathematics.

Square and Cube Roots

In *The Nine Chapters*, algorithms for finding integral parts of square roots or cube roots on the counting surface are based on the same idea as the arithmetic ones used today. These algorithms are set up on the surface in the same way as is a division: at the top, the "quotient"; under it, the "dividend"; one row below, the "divisor"; at the bottom, auxiliary computations. Moreover, the algorithms are written out, sentence by sentence, parallel to each other, so that their similarities and differences become clear.

Commenting on these algorithms, Liu Hui suggested that one could continue computing the nonintegral portion of a root in the same way, setting 10 as denominator for the first subsequent digit, 100 as denominator for the first two digits, and so on. He thus gave the root in terms comparable to decimal fractions. Moreover, in case the algorithm, which generates digit-by-digit the root of an integer N, did not stop with the digit for the units (N was not a perfect square), *The Nine Chapters* stated that another way of providing the result of the square root algorithm should be used: the root should be given in the form "side of N," which should be understood to mean "square root of N." Thus, quadratic irrationals (an irrational number that is the solution to some quadratic equation of the kind $x^2 = N$) were introduced in ancient China and the commentaries attest to their use in computations.

The procedure for extracting square roots was also applied to the solution of quadratic equations (in modern notation, equations of the form $x^2 + bx = c$). The quadratic equation appears to have been conceived of as an arithmetic operation with two terms (b and c). Moreover, the equation was thought to have only one root. The theory of equations developed in China within that framework until the 13th century. The solution by radicals that Babylonian mathematicians had already explored has not been found in the Chinese texts that survive. However, the specific approach to equations that developed in China occurs from at least the end of the 12th century onward in Arabic sources, where it is meshed with approaches from other parts of the ancient world.

Problems Involving Right Triangles

Right-angled triangles also constituted a domain in which research continued until the 13th century in China. The so-called Pythagorean theorem is given, under an algorithmic form, in *The Nine Chapters*. Algorithms are provided to solve various problems on right triangles such as the following: "Given the base, and the sum of the height and of the hypotenuse, find the height and the hypotenuse." Other algorithms are given for determining the diameter of an inscribed circle and the side of an inscribed square.

THE COMMENTARY OF LIU HUI

Liu Hui's 3rd-century commentary on *The Nine Chapters* is the most important text dating from before the 13th century that contains proofs in the modern sense. His commentary on the algorithms for computing the volumes of bodies exemplifies the kind of mathematical work that he carried out throughout the book for the sake of exegesis. Liu proved the algorithms already presented in *The Nine Chapters*, and he also provided and proved new algorithms for the same three-dimensional volumes. In addition, he organized these algorithms, given one after the other without comment in *The Nine Chapters*, into a system in which proofs for one algorithm use only algorithms that had already been established independently. He used a small set of proof techniques, including dissection (even into an infinite number of pieces), decomposition into known pieces and recomposition, and a simplified version of what became known later in the West as Cavalieri's principle — which states that, if two solids of the same height are such that their corresponding sections at any level have the same areas, then they have the same volume. More precisely, Liu deduced the volume of a solid whose cross sections are circles by circumscribing each section with a square. (A finer version of Cavalieri's principle was used by Zu Gengzhi in the 5th century to establish the correctness of the algorithm computing the volume of a sphere.)

The great importance of Liu Hui's commentary on *The Nine Chapters* lies in the fact that he proved the correctness of algorithms not only in geometry but also in arithmetic and algebra. In the course of proving algorithms given in various sections of the work, he compared them with one another and demonstrated how the same formal operations, which he called the "key steps" of computation, are brought into play in different algorithms. For example, in comparing the procedures for adding fractions and for solving simultaneous linear equations (described above) — a comparison which is carried out while establishing their correctness — Liu showed that sets of numbers are involved (numerator and denominator for a fraction, the coefficients of an equation for systems of equations) which share the property that all the numbers of a set can be multiplied by the same number without altering the mathematical meaning of that set. Both algorithms, Liu showed, proceed by multiplying the sets of numbers that enter into a problem, each by an appropriate factor, in such a way that some corresponding numbers of the sets are made equal and the other numbers are multiplied to keep intact the meaning of the whole sets. In the case of fractions, the denominators are made equal, and the numerators are changed appropriately. For linear equations, the procedure is the same as if two numbers in the same row but in different columns were made equal by an appropriate multiplication, so that one of them can be eliminated through a column-to-column subtraction. The whole columns are then multiplied by the same number so that the equations remain valid. Liu proceeded from these analogies to state new algorithms for the same problems.

THE "TEN CLASSICS"

For reasons that are still unclear, explications of the mathematical knowledge presupposed by *The Nine Chapters* (such as the numeration system and arithmetic operations) first appeared in later books that eventually were included in the "Ten Classics of Mathematics." Most of the subjects dealt with in the later canonical works of mathematics from ancient China relied on algorithms presented in *The Nine Chapters*, although sometimes they used versions of these algorithms that had a more limited range of applications.

Nevertheless, it is possible to see an ongoing evolution of some of these topics, such as root extraction and the solution of equations. For example, *Sunzi suanjing* ("Sunzi's Mathematical Classic") and *Zhang Qiujian suanjing* ("Zhang Qiujian's Mathematical Classic"), both probably written before the 5th century and included in the "Ten Classics," employed new descriptions of algorithms for the extraction of square and cube roots. The underlying procedures were the same, and they were still described in parallel ways, but the new descriptions showed more clearly the underlying mathematical object that is responsible for their similarity—namely, the equation. What changed in the descriptions was that, just as division involved a single divisor, square root extraction was shown to have two divisors and cube root extraction three divisors. (These divisors actually are coefficients of the equations that underlie the root extractions.) The divisors were shown to play similar roles in the algorithms. Moreover, in setting up the algorithms, the divisors were arranged one above the other, yielding a place-value notation for the underlying equations: the row in which a number occurred was associated with the power of the unknown whose coefficient it was. However, at that time equations were neither written nor conceptualized in terms of such a place-value notation. Early in the 7th century, Wang Xiaotong generalized the cube root extraction method to solve some third-degree equations using counting rods. It was only much later that the concept and representation of equations begat a full-fledged place-value notation.

The "Ten Classics" also attests to research on topics that were not mentioned in *The Nine Chapters* but that were to be the subject of some of the highest mathematical achievements of the Song and Yuan dynasties (960–1368). For example, "Sunzi's Mathematical Classic" presents this congruence problem:

> *Suppose one has an unknown number of objects. If one counts them by threes, there remain two of them. If one counts them by fives, there remain three of them. If one counts them by sevens, there remain two of them. How many objects are there?*

The procedure used to solve the problem is difficult to understand, because it is described in a very condensed manner. But it clearly belongs to the tradition that eventually led to a general algorithm for solving such problems.

SCHOLARLY REVIVAL, 11TH–13TH CENTURIES

Research appears to have resumed in the 11th century with the reediting of the "Ten Classics" and the production of new commentaries. Within this context new developments took place in branches of mathematics that had been explored at least since *The Nine Chapters*, attesting to a continuity of mathematical practice.

THEORY OF ROOT EXTRACTION AND EQUATIONS

One of the most notable developments regarded root extraction. In the 11th century, Jia Xian is said to have given an algorithm for finding a fourth root using a method similar to the one now known as the Ruffini-Horner method. Jia's algorithm operated on a column of rows set up on the counting surface in such a way that it still involved a place-value notation for the underlying equations. The intermediate values obtained in each row (actually the coefficients of the underlying equations) resulted from operations that involved only the numbers located in the rows below. Again, the algorithm made use of the configuration given to this set of numbers in an essential way. In addition, the procedures used to compute the successive numbers in any row were all the same. The new algorithm highlighted that the rows experience the same transformations throughout the procedure—indicating a continued interest in the homogeneity of row operations in the descriptions of square and cube root extraction. As a consequence, division, square root extraction, and cube root extraction now appeared to be particular cases of the same general operation, which also covered extraction of nth roots. In fact, only the number of rows on which the algorithm operated determined the nature of the operation: three rows for a square root, four rows for a cube root, and so on.

More generally, research on the solution of equations also resumed and revealed that the same basic algorithm could be extended to find a root of any algebraic equation. The first step documented in this direction, by the 11th- or

12th-century scholar Liu Yi, was finding roots of quadratic equations that have positive or negative coefficents. The coefficients, whatever their sign, were entered in the table for root extraction, and the square root algorithm was adapted to each situation.

Later, Qin Jiushao's *Shushu jiuzhang* (1247; "Mathematical Treatise in Nine Chapters") attested to the use of an algorithm extending Jia Xian's procedure to find "the" root of any equation. (Most Chinese mathematicians still clung to the idea that an equation had just one proper solution.) By that time, general equations of any degree were used and were represented by a full-fledged place-value notation. This seems to indicate that it was the slow evolution of the algorithms of root extraction and their comparison that produced a fully developed concept of the equation. Similar methods (with a slightly different notation) were well known to Li Ye, and his *Ceyuan haijing* ("Sea Mirror of Circle Measurements"), written only one year after Qin completed his book, takes the search for the root of equations for granted. Li lived in North China, while Qin lived in the South, and is thought to have worked without knowing Qin's achievements. It is thus highly probable that these methods were well known before the middle of the 13th century.

In parallel to Jia Xian's algorithm described above, another method developed for determining an nth root or finding the root of an equation of any degree, using the coefficients of what is now called Pascal's triangle and the same place-value representation.

THE METHOD OF THE CELESTIAL UNKNOWN

Li Ye's book also contains a method, unknown to Qin Jiushao, that seems to have flourished in North China for some decades before Li completed "Sea Mirror of Circle

Measurements." This method explains how to use polynomial arithmetic to find equations to solve a problem. Li's book is the oldest surviving work that explains this method, but it was probably not the first to deal with it. In this book polynomials are also arranged according to a positional notation. Thus, $x^2 - 3x + 5 + 7/x^2$ is represented as

$$
\begin{matrix}
7 \\
o \\
5. \\
-3 \\
1
\end{matrix}
$$

A character is added next to the 5 (in this case, a dot) to indicate that it is a constant term. The location of the coefficient indicates the power of the indeterminate with which it is associated. This indeterminate is called "the celestial unknown."

Research continued on these topics for several decades, as can be seen from the completion in 1299 of *Suanxue qimeng* ("Introduction to Mathematical Science") by Zhu Shijie, which devotes some problems to presenting the "procedure of the celestial unknown." Moreover, it is known that some mathematicians used this representation for polynomials in two or three unknowns. However, their writings are lost. In his second surviving book, *Siyuan yujian* ("Precious Mirror of the Four Elements"), Zhu made use of four unknowns. Starting from the centre of the counting board, in the two horizontal and the two vertical directions, he put in increasing order of their powers what came from each of the four unknowns. As soon as positive and negative powers of the indeterminates or too many mixed terms occurred, however, he had to use tricks that were in conflict with the principles of the place-value notation. In problems where there was more than one unknown, he had to use a method of elimination of a common unknown between two equations.

CHINESE REMAINDER THEOREM

Qin Jiushao's book also contains algorithms for the general congruence problem, an example of which was given in Sunzi's 5th-century treatise, where its solution was too obscure to be understood. This problem amounts to determining a number, the remainders of which are known when it is divided by given numbers (called moduli). There is no extant work between Sunzi's treatise and Qin's book of 1247 that reveals how this algorithm was elaborated. Such problems seem to have been worked out because of calendrical computation. Qin introduced his discussion by saying that his goal was to clarify several procedures used by astronomers who were applying them without understanding them. His solution is known today as the Chinese remainder theorem. He dealt with the case when moduli are relatively prime, and he then reduced the case when they are not by first eliminating common factors. The first case is easily solved when x can be found that satisfies the congruence $xa \equiv 1 \pmod{b}$, a and b being two given relatively prime numbers (suppose $a < b$). Qin gave an algorithm for this, using a sequence of quotients in searching for the greatest common divisor of a and b, which is also the sequence of convergents for the continued fraction for b/a. Having them, he was then able to compute x.

FALL INTO OBLIVION, 14TH–16TH CENTURIES

Little is known about what happened to Chinese mathematics after Zhu Shijie, but surviving books from the following centuries attest to a progressive loss of the great achievements of the Song-Yuan period. In the 16th century, a mathematician's comments on Li Ye's "Sea Mirror of Circle Measurements" show that the method of the celestial unknown was no longer understood. By the 17th century, it seems to have been completely forgotten. Rods were then no longer used as a counting tool, so perhaps Chinese algebraic place-value notations, deprived of the instrument on which they were based, could not be understood.

On the other hand, there was a rapid diffusion of the abacus, for which many books were written. One of them, the *Suanfa tongzong* ("Systematic Treatise on Mathematics") by Cheng Dawei (1592), had a special significance. In addition to its detailed treatment of arithmetic on the abacus, it provided a summa of mathematical knowledge assembled by the author after 20 years of bibliographic research. Re-edited several times through the 19th century, the "Systematic Treatise" was the main source—and still is an important source—available to scholars in China, and more generally in East Asia, concerning mathematics as it developed in China's tradition.

When European missionaries arrived in China at the end of the 16th century, they found people interested in science (so that the missionaries were accepted in China because of their scientific knowledge) but unaware of their own past in mathematics. An era of translations of Western works then started, the first six books of Euclid's *Elements* being translated by the Jesuit Matteo Ricci and Xu Guangqi in 1607. In parallel to this process of translation, Chinese scholars attempted to find ancient books, to understand them, and to synthesize the Chinese and Western traditions. In the 18th century, with the help of Western algebra, Mei Juecheng deciphered the ancient texts dealing with the method of the celestial unknown. This triggered a renewed search for ancient Chinese sources and attempts to revive mathematical research with traditional Chinese methods.

MATHEMATICS IN JAPAN

The history of Japanese mathematics is that of an engagement with the mathematics of China that had managed to enter Japan. The Japanese tradition culminated in the work of Seki.

THE INTRODUCTION OF CHINESE BOOKS

Very little is known about Japanese mathematics before the 17th century. Beginning in the 7th century, at first only indirectly by way of Korea, there was a flow of Chinese science to Japan. For example, the "Ten Classics of Mathematics" was introduced, along with counting rods, probably by the 8th century. Yet no Japanese book dealing with mathematics survives from before the end of the 16th century. At that time another phase of importation began: the abacus and Cheng Dawei's "Systematic Treatise on Mathematics" became known in Japan, though they did not supplant the use of counting rods. Moreover, many books were brought from Korea, and perhaps in that way two Chinese books, *Yang Hui suanfa* (1275; "Yang Hui's Methods of Mathematics") and Zhu Shijie's "Introduction to Mathematical Science," arrived in Japan. In those books, Japanese scholars could find algorithms for solving systems of simultaneous linear equations and for searching for the root of an equation according to methods used in China in the 13th century. They could also find applications of the method of the celestial unknown (although these were not immediately understood). In addition, books on calendrical computations, which also contained mathematical knowledge, were imported. As a result of such infusions, Chinese mathematics greatly influenced the development of Japanese mathematics (for example, its algebraic orientation) and defined the context in which the Japanese tradition later opened to European mathematics.

At the beginning of the Tokugawa period (1603–1867), contacts with foreigners were limited to trade with Chinese and Dutch ships through the port of Nagasaki. Some Chinese books, which by then may have contained Western knowledge, as well as Dutch books entered Japan secretly, but it is difficult to state how much, or what kind of, mathematical knowledge entered through that channel.

THE ELABORATION OF CHINESE METHODS

Although not the first mathematical book written in Japan, *Jingoki* ("Inalterable Treatise"), published in 1627 by Yoshida Mitsuyoshi, seems to be the first book that played an important role in the emerging Japanese tradition. Inspired by the Chinese text "Systematic Treatise on Mathematics," whose importance is stressed above, it described in Japanese the use of the *soroban*, an improvement of the Chinese abacus, and introduced some Chinese knowledge. Its many editions contributed to popularizing mathematics because most of the works on mathematics in Japan were written in Chinese and could not be widely read. In its enlarged edition of 1641, *Jingoki* introduced the method of performing computations with counting rods, which by then were no longer used in China. Moreover, inspired by his Chinese source, Yoshida added "difficult problems" that he left without solutions and recommended be posed to mathematicians. This initiated a tradition of challenges, reminiscent of those that took place in Europe during the Renaissance, that strongly stimulated the development of mathematics in Japan. In this context, mathematicians in the 1650s, relying on counting-rod computations and looking for new methods of solution, began to decipher the original methods of Chinese algebra—hinted at in the 1658 Japanese reprint of "Introduction to Mathematical Science"—which enabled them to advance beyond the classics. This contrasts with the situation in China, where the original methods could be understood only after the introduction of Western algebra.

Various Japanese authors disseminated traditional Chinese methods for the solution of problems. Sawaguchi Kazuyuki's *Kokon sanpoki* (1671; "Ancient and Modern Mathematics") pointed out that "erroneous" problems could have more than one solution (in other words, equations could have more than one root), but he left unanswered difficult problems involving simultaneous equations of the nth degree. Equations for their solution were published in 1674 by Seki Takakazu, now considered to be the founder of the Japanese tradition of mathematics, or *wasan*. Seki founded what became the most important school of mathematics in Japan. (At this time, mathematics was widely practiced in Japan as a leisure activity.) As in other schools, disciples had to keep the school methods secret, and only the best among them knew most of these methods. Only slowly did they publish their secrets, which hindered the free circulation of ideas and which makes any attribution very difficult.

Explanations of how to use Seki's equations to derive Sawaguchi's problems were published in 1685 by one of Seki's disciples, Takebe Katahiro. Seki had designed for this purpose a "literal" written algebra using characters, thus liberating mathematicians from counting rods. He kept for equations the positional notation with respect to one unknown, the coefficients being expressed in terms of numbers, parameters, or other unknowns. In establishing equations among several unknowns for the solution of a problem, he had to introduce procedures equivalent to computations of determinants in order to eliminate unknowns between simultaneous equations. Further research elaborated these procedures.

Seki devised a classification of problems that amounted to a classification of equations, which took into consideration negative roots and multiple roots, the existence of which had been noticed by Sawaguchi. For this purpose he adapted the Chinese algorithms from the 13th century. Seki and his disciples thus improved upon Chinese methods in many ways, opening new directions for the development of mathematics in Japan—as, for example, in their work on infinite series, the subject of research by contemporary European scientists as well.

CHAPTER 4
THE FOUNDATIONS
OF MATHEMATICS

Mathematicians have long studied the logical and philosophical basis of mathematics, including whether the axioms of a given system ensure its completeness and its consistency. Because mathematics has served as a model for rational inquiry in the West and is used extensively in the sciences, foundational studies have far-reaching consequences for the reliability and extensibility of rational thought itself.

ANCIENT GREECE TO THE ENLIGHTENMENT

A remarkable amount of practical mathematics, some of it even fairly sophisticated, was already developed as early as 2000 BCE by the agricultural civilizations of Egypt and Mesopotamia, and perhaps even farther east. However, the first to exhibit an interest in the foundations of mathematics were the ancient Greeks.

ARITHMETIC OR GEOMETRY

Early Greek philosophy was dominated by a dispute as to which is more basic, arithmetic or geometry, and thus whether mathematics should be concerned primarily with the (positive) integers or the (positive) reals, the latter then being conceived as ratios of geometric quantities. (The Greeks confined themselves to positive numbers, as negative numbers were introduced only much later in India by Brahmagupta.) Underlying this dispute was a perceived basic dichotomy, not confined to mathematics but pervading all nature: is the universe made up of discrete atoms (as the philosopher Democritus believed) which hence can be counted, or does it consist of one or more continuous substances (as Thales of Miletus is reputed to have believed) and thus can only be measured? This dichotomy was presumably inspired by a linguistic distinction, analogous to that between English count nouns, such as "apple," and mass nouns, such as "water." As Aristotle later pointed out, in an effort to mediate between these divergent positions, water can be measured by counting cups.

The Pythagorean school of mathematics, founded on the doctrines of the Greek philosopher Pythagoras, originally insisted that only natural and rational numbers exist. Its members only reluctantly accepted the discovery that $\sqrt{2}$, the ratio of the diagonal of a square to its side, could not be expressed as the ratio of whole numbers. The remarkable proof of this fact has been preserved by Aristotle.

The contradiction between rationals and reals was finally resolved by Eudoxus of Cnidus, a disciple of Plato, who pointed out that two ratios of geometric quantities are equal if and only if they partition the set of (positive) rationals in the same way, thus anticipating the German mathematician Richard Dedekind (1831–1916), who defined real numbers as such partitions.

BEING VERSUS BECOMING

Another dispute among pre-Socratic philosophers was more concerned with the physical world. Parmenides claimed that in the real world there is no such thing as change and that the flow of time is an illusion, a view with parallels in the Einstein-Minkowski four-dimensional space-time model of the universe. Heracleitus, on the other hand, asserted that change is all-pervasive and is reputed to have said that one cannot step into the same river twice.

Zeno of Elea, a follower of Parmenides, claimed that change is actually impossible and produced four paradoxes to show this. The most famous of these describes a race between Achilles and a tortoise. Since Achilles can run much faster than the tortoise, let us say twice as fast, the latter is allowed a head start of one mile. When Achilles has run one mile, the tortoise will have run half as far again—that is, half a mile. When Achilles has covered that additional half-mile, the tortoise will have run a further quarter-mile. After $n + 1$ stages, Achilles has run

$$1 + \frac{1}{2} + \cdots + \frac{1}{2^n} = 2 - \frac{1}{2^n}$$

miles and the tortoise has run

$$1 + \frac{1}{2} + \cdots + \frac{1}{2^n} + \frac{1}{2^{n+1}}$$

miles, being still $1/2^{n+1}$ miles ahead. So how can Achilles ever catch up with the tortoise?

Zeno's paradoxes may also be interpreted as showing that space and time are not made up of discrete atoms but are substances which are infinitely divisible. Mathematically speaking, his argument involves the sum of the infinite geometric progression

$$1 + \frac{1}{2} + \frac{1}{4} + \cdots,$$

no finite partial sum of which adds up to 2. As Aristotle would later say, this progression is only potentially infinite. It is now understood that Zeno was trying to come to grips with the notion of limit, which was not formally explained until the 19th century, although a start in that

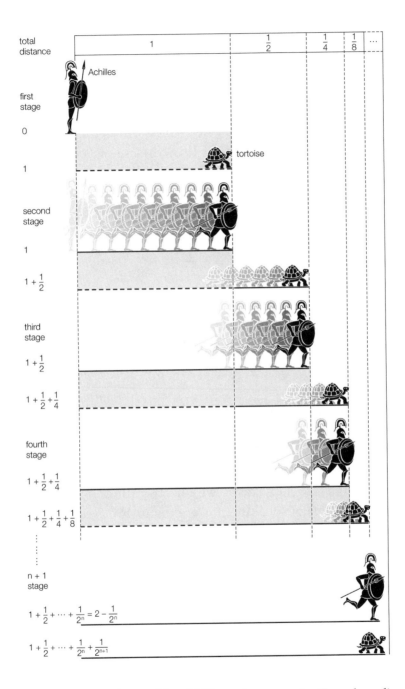

Zeno's paradox, illustrated by Achilles racing a tortoise. Encyclopædia Britannica, Inc.

direction had been made by the French encyclopaedist Jean Le Rond d'Alembert (1717–83).

UNIVERSALS

The Athenian philosopher Plato believed that mathematical entities are not just human inventions but have a real existence. For instance, according to Plato, the number 2 is an ideal object. This is sometimes called an "idea," from the Greek *eide,* or "universal," from the Latin *universalis,*

Plato. Hulton Archive/Getty Images

meaning "that which pertains to all." But Plato did not have in mind a "mental image," as "idea" is usually used. The number 2 is to be distinguished from a collection of two stones or two apples or, for that matter, two platinum balls in Paris.

What, then, are these Platonic ideas? Already in ancient Alexandria some people speculated that they are words. This is why the Greek word *logos,* originally meaning "word," later acquired a theological meaning as denoting the ultimate reality behind the "thing." An intense debate occurred in the Middle Ages over the ontological status of universals. Three dominant views prevailed: realism, from the Latin *res* ("thing"), which asserts that universals have an extra-mental reality—that is, they exist independently of perception; conceptualism, which asserts that universals exist as entities within the mind but have no extra-mental existence; and nominalism, from the Latin *nomen* ("name"), which asserts that universals exist neither in the mind nor in the extra-mental realm but are merely names that refer to collections of individual objects.

It would seem that Plato believed in a notion of truth independent of the human mind. In the *Meno* Plato's teacher Socrates asserts that it is possible to come to know this truth by a process akin to memory retrieval. Thus, by clever questioning, Socrates managed to bring an uneducated person to "remember," or rather to reconstruct, the proof of a mathematical theorem.

THE AXIOMATIC METHOD

Perhaps the most important contribution to the foundations of mathematics made by the ancient Greeks was the axiomatic method and the notion of proof. This was insisted upon in Plato's Academy and reached its high point in Alexandria about 300 BCE with Euclid's *Elements*. This notion survives today, except for some cosmetic changes.

The idea is this: there are a number of basic mathematical truths, called axioms or postulates, from which other true statements may be derived in a finite number of steps. It may take considerable ingenuity to discover a proof. But it is now held that it must be possible to check mechanically, step by step, whether a purported proof is indeed correct, and nowadays a computer should be able to do this. The mathematical statements that can be proved are called theorems, and it follows that, in principle, a mechanical device, such as a modern computer, can generate all theorems.

Two questions about the axiomatic method were left unanswered by the ancients: are all mathematical truths axioms or theorems (this is referred to as completeness), and can it be determined mechanically whether a given statement is a theorem (this is called decidability)? These questions were raised implicitly by David Hilbert (1862–1943) about 1900 and were resolved later in the negative, completeness by the Austrian-American logician Kurt Gödel (1906–78) and decidability by the American logician Alonzo Church (1903–95).

Euclid's work dealt with number theory and geometry, essentially all the mathematics then known. Since the middle of the 20th century, a gradually changing group of mostly French mathematicians under the pseudonym Nicolas Bourbaki has tried to emulate Euclid in writing a new *Elements of Mathematics* based on their theory of structures. Unfortunately, they just missed out on the new ideas from category theory.

NUMBER SYSTEMS

While the ancient Greeks were familiar with the positive integers, rationals, and reals, zero (used as an actual number instead of denoting a missing number) and the negative numbers were first used in India—as far as is known—by Brahmagupta in the 7th century CE. Complex numbers were introduced by the Italian Renaissance mathematician and physician Gerolamo Cardano (1501–76), not just to solve equations such as $x^2 + 1 = 0$ but because they were needed to find real solutions of certain cubic equations with real coefficients. Much later, the German mathematician Carl Friedrich Gauss (1777–1855) proved the fundamental theorem of algebra, that all equations with complex coefficients have complex solutions, thus removing the principal motivation for introducing new numbers. Still, the Irish mathematician Sir William Rowan Hamilton (1805–65) and the French mathematician Olinde Rodrigues (1794–1851) invented quaternions in the mid-19th century, but these proved to be less popular in the scientific community until quite recently.

Currently, a logical presentation of the number system, as taught at the university level, would be as follows: $N \to Z \to Q \to R \to C \to H$. Here the letters, introduced by Nicolas Bourbaki, refer to the natural numbers, integers, rationals, reals, complex numbers, and quaternions, respectively, and the arrows indicate inclusion of each number system into the next. However, as has been shown, the historical development proceeds differently: $N^+ \to Q^+ \to R^+ \to R \to C \to H$, where the plus sign indicates restriction to positive elements. This is the development, up to R, which is often adhered to at the high-school level.

THE REEXAMINATION OF INFINITY

Both Plato and Aristotle shared the general Greek abhorrence of the notion of infinity. Aristotle influenced subsequent thought for more than a millennium with his rejection of "actual" infinity (spatial, temporal, or numerical), which he distinguished from the "potential" infinity of being able to count without end. However, infinity reappeared in mathematics in the 17th century.

CALCULUS REOPENS FOUNDATIONAL QUESTIONS

Although mathematics flourished after the end of the Classical Greek period for 800 years in Alexandria and, after an interlude in India and the Islamic world, again in Renaissance Europe, philosophical questions concerning the foundations of mathematics were not raised until the invention of calculus and then not by mathematicians but by the philosopher George Berkeley (1685–1753).

Sir Isaac Newton in England and Gottfried Wilhelm Leibniz in Germany had independently developed the calculus on a basis of heuristic rules and methods markedly deficient in logical justification. As is the case in many new developments, utility outweighed rigour, and, though Newton's fluxions (or derivatives) and Leibniz's infinitesimals (or differentials) lacked a coherent rational explanation, their power in answering heretofore unanswerable questions was undeniable. Unlike Newton, who made little effort to explain and justify fluxions, Leibniz, as an eminent and highly regarded philosopher, was influential in propagating the idea of infinitesimals, which he described as infinitely small actual numbers — that is, less than $1/n$ in absolute value for each positive integer n and yet not equal to zero. Berkeley, concerned over the deterministic and atheistic implications of philosophical mechanism, set out to reveal contradictions in the calculus in his influential book *The Analyst; or, A Discourse Addressed to an Infidel Mathematician.* There he scathingly wrote about these fluxions and infinitesimals, "They are neither finite quantities, nor quantities infinitely small, nor yet nothing. May we not call them the ghosts of departed quantities?"

and further asked, "Whether mathematicians, who are so delicate in religious points, are strictly scrupulous in their own science? Whether they do not submit to authority, take things upon trust, and believe points inconceivable?"

Berkeley's criticism was not fully met until the 19th century, when it was realized that, in the expression dy/dx, dx and dy need not lead an independent existence. Rather, this expression could be defined as the limit of ordinary ratios $\Delta y/\Delta x$, as Δx approaches zero without ever being zero. Moreover, the notion of limit was then explained quite rigorously, in answer to such thinkers as Zeno and Berkeley.

It was not until the middle of the 20th century that the logician Abraham Robinson (1918–74) showed that the notion of infinitesimal was in fact logically consistent and that, therefore, infinitesimals could be introduced as new kinds of numbers. This led to a novel way of presenting the calculus, called nonstandard analysis, which has, however, not become as widespread and influential as it might have.

Robinson's argument was this: if the assumptions behind the existence of an infinitesimal ξ led to a contradiction, then this contradiction must already be obtainable from a finite set of these assumptions, say from:

$$0 < \xi, \xi < 1, \xi < \frac{1}{2}, \cdots, \xi < \frac{1}{n}.$$

But this finite set is consistent, as is seen by taking $\xi = 1/(n + 1)$.

NON-EUCLIDEAN GEOMETRIES

When Euclid presented his axiomatic treatment of geometry, one of his assumptions, his fifth postulate, appeared to be less obvious or fundamental than the others. As it is now conventionally formulated, it asserts that there is exactly one parallel to a given line through a given point. Attempts to derive this from Euclid's other axioms did not succeed, and, at the beginning of the 19th century, it was realized that Euclid's fifth postulate is, in fact, independent of the others. It was then seen that Euclid had described not the one true geometry but only one of a number of possible geometries.

ELLIPTIC AND HYPERBOLIC GEOMETRIES

Within the framework of Euclid's other four postulates (and a few that he omitted), there were also possible elliptic and hyperbolic geometries. In plane elliptic geometry there are no parallels to a given line through a given point. It may be viewed as the geometry of a spherical surface on which antipodal points have been identified and all lines are great circles. This was not viewed as revolutionary. More exciting was plane hyperbolic geometry, developed

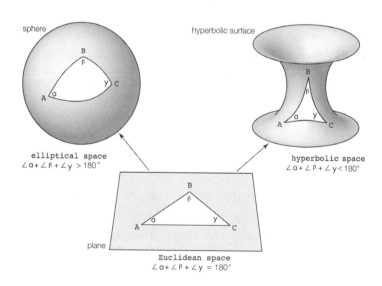

Contrasting triangles in Euclidean, elliptic, and hyperbolic spaces. Encyclopædia Britannica, Inc.

independently by the Hungarian mathematician János Bolyai (1802–60) and the Russian mathematician Nikolay Lobachevsky (1792–1856), in which there is more than one parallel to a given line through a given point. This geometry is more difficult to visualize, but a helpful model presents the hyperbolic plane as the interior of a circle, in which straight lines take the form of arcs of circles perpendicular to the circumference.

Another way to distinguish the three geometries is to look at the sum of the angles of a triangle. It is 180° in Euclidean geometry, as first reputedly discovered by Thales of Miletus (fl. 6th century BCE), whereas it is more than 180° in elliptic and less than 180° in hyperbolic geometry.

RIEMANNIAN GEOMETRY

The discovery that there is more than one geometry was of foundational significance and contradicted the German philosopher Immanuel Kant (1724–1804). Kant had argued that there is only one true geometry, Euclidean, which is known to be true a priori by an inner faculty (or intuition) of the mind. For Kant, and practically all other philosophers and mathematicians of his time, this belief in the unassailable truth of Euclidean geometry formed the foundation and justification for further explorations into the nature of reality. With the discovery of consistent non-Euclidean geometries, there was a subsequent loss of certainty and trust in this innate intuition, and this was fundamental in separating mathematics from a rigid adherence to an external sensory order (no longer vouchsafed as "true") and led to the growing abstraction of mathematics as a self-contained universe. This divorce from geometric intuition added impetus to later efforts to rebuild assurance of truth on the basis of logic.

What then is the correct geometry for describing the space (actually space-time) we live in? It turns out to be none of the above, but a more general kind of geometry, as was first discovered by the German mathematician Bernhard Riemann (1826–66). In the early 20th century, Albert Einstein showed, in the context of his general theory of relativity, that the true geometry of space is only approximately Euclidean. It is a form of Riemannian geometry in which space and time are linked in a four-dimensional manifold, and it is the curvature at each point that is responsible for the gravitational "force" at that point. Einstein spent the last part of his life trying to extend this idea to the electromagnetic force, hoping to reduce all physics to geometry, but a successful unified field theory eluded him.

CANTOR

In the 19th century, the German mathematician Georg Cantor (1845–1918) returned once more to the notion of infinity and showed that, surprisingly, there is not just one kind of infinity but many kinds. In particular, while the set N of natural numbers and the set of all subsets of N are both infinite, the latter collection is more numerous, in a way that Cantor made precise, than the former. He proved that N, Z, and $\mathcal{Q}$ all have the same size, since it is possible to put them into one-to-one correspondence with one another, but that R is bigger, having the same size as the set of all subsets of N.

However, Cantor was unable to prove the so-called continuum hypothesis, which asserts that there is no set that is larger than N yet smaller than the set of its subsets. It was shown only in the 20th century, by Gödel and the American logician Paul Cohen (1934–2007), that the continuum hypothesis can be neither proved nor disproved from the usual axioms of set theory. Cantor had his detractors, most notably the German mathematician Leopold Kronecker (1823–91), who felt that Cantor's theory was too metaphysical and that his methods were not sufficiently constructive.

THE QUEST FOR RIGOUR

The discovery in the 19th century of consistent alternative geometries, however, precipitated a crisis. It showed that Euclidean geometry, based on seemingly the most intuitively obvious axiomatic assumptions, did not correspond with reality as mathematicians had believed. This, together with the bold discoveries of the German mathematician Georg Cantor in set theory, made it clear that, to avoid further confusion and satisfactorily answer paradoxical results, a new and more rigorous foundation for mathematics was necessary.

FORMAL FOUNDATIONS

SET THEORETIC BEGINNINGS

While laying rigorous foundations for mathematics, 19th-century mathematicians discovered that the language of mathematics could be reduced to that of set theory (developed by Cantor), dealing with membership ($\in$) and equality ($=$), together with some rudimentary arithmetic, containing at least symbols for zero (o) and successor (S). Underlying all this were the basic logical concepts: conjunction ($\wedge$), disjunction ($\vee$), implication ($\supset$), negation ($\neg$), and the universal ($\forall$) and existential ($\exists$) quantifiers (formalized by the German mathematician Gottlob Frege [1848–1925]). (The modern notation owes more to the influence of the English logician Bertrand Russell [1872–1970] and the Italian mathematician Giuseppe Peano [1858–1932] than to that of Frege.)

For some time, logicians were obsessed with a principle of parsimony, called Ockham's razor, which justified them in reducing the number of these fundamental concepts, for example, by defining $p \supset q$ (read p implies q) as $\neg p \vee q$ or even as $\neg(p \wedge \neg q)$. While this definition, even if unnecessarily cumbersome, is legitimate classically, it is not permitted in intuitionistic logic. In the same spirit, many mathematicians adopted the Wiener-Kuratowski definition of the ordered pair $< a, b>$ as $\{\{a\}, \{a, b\}\}$, where $\{a\}$ is the set whose sole element is a, which disguises its true significance.

Logic had been studied by the ancients, in particular by Aristotle and the Stoic philosophers. Philo of Megara (fl. c. 250 BCE) had observed (or postulated) that $p \supset q$ is false if and only if p is true and q is false. Yet the intimate connection between logic and mathematics had to await the insight of 19th-century thinkers, in particular Frege.

Frege was able to explain most mathematical notions with the help of his comprehension scheme, which asserts that, for every ϕ (formula or statement), there should exist a set X such that, for all x, $x \in X$ if and only if $\phi(x)$ is true. Moreover, by the axiom of extensionality, this set X is uniquely determined by $\phi(x)$. A flaw in Frege's system was uncovered by Russell, who pointed out some obvious contradictions involving sets that contain themselves as elements—e.g., by taking $\phi(x)$ to be $\neg(x \in x)$. Russell illustrated this by what has come to be known as the barber paradox: A barber states that he shaves all who do not shave themselves. Who shaves the barber? Any answer contradicts the barber's statement. To avoid these contradictions Russell introduced the concept of types, a hierarchy (not necessarily linear) of elements and sets such that definitions always proceed from more basic elements (sets) to more inclusive sets, hoping that self-referencing and circular definitions would then be excluded. With this type distinction, $x \in X$ only if X is of an appropriate higher type than x.

The type theory proposed by Russell, later developed in collaboration with the English mathematician Alfred North Whitehead (1861–1947) in their monumental *Principia Mathematica* (1910–13), turned out to be too cumbersome to appeal to mathematicians and logicians, who managed to avoid Russell's paradox in other ways. Mathematicians made use of the Neumann-Gödel-Bernays set theory, which distinguishes between small sets and large classes, while logicians preferred an essentially equivalent first-order language, the Zermelo-Fraenkel axioms, which allow one to construct new sets only as subsets of given old sets. Mention should also be made of the system of the American philosopher Willard Van Orman Quine (1908–2000), which admits a universal set. (Cantor had not allowed such a "biggest" set, as the set of all its subsets would have to be still bigger.) Although type theory was greatly simplified by Alonzo Church and the American mathematician Leon Henkin (1921–2006), it came into its own only with the advent of category theory.

FOUNDATIONAL LOGIC

The prominence of logic in foundations led some people, referred to as logicists, to suggest that mathematics is a branch of logic. The concepts of membership and equality could reasonably be incorporated into logic, but what about the natural numbers? Kronecker had suggested that, while everything else was made by man, the natural numbers were given by God. The logicists, however, believed that the natural numbers were also man-made, inasmuch as definitions may be said to be of human origin.

Russell proposed that the number 2 be defined as the set of all two-element sets, that is, $X \in 2$ if and only if X has distinct elements x and y and every element of X is either

x or y. The Hungarian-born American mathematician John von Neumann (1903–57) suggested an even simpler definition, namely that $X \in 2$ if and only if $X = 0$ or $X = 1$, where 0 is the empty set and 1 is the set consisting of 0 alone. Both definitions require an extralogical axiom to make them work—the axiom of infinity, which postulates the existence of an infinite set. Since the simplest infinite set is the set of natural numbers, one cannot really say that arithmetic has been reduced to logic. Most mathematicians follow Peano, who preferred to introduce the natural numbers directly by postulating the crucial properties of 0 and the successor operation S, among which one finds the principle of mathematical induction.

The logicist program might conceivably be saved by a 20th-century construction usually ascribed to Church, though he had been anticipated by the Austrian philosopher Ludwig Wittgenstein (1889–1951). According to Church, the number 2 is the process of iteration; that is, 2 is the function which to every function f assigns its iterate $2(f) = f \bigcirc f$, where $(f \bigcirc f)(x) = f(f(x))$. There are some type-theoretical difficulties with this construction, but these can be overcome if quantification over types is allowed. This is finding favour in theoretical computer science.

IMPREDICATIVE CONSTRUCTIONS

A number of 19th-century mathematicians found fault with the program of reducing mathematics to arithmetic and set theory as suggested by the work of Cantor and Frege. In particular, the French mathematician Henri Poincaré (1854–1912) objected to impredicative constructions, which construct an entity of a certain type in terms of entities of the same or higher type—i.e., self-referencing constructions and definitions. For example, when proving that every bounded nonempty set X of real numbers has a least upper bound a, one proceeds as follows. (For this purpose, it will be convenient to think of a real number, following Dedekind, as a set of rationals that contains all the rationals less than any element of the set.) One lets $x \in a$ if and only if $x \in y$ for some $y \in X$; but here y is of the same type as a.

It would seem that to do ordinary analysis one requires impredicative constructions. Russell and Whitehead tried unsuccessfully to base mathematics on a predicative type theory. But, though reluctant, they had to introduce an additional axiom, the axiom of reducibility, which rendered their enterprise impredicative after all. More recently, the Swedish logician Per Martin-Löf presented a new predicative type theory, but no one claims that this is adequate for all of classical analysis. However, the German-American mathematician Hermann Weyl (1885–1955) and the American mathematician Solomon Feferman have shown that impredicative arguments such as the above can often be circumvented and are not needed for most, if not all, of analysis. On the other hand, as was pointed out by the Italian computer scientist Giuseppe Longo (b. 1929), impredicative constructions are extremely useful in computer science—namely, for producing fixpoints (entities that remain unchanged under a given process).

NONCONSTRUCTIVE ARGUMENTS

Another criticism of the Cantor-Frege program was raised by Kronecker, who objected to nonconstructive arguments, such as the following proof that there exist irrational numbers a and b such that a^b is rational. If $\sqrt{2}^{\sqrt{2}}$ is rational, then the proof is complete; otherwise take $\sqrt{2}^{\sqrt{2}}$ and b = $\sqrt{2}$, so that $a^b = 2$. The argument is nonconstructive, because it does not tell us which alternative holds, even though more powerful mathematics will, as was shown by the Russian mathematician Aleksandr Osipovich Gelfond (1906–68). In the present case, the result can be proved constructively by taking $a = \sqrt{2}$ and $b = 2\log_2 3$. But there are other classical theorems for which no constructive proof exists.

Consider, for example, the statement $\exists_x(\exists_y \phi(y) \supset \phi(x))$, which symbolizes the statement that there exists a person who is famous if there are any famous people. This can be proved with the help of De Morgan's laws, named after the English mathematician and logician Augustus De Morgan (1806–71). It asserts the equivalence of $\exists_y \phi(y)$ with $\neg\forall_y \neg\phi(y)$, using classical logic, but there is no way one can construct such an x, for example, when $\phi(x)$ asserts the existence of a well-ordering of the reals, as was proved by Feferman. An ordered set is said to be well-ordered if every nonempty subset has a least element. It had been shown by the German mathematician Ernst Zermelo (1871–1951) that every set can be well-ordered, provided one adopts another axiom, the axiom of choice, which says that, for every nonempty family of nonempty sets, there is a set obtainable by picking out exactly one element from each of these sets. This axiom is a fertile source of nonconstructive arguments.

INTUITIONISTIC LOGIC

The Dutch mathematician L.E.J. Brouwer (1881–1966) in the early 20th century had the fundamental insight that such nonconstructive arguments will be avoided if one abandons a principle of classical logic which lies behind De Morgan's laws. This is the principle of the excluded third (or excluded middle), which asserts that, for every proposition p, either p or not p; and equivalently that, for every p, not not p implies p. This principle is basic to classical logic and had already been enunciated by Aristotle, though with some reservations, as he pointed out that the statement "there will be a sea battle tomorrow" is neither true nor false.

Brouwer did not claim that the principle of the excluded third always fails, only that it may fail in the presence of infinite sets. Of two natural numbers x and y one can always decide whether $x = y$ or $x \neq y$, but of two real numbers this may not be possible, as one might have to know an infinite number of digits of their decimal expansions. Similar objections apply to De Morgan's laws, a consequence of the principle of the excluded third. For a finite set A, if it has been shown that the assertion $\forall_{x \in A} \neg \phi(x)$ leads to a contradiction, $\exists_{x \in A} \phi(x)$ can be verified by looking at each element of A in turn; i.e., the statement that no members of a given set have a certain property can be disproved by examining in turn each element of the set. For an infinite set A, there is no way in which such an inspection can be carried out.

Brouwer's philosophy of mathematics is called intuitionism. Although Brouwer himself felt that mathematics was language-independent, his disciple Arend Heyting (1898–1980) set up a formal language for first-order intuitionistic arithmetic. Some of Brouwer's later followers even studied intuitionistic type theory, which differs from classical type theory only by the absence of a single axiom (double negation): $\forall_{x \in \Omega} (\neg\neg x \supset x)$, where Ω is the type of truth-values.

While it cannot be said that many practicing mathematicians have followed Brouwer in rejecting this principle on philosophical grounds, it came as a great surprise to people working in category theory that certain important categories called topoi (singular: topos) have associated with them a language that is intuitionistic in general. In consequence of this fact, a theorem about sets proved constructively was immediately seen to be valid not only for sets but also for sheaves, which, however, lie beyond the scope of this book.

The moderate form of intuitionism considered here embraces Kronecker's constructivism but not the more extreme position of finitism. According to this view, which goes back to Aristotle, infinite sets do not exist, except potentially. In fact, it is precisely in the presence of infinite sets that intuitionists drop the classical principle of the excluded third.

An even more extreme position, called ultrafinitism, maintains that even very large numbers do not exist, say numbers greater than $10^{(10^{10})}$. Of course, the vast majority of mathematicians reject this view by referring to $10^{(10^{10})} + 1$, but the true believers have subtle ways of getting around this objection, which, however, lie beyond the scope of this discussion.

OTHER LOGICS

While intuitionistic logic is obtained from classical logic by dropping the principle of the excluded third, other logics have also been proposed, though none has had a comparable impact on the foundations of mathematics. One may mention many-valued, or multivalued, logics, which admit a finite number of truth-values; fuzzy logic, with an imprecise membership relationship (though, paradoxically, a precise equality relation); and quantum logic, where conjunction may be only partially defined and implication may not be defined at all. Perhaps more important have been various so-called substructural logics in which the usual properties of the deduction symbol are weakened: relevance logic is studied by philosophers, linear logic by computer scientists, and a noncommutative version of the latter by linguists.

FORMALISM

Russell's discovery of a hidden contradiction in Frege's attempt to formalize set theory, with the help of his simple comprehension scheme, caused some mathematicians to wonder how one could make sure that no other contradictions existed. Hilbert's program, called formalism, was to concentrate on the formal language of mathematics and to study its syntax. In particular, the consistency of mathematics, which may be taken, for instance, to be the metamathematical assertion that the mathematical statement $0 = 1$ is not provable, ought to be a metatheorem—that is, provable within the syntax of mathematics. This formalization project made sense only if the syntax of mathematics was consistent, for otherwise every syntactical statement would be provable, including that which asserts the consistency of mathematics.

Unfortunately, a consequence of Gödel's incompleteness theorem is that the consistency of mathematics can be proved only in a language which is stronger than the language of mathematics itself. Yet, formalism is not dead—in fact, most pure mathematicians are tacit formalists—but the naive attempt to prove the consistency of mathematics in a weaker system had to be abandoned.

While no one, except an extremist intuitionist, will deny the importance of the language of mathematics, most mathematicians are also philosophical realists who believe that the words of this language denote entities in the real world. Following the Swiss mathematician Paul Bernays (1888–1977), this position is also called Platonism, since Plato believed that mathematical entities really exist.

GÖDEL

Implicit in Hilbert's program had been the hope that the syntactic notion of provability would capture the semantic notion of truth. Gödel came up with the surprising discovery that this was not the case for type theory and related languages adequate for arithmetic, as long as the following assumptions are insisted upon:

1. The set of theorems (provable statements) is effectively enumerable, by virtue of the notion of proof being decidable.

2. The set of true statements of mathematics is ω-complete in the following sense: given any formula $\phi(x)$, containing a free variable x of type N, the universal statement $\forall_{x \in N} \phi(x)$ will be true if $\phi(n)$ is true for each numeral n—that is, for $n = 0$, $n = S0$, $n = SS0$, and so on.
3. The language is consistent.

Actually, Gödel also made a somewhat stronger assumption, which, as the American mathematician J. Barkley Rosser later showed, could be replaced by assuming consistency. Gödel's ingenious argument was based on the observation that syntactical statements about the language of mathematics can be translated into statements of arithmetic, hence into the language of mathematics. It was partly inspired by an argument that supposedly goes back to the ancient Greeks and which went something like this: Epimenides says that all Cretans are liars; Epimenides is a Cretan; hence Epimenides is a liar. Under the assumptions 1 and 2, Gödel constructed a mathematical statement g that is true but not provable. If it is assumed that all theorems are true, it follows that neither g nor $\neg g$ is a theorem.

No mathematician doubts assumption 1. By looking at a purported proof of a theorem, suitably formalized, it is possible for a mathematician, or even a computer, to tell whether it is a proof. By listing all proofs in, say, alphabetic order, an effective enumeration of all theorems is obtained. Classical mathematicians also accept assumption 2 and therefore reluctantly agree with Gödel that, contrary to Hilbert's expectation, there are true mathematical statements which are not provable.

However, moderate intuitionists could draw a different conclusion, because they are not committed to assumption 2. To them, the truth of the universal statement $\forall_{x \in N} \phi(x)$ can be known only if the truth of $\phi(n)$ is

Kurt Gödel. Alfred Eisenstaedt/Time & Life Pictures/Getty Images

known, for each natural number n, in a uniform way. This would not be the case, for example, if the proof of $\phi(n)$ increases in difficulty, hence in length, with n. Moderate intuitionists might therefore identify truth with provability and not be bothered by the fact that neither g nor $\neg g$ is true, as they would not believe in the principle of the excluded third in the first place.

Intuitionists have always believed that, for a statement to be true, its truth must be knowable. Moreover, moderate intuitionists might concede to formalists that to say that a statement is known to be true is to say that it has been proved. Still, some intuitionists do not accept the above argument. Claiming that mathematics is language-independent, intuitionists would state that in Gödel's metamathematical proof of his incompleteness theorem, citing ω-completeness to establish the truth of a universal statement yields a uniform proof of the latter after all.

Gödel considered himself to be a Platonist, inasmuch as he believed in a notion of absolute truth. He took it for granted, as do many mathematicians, that the set of true statements is ω-complete. Other logicians are more skeptical and want to replace the notion of truth by that of truth in a model. In fact, Gödel himself, in his completeness theorem, had shown that for a mathematical statement to be provable it is necessary and sufficient that it be true in every model. His incompleteness theorem now showed that truth in every ω-complete model is not sufficient for provability. This point will be returned to later, as the notion of model for type theory is most easily formulated with the help of category theory, although this is not the way Gödel himself proceeded.

RECURSIVE DEFINITIONS

Peano had observed that addition of natural numbers can be defined recursively thus: $x + 0 = x, x + Sy = S(x + y)$. Other numerical functions $N^k \to N$ that can be defined with the help of such a recursion scheme (and with the help of o, S, and substitution) are called primitive recursive. Gödel used this concept to make precise what he meant by "effectively enumerable." A set of natural numbers is said to be recursively enumerable if it consists of all $f(n)$ with $n \in N$, where $f : N \to N$ is a primitive recursive function.

This notion can easily be extended to subsets of N^k and, by a simple trick called arithmetization, to sets of strings of words in a language. Thus Gödel was able to assert that the set of theorems of mathematics is recursively enumerable, and, more recently, the American linguist Noam Chomsky (b. 1928) could say that the set of grammatical sentences of a natural language, such as English, is recursively enumerable.

It is not difficult to show that all primitive recursive functions can be calculated. For example, to calculate $x + y$ when $x = 3$ and $y = 2$, making use of Peano's recursive definition of $x + y$ and of the definitions $1 = S\text{o}$, $2 = S1$, and so on, one proceeds as follows:

$$3 + 2 = S2 + S1 = S(S2 + 1) = S(S2 + S\text{o})$$
$$= SS(S2 + \text{o}) = SSS2 = SS3 = S4 = 5.$$

But primitive recursive functions are not the only numerical functions that can be calculated. More general are the recursive functions, where $f : N \to N$ is said to be recursive if its graph is recursively enumerable—that is, if there exist primitive recursive functions $u, v : N \to N$ such that, for all natural numbers x and y, $y = f(x)$ if and only if, for some $z \in N$, $x = u(z)$ and $y = v(z)$.

All recursive functions can be calculated with pencil and paper or, even more primitively, by moving pebbles (*calculi* in Latin) from one location to another, using some finite set of instructions, nowadays called a program. Conversely, only recursive functions can be so calculated, or computed by a theoretical machine introduced by the English mathematician Alan Turing (1912–54), or by a modern computer, for that matter. The Church-Turing thesis asserts that the informal notion of calculability is completely captured by the formal notion of recursive functions and hence, in theory, replicable by a machine.

Gödel's incompleteness theorem had proved that any useful formal mathematical system will contain undecidable propositions—propositions which can be neither proved nor disproved. Church and Turing, while seeking an algorithmic (mechanical) test for deciding theoremhood and thus potentially deleting nontheorems, proved independently, in 1936, that such an algorithmic method was impossible for the first-order predicate logic. The Church-Turing theorem of undecidability, combined with the related result of the Polish-born American mathematician Alfred Tarski (1902–83) on undecidability of truth, eliminated the possibility of a purely mechanical device replacing mathematicians.

COMPUTERS AND PROOF

While many mathematicians use computers only as word processors and for the purpose of communication, computer-assisted computations can be useful for discovering potential theorems. For example, the prime number theorem was first suggested as the result of extensive hand calculations on the prime numbers up to 3,000,000 by the Swiss mathematician Leonhard Euler (1707–83), a process that would have been greatly facilitated by the availability of a modern computer. Computers may also be helpful in completing proofs when there are a large number of cases to be considered. The renowned computer-aided proof of the four-colour mapping theorem by the American mathematicians Kenneth Appel (b. 1932) and Wolfgang Haken (b. 1928) even goes beyond this, as the computer helped to determine which cases were to be considered in the next step of the proof. Yet, in principle, computers cannot be asked to discover proofs, except in very restricted areas of mathematics — such as elementary Euclidean geometry — where the set of theorems happens to be recursive, as was proved by Tarski.

As the result of earlier investigations by Turing, Church, the American mathematician Haskell Brooks Curry (1900–82), and others, computer science has itself become a branch of mathematics. Thus, in theoretical computer science, the objects of study are not just theorems but also their proofs, as well as calculations, programs, and algorithms. Theoretical computer science turns out to have a close connection to category theory.

CATEGORY THEORY

ABSTRACTION IN MATHEMATICS

One recent tendency in the development of mathematics has been the gradual process of abstraction. The Norwegian mathematician Niels Henrik Abel (1802–29) proved that equations of the fifth degree cannot, in general, be solved by radicals. The French mathematician Évariste Galois (1811–32), motivated in part by Abel's work, introduced certain groups of permutations to determine the necessary conditions for a polynomial equation to be solvable. These concrete groups soon gave rise to abstract groups, which were described axiomatically. Then it was realized that to study groups it was necessary to look at the relation between different groups — in particular, at the homomorphisms which map one group into another while preserving the group operations. Thus, people began to study what is now called the concrete category of groups, whose objects are groups and whose arrows are homomorphisms. It did not take long for concrete categories to be replaced by abstract categories, again described axiomatically.

The important notion of a category was introduced by Samuel Eilenberg and Saunders Mac Lane at the end of World War II. These modern categories must be distinguished from Aristotle's categories, which are better called types in the present context. A category has not only objects but also arrows (referred to also as morphisms, transformations, or mappings) between them.

Many categories have as objects sets endowed with some structure and arrows, which preserve this structure. Thus, there exist the categories of sets (with empty structure) and mappings, of groups and group-homomorphisms, of rings and ring-homomorphisms, of vector spaces and linear transformations, of topological spaces and continuous mappings, and so on. There even exists, at a still more abstract level, the category of (small) categories and functors, as the morphisms between categories are called, which preserve relationships among the objects and arrows.

Not all categories can be viewed in this concrete way. For example, the formulas of a deductive system may be seen as objects of a category whose arrows $f : A \to B$ are deductions of B from A. In fact, this point of view is important in theoretical computer science, where formulas are thought of as types and deductions as operations.

More formally, a category consists of (1) a collection of objects $A, B, C, \ldots$, (2) for each ordered pair of objects in the collection an associated collection of transformations including the identity $I_A : A \to A$, and (3) an associated law of composition for each ordered triple of objects in the category such that for $f : A \to B$ and $g : B \to C$ the composition gf (or $g \bigcirc f$) is a transformation from A to C—i.e., $gf : A \to C$. Additionally, the associative law and the identities are required to hold (where the compositions are defined)—i.e., $h(gf) = (hg)f$ and $1_B f = f = f 1_A$.

In a sense, the objects of an abstract category have no windows, like the monads of Leibniz. To infer the interior of an object A one need only look at all the arrows from other objects to A. For example, in the category of sets, elements of a set A may be represented by arrows from a typical one-element set into A. Similarly, in the category of small categories, if *bi1* is the category with one object and no nonidentity arrows, the objects of a category *biA* may be identified with the functors *bi1* $\to$ *biA*. Moreover, if *bi2* is the category with two objects and one nonidentity arrow, the arrows of *biA* may be identified with the functors *bi2* $\to$ *biA*.

ISOMORPHIC STRUCTURES

An arrow $f : A \to B$ is called an isomorphism if there is an arrow $g : B \to A$ inverse to f—that is, such that $g \bigcirc f = 1_A$ and $f \bigcirc g = 1_B$. This is written $A \cong B$, and A and B are called isomorphic, meaning that they have essentially the same structure and that there is no need to distinguish between them. Inasmuch as mathematical entities are objects of categories, they are given only up to isomorphism. Their traditional set-theoretical constructions, aside from serving a useful purpose in showing consistency, are really irrelevant.

For example, in the usual construction of the ring of integers, an integer is defined as an equivalence class of pairs (m,n) of natural numbers, where (m,n) is equivalent to (m',n') if and only if $m + n' = m' + n$. The idea is that the equivalence class of (m,n) is to be viewed as $m - n$. What is important to a categorist, however, is that the ring Z of integers is an initial object in the category of rings and homomorphisms — that is, that for every ring R there is a unique homomorphism $Z \to R$. Seen in this way, Z is given only up to isomorphism. In the same spirit, it should be said not that Z is contained in the field Q of rational numbers but only that the homomorphism $Z \to Q$ is one-to-one. Likewise, it makes no sense to speak of the set-theoretical intersection of π and $\sqrt{-1}$, if both are expressed as sets of sets of sets (ad infinitum).

Of special interest in foundations and elsewhere are adjoint functors (F,G). These are pairs of functors between two categories $\mathcal{A}$ and B, which go in opposite directions such that a one-to-one correspondence exists between the set of arrows $F(A) \to B$ in B and the set of arrows $A \to G(B)$ in $\mathcal{A}$ — that is, such that the sets are isomorphic.

TOPOS THEORY

The original purpose of category theory had been to make precise certain technical notions of algebra and topology and to present crucial results of divergent mathematical fields in an elegant and uniform way, but it soon became clear that categories had an important role to play in the foundations of mathematics. This observation was largely the contribution of the American mathematician F.W. Lawvere (b. 1937), who elaborated on the seminal work of the German-born French mathematician Alexandre Grothendieck (b. 1928) in algebraic geometry. At one time he considered using the category of (small) categories (and functors) itself for the foundations of mathematics. Though he did not abandon this idea, later he proposed a generalization of the category of sets (and mappings) instead.

Among the properties of the category of sets, Lawvere singled out certain crucial ones, only two of which are mentioned here:

- There is a one-to-one correspondence between subsets B of A and their characteristic functions $\chi : A \to \{true, false\}$, where, for each element a of A, $\chi(a) = true$ if and only if a is in B.
- Given an element a of A and a function $h : A \to A$, there is a unique function $f : N \to A$ such that $f(n) = h^n(a)$.

Suitably axiomatized, a category with these properties is called an (elementary) topos. However, in general, the two-element set $\{true, false\}$ must be replaced by an object Ω with more than two truth-values, though a distinguished arrow into Ω is still labeled as *true*.

INTUITIONISTIC TYPE THEORIES

Topoi are closely related to intuitionistic type theories. Such a theory is equipped with certain types, terms, and theorems.

Among the types there should be a type Ω for truth-values, a type N for natural numbers, and, for each type A, a type $\wp(A)$ for all sets of entities of type A.

Among the terms there should be in particular the following:

- The formulas $a = a'$ and $a \in \alpha$ of type Ω, if a and a' are of type A and α is of type $\wp(A)$.
- The numerals o and Sn of type N, if the numeral n is of type N.
- The comprehension term $\{x \in A | \phi(x)\}$ of type $\wp(A)$, if $\phi(x)$ is a formula of type Ω containing a free variable x of type A.

The set of theorems should contain certain obvious axioms and be closed under certain obvious rules of inference, neither of which will be spelled out here.

At this point the reader may wonder what happened to the usual logical symbols. These can all be defined—for example, universal quantification $\forall_{x \in A}\phi(x)$ as $\{x \in A | \phi(x)\} = \{x \in A | x = x\}$ and disjunction p $\vee$ q as $\forall_{t \in \Omega}((p \supset t) \supset ((q \supset t) \supset t))$.

In general, the set of theorems will not be recursively enumerable. However, this will be the case for pure intuitionistic type theory L_0, in which types, terms, and theorems are all defined inductively. In L_0 there are no types, terms, or theorems other than those that follow from the definition of type theory. L_0 is adequate for the constructive part of the usual elementary mathematics—arithmetic and analysis—but not for metamathematics, if this is to include a proof of Gödel's completeness theorem, and not for category theory, if this is to include the Yoneda embedding of a small category into a set-valued functor category.

INTERNAL LANGUAGE

It turns out that each topos $\mathscr{T}$ has an internal language $L(\mathscr{T})$, an intuitionistic type theory whose types are objects and whose terms are arrows of $\mathscr{T}$. Conversely, every type theory L generates a topos $T(L)$, by the device of turning (equivalence classes of) terms into objects, which may be thought of as denoting sets.

Nominalists may be pleased to note that every topos $\mathscr{T}$ is equivalent (in the sense of category theory) to the topos generated by a language—namely, the internal language of $\mathscr{T}$. On the other hand, Platonists may observe that every type theory L has a conservative extension to the internal language of a topos—namely, the topos generated by L, assuming that this topos exists in the real (ideal) world. Here, the phrase "conservative extension" means that L can be extended to $LT(L)$ without creating new theorems. The types of $LT(L)$ are names of sets in L and the terms of $LT(L)$ may be identified with names of sets in L for which it can be proved that they have exactly one element. This last observation provides a categorical version of Russell's theory of descriptions: if one can prove the unique existence of an x of type A in L such that $\phi(x)$, then this unique x has a name in $LT(L)$.

The interpretation of a type theory L in a topos $\mathcal{T}$ means an arrow $L \to L(\mathcal{T})$ in the category of type theories or, equivalently, an arrow $T(L) \to \mathcal{T}$ in the category of topoi. Indeed, T and L constitute a pair of adjoint functors.

GÖDEL AND CATEGORY THEORY

It is now possible to reexamine Gödel's theorems from a categorical point of view. In a sense, every interpretation of L in a topos $\mathcal{T}$ may be considered as a model of L, but this notion of model is too general—for example, when compared with the models of classical type theories studied by Henkin. Therefore, it is preferable to restrict $\mathcal{T}$ to being a special kind of topos called local. Given an arrow p into Ω in $\mathcal{T}$, then, p is true in $\mathcal{T}$ if p coincides with the arrow *true* in $\mathcal{T}$, or, equivalently, if p is a theorem in the internal language of $\mathcal{T}$. $\mathcal{T}$ is called a local topos provided that (1) $0 = 1$ is not true in $\mathcal{T}$, (2) $p \vee q$ is true in $\mathcal{T}$ only if p is true in $\mathcal{T}$ or q is true in $\mathcal{T}$, and (3) $\exists_{x \in A} \phi(x)$ is true in $\mathcal{T}$ only if $\phi(a)$ is true in $\mathcal{T}$ for some arrow $a : 1 \to A$ in $\mathcal{T}$. Here the statement $0 = 1$ in provision 1 can be replaced by any other contradiction— e.g., by $\forall_{t \in \Omega} t$, which says that every proposition is true.

A model of L is an interpretation of L in a local topos $\mathcal{T}$. Gödel's completeness theorem, generalized to intuitionistic type theory, may now be stated as follows: A closed formula of L is a theorem if and only if it is true in every model of L.

Gödel's incompleteness theorem, generalized like-wise, says that, in the usual language of arithmetic, it is not enough to look only at ω-complete models: Assuming that L is consistent and that the theorems of L are recursively enumerable, with the help of a decidable notion of proof, there is a closed formula g in L, which is true in every ω-complete model, yet g is not a theorem in L.

The Search for a Distinguished Model

A Platonist might still ask whether, among all the models of the language of mathematics, there is a distinguished model, which may be considered to be the world of mathematics. Take as the language L_o pure intuitionistic type theory. It turns out, somewhat surprisingly, that the topos generated by L_o is a local topos. Hence, the unique interpretation of L_o in the topos generated by it may serve as a distinguished model.

This so-called free topos has been constructed linguistically to satisfy any formalist, but it should also satisfy a moderate Platonist, one who is willing to abandon the principle of the excluded third, inasmuch as the free topos is the initial object in the category of all topoi. Hence, the free topos may be viewed, in the words of Leibniz, as the best of all possible worlds. More modestly speaking, the free topos is to an arbitrary topos like the ring of integers is to an arbitrary ring.

The language L_o should also satisfy any constructivist: if an existential statement $\exists_{x \in A} \phi(x)$ can be proved in L_o, then $\phi(a)$ can be proved for some term a of type A. Moreover, if $p \vee q$ can be proved, then either p can be proved or q can be proved.

The above argument would seem to make a strong case for the acceptance of pure intuitionistic type theory as the language of elementary mathematics—that is, of arithmetic and analysis—and hence for the acceptance of the free topos as the world of mathematics. Nonetheless, most practicing mathematicians prefer to stick to classical mathematics. In fact, classical arguments seem to be necessary for metamathematics—for example, in the usual proof of Gödel's completeness theorem—even for intuitionistic type theory.

In this connection, one celebrated consequence of Gödel's incompleteness theorem may be recalled, to wit: the consistency of L cannot be proved (via arithmetization) within L. This is not to say that it cannot be proved in a stronger metalanguage. Indeed, to exhibit a single model of L would constitute such a proof.

It is more difficult to make a case for the classical world of mathematics, although this is what most mathematicians believe in. This ought to be a distinguished model of pure classical type theory L_1. Unfortunately, Gödel's argument shows that the interpretation of L_1 in the topos generated by it is not a model in this sense.

BOOLEAN LOCAL TOPOI

A topos is said to be Boolean if its internal language is classical. It is named after the English mathematician George Boole (1815–64), who was the first to give an algebraic presentation of the classical calculus of propositions. A Boolean topos is local under the following circumstances. The disjunction property (2) holds in a Boolean topos if and only if, for every closed formula p, either p is true or $\neg p$ is true. Moreover, with the help of De Morgan's laws, the existence property (3) may then be rephrased thus: if $\phi(a)$ is true for all closed terms a of type A, then $\forall_{x \in A} \phi(x)$ is true. As it turns out, a Boolean local topos may be described more simply, without referring to the internal language, as a topos with the following property: if $f, g : A \to B$ are arrows such that $fa = ga$ for all $a : 1 \to A$, then $f = g$.

(Here 1 is the so-called terminal object, with the property that, for each object C, there is a unique arrow $C \to 1$.) For the Boolean topos to be ω-complete requires furthermore that all numerals—that is, closed terms of type N in its internal language—be standard—that is, have the form o, So, SSo, and so on.

Of course, Gödel's completeness theorem shows that there are plenty of Boolean local topoi to model pure classical type theory in, but the usual proof of their existence requires nonconstructive arguments. It would be interesting to exhibit at least one such model constructively.

As a first step toward constructing a distinguished ω-complete Boolean model of L_1 one might wish to define the notion of truth in L_1, as induced by this model. Tarski had shown how truth can be defined for classical first-order arithmetic, a language that admits, aside from formulas, only terms of type N. Tarski achieved this essentially by incorporating ω-completeness into the definition of truth. It is not obvious whether his method can be extended to classical higher-order arithmetic—that is, to classical type theory. In fact, Tarski himself showed that the notion of truth is not definable (in a technical sense) in such a system. If his notion of definability corresponds to what is here meant by constructibility, then it is possible to conclude that, indeed, no Boolean model can be constructed.

One may be tempted to consider as a candidate for the distinguished Boolean local topos the so-called von Neumann universe. This is defined as the union of a class of sets containing the empty set (the initial object in the category of sets) and closed under the power-set operation and under transfinite unions—thus, as a subcategory of the category of sets. But what is the category of sets if not the distinguished Boolean local topos being sought?

A better candidate may be Gödel's constructible universe, whose original purpose was to serve as a model of Zermelo-Fraenkel set theory in which the continuum hypothesis holds. It is formed like the von Neumann universe, except that the notion of subset, implicit in the power-set operation, is replaced by that of definable subset. Is it possible that this universe can be constructed syntactically, like the free topos, without reference to any previously given category of sets, or by a universal property?

In the internal language of a Boolean local topos, the logical connectives and quantifiers have their natural meanings. In particular, quantifiers admit a substitutional interpretation, a desirable property that has been discussed by philosophers (among them, Russell and the American logician Saul Kripke [b. 1940])—to wit: if an existential statement is true, then it can be witnessed by a term of appropriate type in the language; and a universal statement is true if it is witnessed by all terms of the appropriate type.

Note that, in the internal language of the free topos, and therefore in pure intuitionistic type theory, the substitutional interpretation is valid for existential quantifiers, by virtue of the free topos being local, but that it fails for universal quantifiers, in view of the absence of ω-completeness and the fact that in the free topos all numerals are standard. For a Boolean local topos, ω-completeness will also ensure that all numerals are standard, so that numerals mean exactly what they are intended to mean.

ONE DISTINGUISHED MODEL OR MANY MODELS

Some mathematicians do not believe that a distinguished world of mathematics should be sought at all, but rather that the multiplicity of such worlds should be looked at simultaneously. A major result in algebraic geometry, due to

Alexandre Grothendieck, was the observation that every commutative ring may be viewed as a continuously variable local ring, as Lawvere would put it. In the same spirit, an amplified version of Gödel's completeness theorem would say that every topos may be viewed as a continuously variable local topos, provided sufficiently many variables (Henkin constants) are adjoined to its internal language. Put in more technical language, this makes the possible worlds of mathematics stalks of a sheaf. However, the question still remains as to where this sheaf lives if not in a distinguished world of mathematics or—perhaps better to say—metamathematics.

These observations suggest that the foundations of mathematics have not achieved a definitive shape but are still evolving. They form the subject of a lively debate among a small group of interested mathematicians, logicians, and philosophers.

CHAPTER 5
THE PHILOSOPHY
OF MATHEMATICS

There is a branch of philosophy that is concerned with two major questions: one concerning the meanings of ordinary mathematical sentences and the other concerning the issue of whether abstract objects exist. The first is a straightforward question of interpretation: What is the best way to interpret standard mathematical sentences and theories? In other words, what is really meant by ordinary mathematical sentences such as "3 is prime," "2 + 2 = 4," and "There are infinitely many prime numbers." Thus, a central task of the philosophy of mathematics is to construct a semantic theory for the language of mathematics. Semantics is concerned with what certain expressions mean (or refer to) in ordinary discourse. So, for instance, the claim that in English the term *Mars* denotes the Mississippi River is a false semantic theory; and the claim that in English *Mars* denotes the fourth planet from the Sun is a true semantic theory. Thus, to say that philosophers of mathematics are interested in figuring out how to interpret mathematical sentences is just to say that they want to provide a semantic theory for the language of mathematics.

Philosophers are interested in this question for two main reasons: 1) it is not at all obvious what the right answer is, and 2) the various answers seem to have deep philosophical implications. More specifically, different interpretations of mathematics seem to produce different metaphysical views about the nature of reality. These points can be brought out by looking at the sentences of arithmetic, which seem to make straightforward claims about certain objects. Consider, for instance, the sentence

"4 is even." This seems to be a simple subject-predicate sentence of the form "*S* is *P*"—like, for instance, the sentence "The Moon is round." This latter sentence makes a straightforward claim about the Moon, and likewise, "4 is even" seems to make a straightforward claim about the number 4. This, however, is where philosophers get puzzled. For it is not clear what the number 4 is supposed to be. What kind of thing is a number? Some philosophers (antirealists) have responded here with disbelief—according to them, there are simply no such things as numbers. Others (realists) think that there are such things as numbers (as well as other mathematical objects). Among the realists, however, there are several different views of what kind of thing a number is. Some realists think that numbers are mental objects (something like ideas in people's heads). Other realists claim that numbers exist outside of people's heads, as features of the physical world. There is, however, a third view of the nature of numbers, known as Platonism or mathematical Platonism, that has been more popular in the history of philosophy. This is the view that numbers are abstract objects, where an abstract object is both nonphysical and nonmental. According to Platonists, abstract objects exist but not anywhere in the physical world or in people's minds. In fact, they do not exist in space and time at all.

In what follows, more will be said to clarify exactly what Platonists have in mind by an abstract object. However, it is important to note that many philosophers simply do not believe in abstract objects. They think that to believe in abstract objects—objects that are wholly nonspatiotemporal, nonphysical, and nonmental—is to believe in weird, occult entities. In fact, the question of whether abstract objects exist is one of the oldest and most controversial questions of philosophy. The view that there do exist such things goes back to Plato, and serious resistance to the view can be traced back at least to Aristotle. This ongoing controversy has survived for more than 2,000 years.

The second major question with which the philosophy of mathematics is concerned is this: "Do abstract objects exist?" This question is deeply related to the semantic question about how the sentences and theories of mathematics should be interpreted. For if Platonism is right that the best interpretation of mathematics is that sentences such as "4 is even" are about abstract objects (and it will become clear below that there are some very good reasons for endorsing this interpretation), and if (what seems pretty obvious) sentences such as "4 is even" are true, then it would seem natural to endorse the view that abstract objects exist.

MATHEMATICAL PLATONISM

TRADITIONAL PLATONISM

Mathematical Platonism, formally defined, is the view that (a) there exist abstract objects—objects that are wholly nonspatiotemporal, nonphysical, and nonmental—and (b) there are true mathematical sentences that provide true descriptions of such objects. The discussion of Platonism that follows will address both (a) and (b).

It is best to start with what is meant by an abstract object. Among contemporary Platonists, the most common view is that the really defining trait of an abstract object is nonspatiotemporality. That is, abstract objects are not located anywhere in the physical universe, and they are also entirely nonmental, yet they have always existed and they always will exist. This does not preclude having mental ideas of abstract objects; according to Platonists, one can—e.g., one might have a mental idea of the number 4. It does not follow from this, though, that the number 4 is just a mental idea. After all, people have ideas of the Moon in their heads too, but it does not follow from this that the Moon is just an idea, because the Moon and people's ideas of the Moon are distinct things. Thus, when Platonists say that the number 4 is an abstract object, they mean to say that it is a real and objective thing that, like the Moon, exists independently of people and their thinking but, unlike the Moon, is nonphysical.

Abstract objects are also, according to Platonists, unchanging and entirely noncausal. Because abstract objects are not extended in space and not made of physical matter, it follows that they cannot enter into cause-and-effect relationships with other objects.

Platonists also claim that mathematical theorems provide true descriptions of such objects. What does this claim amount to? Consider the positive integers (1, 2, 3,...). According to Platonists, the theory of arithmetic says what this sequence of abstract objects is like. Over the years, mathematicians have discovered all sorts of interesting facts about this sequence. For instance, Euclid proved more than 2,000 years ago that there are infinitely many prime numbers among the positive integers. Thus, according to Platonists, the sequence of positive integers is an object of study, just like the solar system is an object of study for astronomers.

Now, so far, only one kind of mathematical object has been discussed, namely, numbers. But there are many different kinds of mathematical objects—functions, sets, vectors, circles, and so on—and for Platonists these are all abstract objects. Moreover, Platonists also believe that there are such things as set-theoretic hierarchies and that set theory describes these structures. And so on for all the various branches of mathematics. In general, according to Platonists, mathematics is the study of the nature of various mathematical structures, which are abstract in nature.

Platonism has been around for over two millennia, and over the years it has been one of the most popular views among philosophers of mathematics. Yet, for most of the history of philosophy, mathematical Platonism was stagnant. In the late 19th century, Gottlob Frege of Germany, who founded modern mathematical logic, developed what is widely thought to be the most powerful argument in favour of Platonism. But he did not alter the formulation of the view. Likewise, in the 20th century Kurt Gödel of Austria and Willard Van Orman Quine of the United States introduced hypotheses in an attempt to explain how human beings could acquire knowledge of abstract objects—but again, neither of these thinkers altered the Platonist view itself. (Gödel's hypothesis was about the nature of human beings, and Quine's hypothesis was about the nature of empirical evidence.)

NONTRADITIONAL VERSIONS

During the 1980s and '90s, various Americans developed three nontraditional versions of mathematical Platonism: one by Penelope Maddy, a second by Mark Balaguer and Edward Zalta, and a third by Michael Resnik and Stewart Shapiro. All three versions were inspired by concerns over how humans could acquire knowledge of abstract objects.

According to Maddy, mathematics is about abstract objects, and abstract objects are, in some important sense, nonphysical and nonmental, though they are located in space and time. Maddy developed this idea most fully in connection with sets. For her, a set of physical objects is located right where the physical objects themselves are located. For instance, if there are three eggs in a refrigerator, then the set containing those eggs is also in the refrigerator. This might seem eminently sensible, and one might wonder why Maddy counts as a Platonist at all. That is, one might wonder why a set of eggs counts as a nonphysical object in Maddy's view. In order to appreciate why Maddy is a Platonist (in some nontraditional sense), it is necessary to know something about set theory—most notably, that for every physical object, or pile of physical objects, there are infinitely many sets. For instance, if there are three eggs in a refrigerator, then corresponding to these eggs there exists the set containing the eggs, the set containing that set, the set containing that set, and so on. Moreover, there is also a set containing two different sets—namely, the set containing the eggs and the set containing the set containing the eggs—and so on without end. Thus, combining the principles of set theory (which Maddy wants to preserve) with Maddy's thesis that sets are spatiotemporally located implies that if there are three eggs in a given refrigerator, then there are also infinitely many sets in the refrigerator. Of course there is only a finite amount of physical stuff in the refrigerator. More specifically, it contains a rather small aggregate of egg-stuff. Thus, for Maddy the various sets built up out of this egg-stuff are all distinct from the aggregate itself. In order to avoid contradicting the principles of set theory, Maddy has to say that the sets are distinct from the egg-aggregate, and so even though she wants to maintain that all these sets are located in the refrigerator, she has to say that they are nonphysical in some sense. (Again, the reason that Maddy altered the Platonist view by giving sets spatiotemporal existence is that she thought it was necessary in order to explain how anyone could acquire knowledge of abstract objects.)

According to Balaguer and Zalta, on the other hand, the only versions of Platonism that are tenable are those that maintain not just the existence of abstract objects but the existence of as many abstract objects as there can possibly be. If this is right, then any system of mathematical objects that can consistently be conceived of must actually exist. Balaguer called this view "full-blooded Platonism," and he argued that it is only by endorsing this view that Platonists can explain how humans could acquire knowledge of abstract objects.

Finally, the nontraditional version of Platonism developed by Resnik and Shapiro is known as structuralism. The essential ideas here are that the real objects of study in mathematics are structures, or patterns—things such as infinite series, geometric spaces, and set-theoretic hierarchies—and that individual mathematical objects (such as the number 4) are not really objects at all in the ordinary sense of the term. Rather, they are simply positions in structures, or patterns. This idea can be clarified by thinking first about nonmathematical patterns.

Consider a baseball defense, which can be thought of as a certain kind of pattern. There is a left fielder, a right fielder, a shortstop, a pitcher, and so on. These are all positions in the overall pattern, or structure, and they are all associated with certain regions on a baseball field. Now, when a specific team takes the field, real players occupy these positions. For instance, during the early 1900s, Honus Wagner usually occupied the shortstop position for the Pittsburgh Pirates. He was a specific object, with spatiotemporal location. However, one can also think about the shortstop position itself. It is not an object in the ordinary sense of the term; rather, it is a role that can be filled by different people. According to Resnik and Shapiro, similar things can be said about mathematical structures. They are something like patterns, made up of positions that can be filled by objects. The number 4, for instance, is just the fourth position in the positive integer pattern. Different objects can be put into this position, but the number itself is not an object at all; it is merely a position. Structuralists sometimes express this idea by saying that numbers have no internal properties or that their only properties are those they have because of the relations they bear to other numbers in the structure; e.g., 4 has the property of being between 3 and 5. This is analogous to saying that the shortstop position does not have internal properties in the way that actual shortstops do. For instance, it does not have a height or a weight or a nationality. The only properties that it has are structural, such as the property of being located in or near the infield between the third baseman and the second baseman.

MATHEMATICAL ANTI-PLATONISM

Many philosophers cannot bring themselves to believe in abstract objects. However, there are not many tenable alternatives to mathematical Platonism. One option is to maintain that there do exist such things as numbers and sets (and that mathematical theorems provide true descriptions of these things) while denying that these things are abstract objects. Views of this kind can be called realistic versions of anti-Platonism. Like Platonism, they are still versions of mathematical realism because they maintain that mathematical theorems provide true descriptions of some part of the world.

In contrast to realistic versions of anti-Platonism, there is also an antirealist view known as mathematical nominalism. This view rejects the belief in the existence of numbers, sets, and so on and also rejects the belief that mathematical theorems provide true descriptions of some part of the world. The two main alternatives to Platonism, then, are realistic anti-Platonism and nominalism.

REALISTIC ANTI-PLATONISM

There are two different versions of realistic anti-Platonism, namely, psychologism and physicalism. Psychologism is the view that mathematical theorems are about concrete mental objects of some sort. In this view, numbers and circles and so on do exist, but they do not exist independently of people. Instead, they are concrete mental objects—in particular, ideas in people's heads. As will become clearer below, psychologism has serious problems and is no longer endorsed by many philosophers. Nonetheless, it was popular during the late 19th and early 20th centuries, the most notable proponents being the German philosopher Edmund Husserl and the Dutch mathematicians L.E.J. Brouwer and Arend Heyting.

Physicalism, on the other hand, is the view that mathematics is about concrete physical objects of some sort. Advocates of this view agree with Platonists that there exist such things as numbers and sets, and, unlike adherents of psychologism, they also agree that these things exist independently of people and their thoughts. Physicalists differ from Platonists, however, in holding that mathematics is about ordinary physical objects. There are a few different versions of this view. For example, one might hold that geometric objects, such as circles, are regions of actual physical space. Similarly, sets might be claimed to be piles of actual physical objects—thus, a set of eggs would be nothing more than the aggregate of physical matter that makes up the eggs. Moving on to numbers, one strategy is to take them to be physical properties of some sort—for example, properties of piles of physical objects, so that, for instance, the number 3 might be a property of a pile of three eggs. It should be noted here that many people have endorsed a Platonistic view of properties. In particular, Plato thought that, in addition to all the red things he observed in the world, there exists an independent property of redness and that this property was an abstract object. Aristotle, on the other hand, thought that properties exist in the physical world. Thus, in his view, redness

Edmund Husserl. Imagno/Hulton Archvie/Getty Images

exists in particular objects, such as red houses and red apples, rather than as an abstract object outside of space and time. So in order to motivate a physicalistic view of mathematics by claiming that numbers are properties, one would also have to argue for an Aristotelian, or physicalistic, view of properties. One person who has developed a view of this sort since Aristotle is the Australian philosopher David Armstrong.

Another strategy for interpreting talk of numbers to be about the physical world is to interpret it as talk about actual piles of physical objects rather than properties of such piles. For instance, one might maintain that the sentence "2 + 3 = 5" is not really about specific entities (the numbers 2, 3, and 5). Rather, it says that whenever a pile of two objects is pushed together with a pile of three objects, the result is a pile of five objects. A view of this sort was developed by the English philosopher John Stuart Mill in the 19th century.

NOMINALISM

Nominalism is the view that mathematical objects such as numbers and sets and circles do not really exist. Nominalists do admit that there are such things as piles of three eggs and ideas of the number 3 in people's heads, but they do not think that any of these things is the number 3. Of course, when nominalists deny that the number 3 is a physical or mental object, they are in agreement with Platonists. They admit that if there were any such thing as the number 3, then it would be an abstract object. But, unlike mathematical Platonists, they do not believe in abstract objects, and so they do not believe in numbers. There are three different versions of mathematical nominalism: paraphrase nominalism, fictionalism, and what can be called neo-Meinongianism.

The paraphrase nominalist view can be elucidated by returning to the sentence "4 is even." Paraphrase nominalists agree with Platonists that if this sentence is interpreted at face value—i.e., as saying that the object 4 has the property of being even—then it makes a straightforward claim about an abstract object. However, paraphrase nominalists do not think that ordinary mathematical sentences such as "4 is even" should be interpreted at face value. They think that what these sentences really say is different from what they seem to say on the surface. More specifically, paraphrase nominalists think that these sentences do not make straightforward claims about objects. There are several different versions of paraphrase nominalism, of which the best known is "if-thenism," or deductivism. According to this view, the sentence "4 is even" can be paraphrased by the sentence "If there were such things as numbers, then 4 would be even." In this view, even if there are no such things as numbers, the sentence "4 is even" is still true. For, of course, even if there is no such thing as the number 4, it is still true that, if there were such a thing, it would be even. Deductivism has roots in the thought of David Hilbert, a brilliant German mathematician from the late 19th and early 20th centuries, but it was developed more fully by the American philosophers Hilary Putnam and Geoffrey Hellman. Other versions of paraphrase nominalism have been developed by the American philosophers Haskell Curry and Charles Chihara.

Mathematical fictionalists agree with paraphrase nominalists that there are no such things as abstract objects and, hence, no such things as numbers. They think that paraphrase nominalists are mistaken, however, in their claims about what mathematical sentences such as "4 is even" really mean. Fictionalists think that Platonists are right that these sentences should be read at face value. They think that "4 is even" should be taken as saying just what it seems to say—namely, that the number 4 has the property of being even. Moreover, fictionalists also agree with Platonists that if there really were such a thing as the number 4, then it would be an abstract object. But, again, fictionalists do not believe that there is such a thing as the number 4, and so they maintain that sentences like "4 is even" are not literally true. Fictionalists think that sentences such as "4 is even" are analogous in a certain way to sentences like "Santa Claus lives at the North Pole." They are not literally true descriptions of the world, but they are true in a certain well-known story. Thus, according to fictionalism, arithmetic is something like a story, and it involves a sort of fiction, or pretense, to the effect that there are such things as numbers. Given this pretense, the theory says what numbers are like, or what they would be like if they existed. Fictionalists then argue that it is not a bad thing that mathematical sentences are not literally true. Mathematics is not supposed to be literally true, say the fictionalists, and they have a long explanation of why mathematics is pragmatically useful and intellectually interesting despite the fact that it is not literally true. Fictionalism was first proposed by the American philosopher Hartry Field. It was then developed in a somewhat different way by Balaguer, the American philosopher Gideon Rosen, and the Canadian philosopher Stephen Yablo.

The last version of nominalism is neo-Meinongianism, which derives from Alexius Meinong, a late-19th century Austrian philosopher. Meinong endorsed a view that was supposed to be distinct from Platonism, but most philosophers now agree that it is in fact equivalent to Platonism. In particular, Meinong held that there are such things as abstract objects but that these things do not have full-blown existence. Philosophers have responded to Meinong's claims by making a pair of related points. First, since Meinong thought there are such things as numbers, and since he thought that these things are nonspatiotemporal, it follows that he was a Platonist. Second, Meinong simply used the word *exist* in a nonstandard way. According to ordinary English, anything that is exists, and so it is contradictory to say that numbers are but do not exist.

Advocates of neo-Meinongianism agree with Platonists and fictionalists that the sentence "4 is even" should be interpreted at face value, as making (or purporting to make) a straightforward claim about a certain object—namely, the number 4. Moreover, they also agree that if there were any such thing as the number 4, then it would be an abstract object. Finally, they agree with fictionalists that there are no such things as abstract objects. In spite of this, neo-Meinongians claim that "4 is even" is literally true, for they maintain that a sentence of the form "The object O has the property P" can be literally true, even if there is no such thing as the object O. Thus, neo-Meinongianism consists in the following (seemingly awkward) trio of claims: (1) mathematical sentences should be read at face value, as purporting to make claims about mathematical objects such as numbers; (2) there are no such things as mathematical objects; and yet (3) mathematical sentences are still literally true. Neo-Meinongianism, in the form described here, was first introduced by the New Zealand philosopher Richard Sylvan, but related views were held much earlier by the German philosophers Rudolf Carnap and Carl Gustav Hempel and the British philosopher Sir Alfred Ayer. Views along these lines have been endorsed by Graham Priest of England, Jody Azzouni of the United States, and Otavio Bueno of Brazil.

In sum, then, there are essentially five alternatives to Platonism. If one does not want to claim that mathematics is about nonphysical, nonmental, nonspatiotemporal objects, then one must claim (1) that mathematics is about concrete mental objects in people's heads (psychologism); or (2) that it is about concrete physical objects (physicalism); or (3) that, contrary to first appearances, mathematical sentences do not make claims about objects at all (paraphrase nominalism); or (4) that, while mathematics does purport to be about abstract objects, there are in fact no such things, and so mathematics is not literally true (fictionalism); or (5) that mathematical sentences purport to be about abstract objects, and there are no such things as abstract objects, and yet these sentences are still literally true (neo-Meinongianism).

LOGICISM, INTUITIONISM, AND FORMALISM

During the first half of the 20th century, the philosophy of mathematics was dominated by three views: logicism, intuitionism, and formalism. Given this, it might seem odd that none of these views has been mentioned yet. The reason is that (with the exception of certain varieties of formalism) these views are not views of the kind discussed above. The views discussed above concern what the sentences of mathematics are really saying and what they are really about. But logicism and intuitionism are not views of this kind at all, and insofar as certain versions of formalism are views of this kind, they are versions of the views described above. How then should logicism, intuitionism, and formalism be characterized? In order to understand these views, it is important to understand the intellectual climate in which they were developed. During the late 19th and early 20th centuries, mathematicians and philosophers of mathematics became preoccupied with the idea of securing a firm foundation of mathematics. That is, they wanted to show that mathematics, as ordinarily practiced, was reliable or trustworthy or certain. It was in connection with this project that logicism, intuitionism, and formalism were developed.

The desire to secure a foundation for mathematics was brought on in large part by the British philosopher Bertrand Russell's discovery in 1901 that naive set theory contained a contradiction. It had been naively thought that for every concept, there exists a set of things that fall under that concept. For instance, corresponding to the concept "egg" is the set of all the eggs in the world. Even concepts such as "mermaid" are associated with a set—namely, the empty set. Russell noticed, however, that there is no set corresponding to the concept "not a member of itself." For suppose that there were such a set—i.e., a set of all the sets that are not members of themselves. Call this set S. Is S a member of itself? If it is, then it is not (because all the sets in S are not members of themselves). If S is not a member of itself, then it is (because all the sets not in S are members of themselves). Either way, a contradiction follows. Thus, there is no such set as S.

Logicism is the view that mathematical truths are ultimately logical truths. This idea was introduced by Frege. He endorsed logicism in conjunction with Platonism, but logicism is consistent with various anti-Platonist views as well. Logicism was also endorsed at about the same time by Russell and his associate, British philosopher Alfred North Whitehead. Few people still endorse this view, although there is a neologicist school, the main proponents of which are the British philosophers Crispin Wright and Robert Hale.

Intuitionism is the view that certain kinds of mathematical proofs (namely, nonconstructive arguments) are unacceptable. More fundamentally, intuitionism is best seen as a theory about mathematical assertion and denial. Intuitionists embrace the nonstandard view that mathematical sentences of the form "The object O has the property P" really mean that there is a proof that the object O has the property P, and they also embrace the view that mathematical sentences of the form "not-P" mean that a contradiction can be proven from P. Because intuitionists accept both of these views, they reject the traditionally accepted claim that for any mathematical sentence P, either P or not-P is true; and because of this, they reject nonconstructive proofs. Intuitionism was introduced by L.E.J. Brouwer, and it was developed by Brouwer's student Arend Heyting and somewhat later by the British philosopher Michael Dummett. Brouwer and Heyting endorsed intuitionism in conjunction with psychologism, but Dummett did not, and the view is consistent with various nonpsychologistic views—e.g., Platonism and nominalism.

There are a few different versions of formalism. Perhaps the simplest and most straightforward is metamathematical formalism, which holds that ordinary mathematical sentences that seem to be about things such as numbers are really about mathematical sentences and theories. In this view, "4 is even" should not be literally taken to mean that the number 4 is even but that the sentence "4 is even" follows from arithmetic axioms. Formalism can be held simultaneously with Platonism or various versions of anti-Platonism, but it is usually conjoined with nominalism. Metamathematical formalism was developed by Haskell Curry, who endorsed it in conjunction with a sort of nominalism.

MATHEMATICAL PLATONISM: FOR AND AGAINST

Philosophers have come up with numerous arguments for and against Platonism, but one of the arguments for Platonism stands out above the rest, and one of the arguments against Platonism also stands out as the best. These arguments have roots in the writings of Plato, but the pro-Platonist argument was first clearly formulated by Frege, and the locus classicus of the anti-Platonist argument is a 1973 paper by the American philosopher Paul Benacerraf.

THE FREGEAN ARGUMENT FOR PLATONISM

Frege's argument for mathematical Platonism boils down to the assertion that it is the only tenable view of mathematics. (The version of the argument presented here includes numerous points that Frege himself never made. Nonetheless, the argument is still Fregean in spirit.)

From the Platonist point of view, the weakest anti-Platonist views are psychologism, physicalism, and paraphrase nominalism. These three views make controversial claims about how the language of mathematics should be interpreted, and Platonists rebut their claims by carefully examining what people actually mean when they make mathematical utterances. The following brings out some of the arguments against these three views.

Psychologism can be thought of as involving two central claims: (1) number-ideas exist inside people's heads and (2) ordinary mathematical sentences and theories are best interpreted as being about these ideas. Very few people would reject the first of these theses, but there are several well-known arguments against accepting the second view. Three are presented here. First is the argument that psychologism makes mathematical truth contingent upon psychological truth. Thus, if every human being died, the sentence "2 + 2 = 4" would suddenly become untrue. This seems blatantly wrong. The second argument is that psychologism seems incompatible with standard arithmetical theory, which insists that infinitely many numbers actually exist, because clearly there are only a finite number of ideas in human heads. This is not to say that humans cannot conceive of an infinite set. The point is, rather, that infinitely many actual objects (i.e., distinct number-ideas) cannot reside in human heads. Therefore, numbers cannot be ideas in human heads. Third, psychologism suggests that the proper methodology for mathematics is that of empirical psychology. If psychologism were true, then the proper way to discover whether, say, there is a prime number between 10,000,000 and 10,000,020 would be to do an empirical study of humans to ascertain whether such a number existed in someone's head. This, however, is obviously not the proper methodology for mathematics. The proper methodology involves mathematical proof, not empirical psychology.

Physicalism does not fare much better in the eyes of Platonists. The easiest way to bring out the arguments against physicalistic interpretations of mathematics is to focus on set theory. According to physicalism, sets are just piles of physical objects. But, as has been previously shown, sets cannot be piles of physical stuff—or at any rate, when mathematicians talk about sets, they are not talking about physical piles—because it follows from the principles of set theory that for every physical pile, there corresponds infinitely many sets. A second problem with physicalistic views is that they seem incapable of accounting for the sheer size of the infinities involved in set theory. Standard set theory holds not just that there are infinitely large sets but also that there are infinitely many sizes of infinity, that these sizes get larger and larger with no end, and that there actually exist sets of all of these different sizes of infinity. There is simply no plausible way to take this sort of mathematical theorizing about the infinite to be about the physical world. Finally, a third problem with physicalism in Platonists' eyes is that it also seems to imply that mathematics is an empirical science, contingent on physical facts and susceptible to empirical falsification. This seems to contradict mathematical methodology. Mathematics is not empirical (at least not usually), and most mathematical truths (e.g., "2 + 3 = 5") cannot be empirically falsified by discoveries about the nature of the physical world.

Platonists argue against the various versions of paraphrase nominalism by pointing out that they are also out of step with actual mathematical discourse. These views are all committed to implausible hypotheses about the intentions of mathematicians and ordinary folk. For instance, deductivism is committed to the thesis that when people utter sentences such as "4 is even," what they really mean to say is that, if there were numbers, then 4 would be even. However, there simply is no evidence for this thesis, and, what is more, it seems obviously false. Similar remarks can be made about the other versions of paraphrase nominalism. All of these views involve the same idea that mathematical statements are not used literally. There is no evidence, however, that people use mathematical sentences nonliterally. It seems that the best interpretation of mathematical discourse takes it to be about (or at any rate, to purport to be about) certain kinds of objects. Furthermore, as has already been shown, there are good reasons to think that the objects in question could not be physical or mental objects. Thus, the arguments outlined here seem to lead to the Platonistic conclusion that mathematical discourse is about abstract objects.

It does not follow from this that Platonism is true, however, because anti-Platonists can concede all these arguments and still endorse fictionalism or neo-Meinongianism. Advocates of the neo-Meinongian view accept the eminently plausible Platonistic interpretation of mathematical sentences while also denying that there are any such things as numbers and functions and sets. But then neo-Meinongians want to claim that mathematics is true anyway. Platonists argue that this reasoning is absurd.

For instance, if mermaids do not exist, then the sentence "There are some mermaids with red hair" cannot be literally true. Likewise, if there are no such things as numbers, then the sentence "There are some prime numbers larger than 20" cannot be literally true either. Perhaps the best thing to say here is that neo-Meinongianism warps the meaning of the word *true*.

The one remaining group of anti-Platonists, the fictionalists, agree with Platonists on how to interpret mathematical sentences. In fact, the only point on which fictionalists disagree with Platonists is the bare question of whether there exist any such things as abstract objects (and, as a result, the question about whether mathematical sentences are literally true). However, since abstract objects must be nonphysical and nonmental if they exist at all, it is not obvious how one could ever determine whether they exist. This is the beauty of the fictionalists' view: they endorse all of the Platonists' arguments that mathematics is best interpreted as being about abstract objects, and then they simply assert that they do not believe in abstract objects. It might seem very easy to dispense with fictionalism, because it might seem utterly obvious that sentences such as "2 + 2 = 4" are true. On closer inspection, however, this is not at all obvious. If the arguments discussed above are correct—and Platonists and fictionalists both accept them—then in order for "2 + 2 = 4" to be true, abstract objects must exist. But one might very well doubt that there really do exist such things. After all, they seem more than a bit strange, and what is more, there does not seem to be any evidence that they really exist.

Or maybe some evidence does exist. This, at any rate, is what Platonists want to claim. Platonists have offered a few different arguments as refutations of fictionalism, but only one of them, known as the indispensability argument, has gained any real currency. According to the indispensability argument, well-established mathematical theorems must be true because they are inextricably woven into the empirical theories that have been developed and accepted in the natural sciences, and there are good reasons to think that these empirical theories are true. (This argument has roots in the work of Frege and has been developed by Quine and Putnam.) Fictionalists have offered two responses to this argument. Field has argued that mathematics is not inextricably woven into the empirical theories that scientists have developed. If scientists wanted, he has argued, they could extract mathematics from their theories. Furthermore, Balaguer, Rosen, and Yablo have argued that it does not matter whether mathematics is indispensable to empirical science because even if it is, and even if mathematical theorems are not literally true (because there are no such things as abstract objects), the empirical theories that use these mathematical theorems could still provide essentially accurate pictures of the physical world.

THE EPISTEMOLOGICAL ARGUMENT AGAINST PLATONISM

The epistemological argument is very simple. It is based on the idea that, according to Platonism, mathematical knowledge is knowledge of abstract objects, but there does not seem to be any way for humans to acquire knowledge of abstract objects. The argument for the claim that humans could not acquire knowledge of abstract objects proceeds as follows:

1. Humans exist entirely within space-time.
2. If there exist any abstract objects, then they exist entirely outside of space-time.
3. Therefore, it seems that humans could never acquire knowledge of abstract objects.

There are three ways for Platonists to respond to this argument. They can reject (1), they can reject (2), or they can accept (1) and (2) and explain why the very plausible sounding (3) is nonetheless false.

Platonists who reject (1) maintain that the human mind is not entirely physical and that it is capable of somehow forging contact with abstract objects and thereby acquiring information about such objects. This strategy was pursued by Plato and Gödel. According to Plato, people have immaterial souls, and before birth their souls acquire knowledge of abstract objects, so that mathematical learning is really just a process of recollection. For Gödel, humans acquire information about abstract objects by means of a faculty of mathematical intuition—in much the same way that information about physical objects is acquired through sense perception.

Platonists who reject (2) alter the traditional Platonic view and maintain that, although abstract objects are nonphysical and nonmental, they are still located in space-time. Hence, according to this view, knowledge of abstract objects can be acquired through ordinary sense perceptions. Maddy developed this idea in connection with sets. She claimed that sets of physical objects are spatiotemporally located and that, because of this, people can perceive them—that is, see them and taste them and so on. For example, suppose that Maddy is looking at three eggs. According to her view, she can see not only the three eggs but also the set containing them. Thus, she knows that this set has three members simply by looking at it—analogous to the way that she knows that one of the eggs is white just by looking at it.

Platonists who accept both (1) and (2) deny that humans have some sort of information-gathering contact with abstract objects in the way proposed by Plato, Gödel, and

Maddy. But these Platonists still think that humans can acquire knowledge of abstract objects. One strategy that Platonists have used here is to argue that people acquire knowledge of abstract mathematical objects by acquiring evidence for the truth of their empirical scientific theories. The idea is that this evidence provides reason to believe all of empirical science, and science includes claims about mathematical objects. Another approach, developed by Resnik and Shapiro, is to claim that humans can acquire knowledge of mathematical structures by means of the faculty of pattern recognition. They claim that mathematical structures are nothing more than patterns, and humans clearly have the ability to recognize patterns.

Another strategy, that of full-blooded Platonism, is based on the claim that Platonists ought to endorse the thesis that all the mathematical objects that possibly could exist actually do exist. According to Balaguer, if full-blooded Platonism is true, then knowledge of abstract objects can be obtained without the aid of any information-transferring contact with such objects. In particular, knowledge of abstract objects could be obtained via the following two-step method (which corresponds to the actual methodology of mathematicians): first, stipulate which mathematical structures are to be theorized about by formulating some axioms that characterize the structures of interest; and second, deduce facts about these structures by proving theorems from the given axioms.

For example, if mathematicians want to study the sequence of nonnegative integers, they can begin with axioms that elaborate its structure. Thus, the axioms might say that there is a unique first number (namely, 0), that every number has a unique successor, that every nonzero number has a unique predecessor, and so on. Then, from these axioms, theorems can be proven—for instance, that there are infinitely many prime numbers. This is, in fact, how mathematicians actually proceed. The point here is that full-blooded Platonists can maintain that by proceeding in this way, mathematicians acquire knowledge of abstract objects without the aid of any information-transferring contact with such objects. Put differently, they maintain that what mathematicians have discovered is that, in the sequence of nonnegative integers (by which is just meant the part or parts of the mathematical realm that mathematicians have in mind when they select the standard axioms of arithmetic), there are infinitely many prime numbers. Without full-blooded Platonism this cannot be said, because traditional Platonists have no answer to the question "How do mathematicians know which axiom systems describe the mathematical realm?" In contrast, this view entails that all internally consistent axiom systems accurately describe parts of the mathematical realm. Therefore, full-blooded Platonists can say that when mathematicians lay down axiom systems, all they are doing is stipulating which parts of the mathematical realm they want to talk about. Then they can acquire knowledge of those parts simply by proving theorems from the given axioms.

Ongoing Impasse

Just as there is no widespread agreement that fictionalists can succeed in responding to the indispensability argument, there is no widespread agreement that Platonists can adequately respond to the epistemological argument. It seems to this writer, though, that both full-blooded Platonism and fictionalism can be successfully defended against all of the traditional arguments brought against them. Recall that Platonism and fictionalism agree on how mathematical sentences should be interpreted—that is, both views agree that mathematical sentences should be interpreted as being statements about abstract objects. On the other hand, Platonism and fictionalism disagree on the metaphysical question of whether abstract objects exist, and an examination of the foregoing debate does not provide any compelling reason to endorse or reject either view (though some reasons have proved plausible and attractive enough to persuade people to take sides on this question). In fact, humanity seems to be cut off in principle from ever knowing whether there are such things as abstract objects. Indeed, it seems to this writer that it is doubtful that a correct answer even exists. For it can be argued that the concept of an abstract object is so unclear that there is no objective, agreed-upon condition that would need to be satisfied in order for it to be true that there are abstract objects. This view of the debate is extremely controversial, however.

GLOSSARY

abacus An early calculating device, often constructed of a board or slab upon which letters could be traced in sand. Later abaci used counters that represented numerical values.

arithmetic Branch of mathematics in which numbers, relations among numbers, and observations on numbers are studied and used to solve problems. This includes measurement and computation including addition, subtraction, multiplication, division, raising to powers, and extraction of roots.

astrology A type of divination wherein events can supposedly be foreseen because of the positions of the Sun, Moon, and planets.

astronomy The study of all objects outside of Earth's atmosphere, including the evolution, physics, chemistry, and motion of celestial objects.

axiom A rule that is generally accepted.

calculus Branch of mathematics, developed by Isaac Newton and Gottfried Wilhelm Leibniz, concerned with the calculation of instantaneous rates of change and the summation of infinitely many small factors to determine some whole.

chord A line segment joining two points on a curve.

density Weight per unit volume of a liquid, solid, or gas.

ellipsoid A symmetrical object of which all plane cross sections are either ellipses or circles; with three mutually perpendicular axes that intersect at the centre.

geometry The branch of mathematics concerned with the shape and size of individual objects, position and distance among various objects, and the properties of surrounding space.

heliocentric Relating to the theory that Earth and the planets revolve around the Sun and that it is stationary and at the centre of the universe.

hieroglyphic A system of writing that uses characters in the form of pictures. These pictures are called hieroglyphs.

hyperbola A two-branched open curve produced by the intersection of a circular cone and a plane that cuts through both halves of the cone.

papyrus Material derived from the papyrus plant that can be pressed into a smooth surface that can be written upon.

parabola Open curve produced by the intersection of a circular cone and a plane parallel to an element of the cone.

paradox A statement that seems to contradict itself, but has an underlying meaning after some consideration, making it true.

postulate Another word for axiom, or a rule that is generally accepted.

proportion A relation between parts, wherein one part is a constant multiple of the other or they share a constant ratio.

Pythagorean theorem Theorem that states that the sum of the squares of the legs of a right triangle is equal to the square of the hypotenuse.

ratio A comparison between two or more things comparing quantity, amount, or size.

reciprocal A multiplicative inverse; for instance the reciprocal of 3 would be 1/3.

sage A wise person or scholar.

sexagesimal Relating to or based on the number sixty; sixty being the smallest number divisible by every number from 1 to 6.

theorem A statement or proposition that is proven by formulas and accepted as truth.

trigonometry The branch of mathematics concerned with the functions of angles and the relationships between the sides and angles of triangles.

velocity Quantity that defines how fast and in what direction an object is moving.

BIBLIOGRAPHY

GENERAL SOURCES

Two standard texts are Carl B. Boyer, *A History of Mathematics*, rev. by Uta C. Merzbach, 2nd ed. rev. (1989, reissued 1991); and, on a more elementary level, Howard Eves, *An Introduction to the History of Mathematics*, 6th ed. (1990). Discussions of the mathematics of various periods may be found in O. Neugebauer, *The Exact Sciences in Antiquity*, 2nd ed. (1957, reissued 1993); Morris Kline, *Mathematical Thought from Ancient to Modern Times*, 3 vol. (1972, reissued 1990); and B.L. van der Waerden, *Science Awakening*, trans. by Arnold Dresden, 4th ed. (1975, reissued 1988; originally published in Dutch, 1950). See also Kenneth O. May, *Bibliography and Research Manual of the History of Mathematics* (1973); and Joseph W. Dauben, *The History of Mathematics from Antiquity to the Present: A Selective Bibliography* (1985). A good source for biographies of mathematicians is Charles Coulston Gillispie (ed.), *Dictionary of Scientific Biography*, 16 vol. (1970–80, reissued 16 vol. in 8, 1981). Those wanting to study the writings of the mathematicians themselves will find the following sourcebooks useful: Henrietta O. Midonick (ed.), *The Treasury of Mathematics: A Collection of Source Material in Mathematics*, new ed. (1968); John Fauvel and Jeremy Gray (eds.), *The History of Mathematics: A Reader* (1987, reissued 1990); D.J. Struik (ed.), *A Source Book in Mathematics, 1200–1800* (1969, reprinted 1986); and David Eugene Smith, *A Source Book in Mathematics* (1929; reissued in 2 vol., 1959). A study of the development of numeric notation can be found in Georges Ifrah, *From One to Zero*, trans. by Lowell Bair (1985; originally published in French, 1981).

MATHEMATICS IN ANCIENT MESOPOTAMIA

O. Neugebauer and A. Sachs, *Mathematical Cuneiform Texts* (1945, reissued 1986), is the principal English edition of mathematical tablets. A brief look at Babylonian mathematics is contained in the first chapter of Asger Aaboe, *Episodes from the Early History of Mathematics* (1964, reissued 1998), pp. 5–31.

MATHEMATICS IN ANCIENT EGYPT

Editions of the basic texts are T. Eric Peet (ed. and trans.), *The Rhind Mathematical Papyrus: British Museum 10057 and 10058* (1923, reprinted 1970); and Arnold Buffam Chace and Henry Parker Manning (trans.), *The Rhind Mathematical Papyrus*, 2 vol. (1927–29, reprinted 2 vol. in 1, 1979). A brief but useful summary appears in G.J. Toomer, "Mathematics and Astronomy," chapter 2 in J.R. Harris (ed.), *The Legacy of Egypt*, 2nd ed. (1971), pp. 27–54. For an extended account of Egyptian mathematics, see Richard J. Gillings, *Mathematics in the Time of the Pharaohs* (1972, reprinted 1982).

GREEK MATHEMATICS

Critical editions of Greek mathematical texts include Dana Densmore (ed.), *Euclid's Elements*, trans. by Thomas L. Heath (2002; also published as *The Thirteen Books of Euclid's Elements*, 1926, reprinted 1956); Thomas L. Heath (ed. and trans.), *The Works of Archimedes* (1897, reissued 2002); E.J. Dijksterhuis, *Archimedes*, trans. by C. Dikshoorn (1956, reprinted 1987; originally published in

Dutch, 1938); Thomas L. Heath, *Apollonius of Perga: Treatise on Conic Sections* (1896, reissued 1961), and *Diophantus of Alexandria: A Study in the History of Greek Algebra*, 2nd ed. (1910, reprinted 1964); and Jacques Sesiano, *Books IV to VII of Diophantus' "Arithmetica" in the Arabic Translation Attributed to Qusta ibn Luq* (1982). General surveys are Thomas L. Heath, *A History of Greek Mathematics*, 2 vol. (1921, reprinted 1993); Jacob Klein, *Greek Mathematical Thought and the Origin of Algebra*, trans. by Eva Brann (1968, reissued 1992; originally published in German, 1934); and Wilbur Richard Knorr, *The Ancient Tradition of Geometric Problems* (1986, reissued 1993). Special topics are examined in O.A.W. Dilke, *Mathematics and Measurement* (1987); Árpád Szabó, *The Beginnings of Greek Mathematics*, trans. by A.M. Ungar (1978; originally published in German, 1969); and Wilbur Richard Knorr, *The Evolution of the Euclidean Elements: A Study of the Theory of Incommensurable Magnitudes and Its Significance for Early Greek Geometry* (1975).

MATHEMATICS IN THE ISLAMIC WORLD

Sources for Arabic mathematics include J.P. Hogendijk (ed. and trans.), *Ibn Al-Haytham's Completion of the Conics*, trans. from Arabic (1985); Martin Levey and Marvin Petruck (eds. and trans.), *Principles of Hindu Reckoning*, trans. from Arabic (1965), the only extant text of Kushyar ibn Labban's work; Martin Levey (ed. and trans.), *The Algebra of Abu Kamil*, trans. from Arabic and Hebrew (1966), with a 13th-century Hebrew commentary by Mordecai Finzi; Daoud S. Kasir (ed. and trans.), *The Algebra of Omar Khayyam*, trans. from Arabic (1931, reprinted 1972); Frederic Rosen (ed. and trans.), *The Algebra of Mohammed ben Musa*, trans. from Arabic (1831, reprinted 1986); and A.S. Saidan (ed. and trans.), *The Arithmetic of al-Uqlidisi*, trans. from Arabic (1978). Islamic mathematics is examined in J.L. Berggren, *Episodes in the*

Mathematics of Medieval Islam (1986); E.S. Kennedy, *Studies in the Islamic Exact Sciences* (1983); and Rushdi Rashid (Roshdi Rashed), *The Development of Arabic Mathematics: Between Arithmetic and Algebra*, trans. by A.F.W. Armstrong (1994; originally published in French, 1984).

EUROPEAN MATHEMATICS DURING THE MIDDLE AGES AND RENAISSANCE

An overview is provided by Michael S. Mahoney, "Mathematics," in David C. Lindberg (ed.), *Science in the Middle Ages* (1978), pp. 145–178. Other sources include Alexander Murray, *Reason and Society in the Middle Ages* (1978, reissued 1990), chapters 6–8; George Sarton, *Introduction to the History of Science* (1927–48, reissued 1975), part 2, "From Rabbi Ben Ezra to Roger Bacon," and part 3, "Science and Learning in the Fourteenth Century"; and, on a more advanced level, Edward Grant and John E. Murdoch (eds.), *Mathematics and Its Applications to Science and Natural Philosophy in the Middle Ages* (1987). For the Renaissance, see Paul Lawrence Rose, *The Italian Renaissance of Mathematics: Studies on Humanists and Mathematicians from Petrarch to Galileo* (1975).

MATHEMATICS IN THE 17TH AND 18TH CENTURIES

An overview of this period is contained in Derek Thomas Whiteside, "Patterns of Mathematical Thought in the Later Seventeenth Century," *Archive for History of Exact Sciences*, 1(3):179–388 (1961). Specific topics are examined in Margaret E. Baron, *The Origins of the Infinitesimal Calculus* (1969, reprinted 1987); Roberto Bonola, *Non-Euclidean Geometry: A Critical and Historical Study of Its Development*, trans. by H.S. Carslaw (1955; originally published in Italian, 1912); Carl B. Boyer, *The Concepts of the Calculus: A Critical and*

Historical Discussion of the Derivative and the Integral (1939; also published as *The History of the Calculus and Its Conceptual Development*, 1949, reprinted 1959); Herman H. Goldstine, *A History of Numerical Analysis from the 16th Through the 19th Century* (1977); Judith V. Grabiner, *The Origins of Cauchy's Rigorous Calculus* (1981); I. Grattan-Guinness, *The Development of the Foundations of Mathematical Analysis from Euler to Riemann* (1970); Roger Hahn, *The Anatomy of a Scientific Institution: The Paris Academy of Sciences, 1666–1803* (1971); and Luboš Nový, *Origins of Modern Algebra*, trans. from the Czech by Jaroslav Tauer (1973).

MATHEMATICS IN THE 19TH AND 20TH CENTURIES

Surveys include Herbert Mehrtens, Henk Bos, and Ivo Schneider (eds.), *Social History of Nineteenth Century Mathematics* (1981); William Aspray and Philip Kitcher (eds.), *History and Philosophy of Modern Mathematics* (1988); and Keith Devlin, *Mathematics: The New Golden Age*, new and rev. ed. (1999). Special topics are examined in Umberto Bottazzini, *The Higher Calculus: A History of Real and Complex Analysis from Euler to Weierstrass*, trans. by Warren Van Egmond (1986; originally published in Italian, 1981); Julian Lowell Coolidge, *A History of Geometrical Methods* (1940, reissued 2003); Joseph Warren Dauben, *Georg Cantor: His Mathematics and Philosophy of the Infinite* (1979, reprinted 1990); Harold M. Edwards, *Fermat's Last Theorem: A Genetic Introduction to Algebraic Number Theory* (1977, reissued 2000); I. Grattan-Guinness (ed.), *From the Calculus to Set Theory, 1630–1910: An Introductory History* (1980, reissued 2000); Jeremy Gray, *Ideas of Space: Euclidian, Non-Euclidean, and Relativistic*, 2nd ed. (1989); Thomas Hawkins, *Lebesgue's Theory of Integration: Its Origins and Development*, 3rd ed. (1979, reissued 2001); Jesper Lützen, *The Prehistory of the Theory of Distributions* (1982); and

Michael Monastyrsky, *Riemann, Topology, and Physics*, trans. from Russian by Roger Cooke, James King, and Victoria King, 2nd ed. (1987).

SOUTH ASIAN MATHEMATICS

The following 19th- and 20th-century classic translations of seminal Sanskrit mathematical texts are still widely relied on: Brahmegupta and Báhscara, *Algebra, with Arithmetic and Mensuration*, trans. by Henry Thomas Colebrooke (1817, reissued 1973); M. Rangacarya, *The Ganita-sara-sangraha of Mahaviracarya: With English Translation and Notes*, trans. by David Eugene Smith (1912); Walter Eugene Clark, *The Aryabhatiya of Aryabhata: An Ancient Indian Work on Mathematics and Astronomy*, trans. from Sanskrit (1930–83); and Bibhutibhusan Datta and Avadhesh Narayan Singh, *History of Hindu Mathematics: A Source Book*, 2 vol. (1935, reissued 2001).

S.N. Sen and A.K. Bag, *The Sulbasutras of Baudhayana, Apastamba, Katyayana, and Manava: With Text, English Translation, and Commentary* (1983), is a modern compilation of several *Sulbasutras* that contain geometry. Takao Hayashi, *The Bakhshali Manuscript: An Ancient Indian Mathematical Treatise* (1995), discusses in detail his translation of the surviving portions of the manuscript and other sources for ancient Indian arithmetic. T.A. Sarasvati Amma, *Geometry in Ancient and Medieval India* (1979, reissued 1999), includes some of the work of the Kerala school.

EAST ASIAN MATHEMATICS

Mathematics in China is discussed in Joseph Needham, *Mathematics and the Sciences of the Heavens and the Earth* (1959, reissued 1979), vol. 3 of *Science and Civilization in China*; Li Yan and Dù Shírán, *Chinese Mathematics: A*

Concise History, trans. by John N. Crossley and Anthony W.-C. Lun (1987; originally published in Chinese, 1963); Jean-Claude Martzloff, *A History of Chinese Mathematics*, trans. by Stephen S. Wilson (1997; originally published in French, 1988); Shen Kangsheng, John N. Crossley, and Anthony W.-C. Lun, *The Nine Chapters on the Mathematical Art: Companion and Commentary* (1999; originally published in Chinese, 1996); Ulrich Libbrecht, *Chinese Mathematics in the Thirteenth Century: The Shu-shu chiu-chang of Ch-in, Chiu-shao* (1973); and Lam Lay Yong, *A Critical Study of the Yang Hui suan fa: A Thirteenth-Century Chinese Mathematical Treatise* (1977).

Overviews of mathematics in Japan include David Eugene Smith and Yoshio Mikami, *A History of Japanese Mathematics* (1914, reissued 2002); and Yoshio Mikami, *The Development of Mathematics in China and Japan*, 2nd ed. (1974).

FOUNDATIONS OF MATHEMATICS

W.S. Anglin and J. Lambek, *The Heritage of Thales* (1995), a textbook aimed primarily at undergraduate mathematics students, deals with the history, philosophy, and foundations of mathematics and includes an elementary introduction to category theory. Collections of important readings and original articles include Paul Benacerraf and Hilary Putnam (eds.), *Philosophy of Mathematics: Selected Readings*, 2nd ed. (1983), treating the foundations of mathematics, the existence of mathematical objects, the notion of mathematical truth, and the concept of set; Jaako Hintikka (ed.), *The Philosophy of Mathematics* (1969), which includes articles by Henkin on completeness, by Feferman on predicativity, by Robinson on the calculus, and by Tarski on elementary geometry; and Jean Van Heijenoort (compiler), *From Frege to Gödel: A Source Book in Mathematical Logic, 1879–1931* (1967, reissued 1977). Bertrand Russell,

A History of Western Philosophy and Its Connection with Political and Social Circumstances from the Earliest Times to the Present Day, 2nd ed. (1961, reprinted 1991), an extremely readable work, portrays the relevant views of the pre-Socratics, Plato, Aristotle, Leibniz, and Kant. Mario Bunge, *Treatise on Basic Philosophy,* vol. 7, *Epistemology & Methodology III: Philosophy of Science and Technology,* part 1, *Formal and Physical Sciences* (1985), contains a discussion by a philosopher of the different philosophical schools in the foundations of mathematics. William Kneale and Martha Kneale, *The Development of Logic* (1962, reprinted 1984), offers a thorough scholarly account of the growth of logic from ancient times to the contributions by Frege, Russell, Brouwer, Hilbert, and Gödel. Saunders Mac Lane, *Mathematics, Form and Function* (1986), records the author's personal views on the form and function of mathematics as a background to the philosophy of mathematics, touching on many branches of mathematics. Michael Hallett, *Cantorian Set Theory and Limitation of Size* (1984), provides a scholarly account of Cantor's set theory and its further development by Fraenkel, Zermelo, and von Neumann. William S. Hatcher, *Foundations of Mathematics* (1968), surveys different systems, including those of Frege, of Russell, of von Neumann, Bernays, and Gödel, and of Quine as well as Lawvere's category of categories. Y.I. Manin (Iu.I. Manin), *A Course in Mathematical Logic,* trans. from Russian (1977), is addressed to mathematicians at a sophisticated level and presents the most significant discoveries up to 1977 concerning the continuum hypothesis, the nonexistence of algorithmic solutions, and other topics. George S. Boolos and Richard C. Jeffrey, *Computability and Logic,* 3rd ed. (1989), for graduate and advanced undergraduate philosophy or mathematics students, deals with computability, Gödel's theorems, and the definability of truth, among other topics. J. Lambek and P.J. Scott, *Introduction to Higher Order Categorical Logic* (1986), is an advanced textbook addressed to graduate students in mathematics and computer science in which the relationship between topoi and type theories is explored in detail and some of the metatheorems cited in this book are proved.

PHILOSOPHY OF MATHEMATICS

Edward A. Maziarz and Thomas Greenwood, *Greek Mathematical Philosophy* (1968, reissued 1995), discusses the evolution of mathematical philosophy from Thales of Miletus and the Pythagoreans through Plato and Aristotle. Bertrand Russell, *Introduction to Mathematical Philosophy*, 2nd ed. (1920, reissued 1993), is perhaps the most famous introductory book on the subject, though it is mainly dedicated to developing Russell's own view. Stephan Körner, *The Philosophy of Mathematics* (1960, reissued 1986), is a classic introductory overview of the debate between logicists, intuitionists, and formalists during the first half of the 20th century. Stewart Shapiro, *Thinking About Mathematics* (2000), is a very good recent book that provides a more general introduction to the philosophy of mathematics. Mark Balaguer, *Platonism and Anti-Platonism in Mathematics* (1998, reissued 2001), provides an overview of various theories in the philosophy of mathematics, while arguing for a very specific, original view of its own. Finally, two works written by mathematicians are G.H. Hardy, *A Mathematician's Apology*, rev. ed. (1969, reissued 1999); and Reuben Hersh, *What Is Mathematics, Really?* (1997).

INDEX

A